T0121248

EXTREME SUDOKU

CAROL VORDERMAN

THREE RIVERS PRESS • NEW YORK

Published in the United States by Three Rivers Press,
an imprint of the Crown Publishing Group,
a division of Random House, Inc., New York.
www.crownpublishing.com

Originally published as *Carol Vorderman's Extreme Sudoku* in
Great Britain by Ebury Press, an imprint of Ebury Publishing,
Random House, Inc., London, in 2006.

Library of Congress Cataloging-in-Publication Data
is available upon request.

ISBN-13: 978-0-307-34646-9
ISBN-10: 0-307-34646-3

First U.S. Edition

CONTENTS

INTRODUCTION

Many millions of us are now hooked on Sudoku, men and women, retirees and children alike. The summer of 2005 will be remembered as the time of sun, sea and Sudoku, as millions of people sat on beaches intrigued and absorbed by a simple grid of numbers. Sales of pencils and erasers have soared and our fascination with pure logic is growing. Here are some quotes from those who've contacted me.

"Bought your book, within an hour I was hooked, so glad it rained at Wimbledon today." - Ros

"Loved your book. I was no good at math when I was at school years ago but now my fear of numbers has disappeared. Hooray for Sudoku." - Natasha

"Oops. Got into Sudoku on holiday and am now suffering with sunburn. I forgot to turn over!" - Brian

"Carol, what have you done to our lives? We've been perfectly happy old-age retirees until we bought your book. Now my wife has become some sort of Sudoku monster. We constantly fight over grids in newspapers and the book. Only joking, Sudoku and your tips on how to solve it has brought us a lot of joy. Thank you." - Jim

I've been asked countless times "why do we love Sudoku so much?" But, even now, I really don't know how to reply to the question.

One day I'm sure psychologists will come up with the reason. They will perform extensive epidemiological research, analyze brain scans and take heart and blood pressure tests while observing Sudokuers in action.

However, until the day dawns when we finally know how to answer the question "WHY?", we Sudoku lovers will just have to happily continue with our obsession and our quest for improvement in times and techniques.

Since we published *Master Sudoku* last year, the response has been amazing. What I've thoroughly enjoyed over the months since then is the emails and conversations I've had with thousands of people who have become hooked on Sudoku. My first book became a bestselling Sudoku book around the world and, I'm proud to say, the Sudoku bible as far as learning techniques are concerned.

But now, after months of mastering the tricks needed to complete all but extreme Sudoku, many of you have asked for more information about how to become a complete Sudoku master, venturing into the territory of the newly crowned champions. You've conquered the basics and now you want more.

I've thoroughly enjoyed putting this book together because it's been yet another excuse to lock myself away with hundreds of Sudoku grids and pretend that it's work. Rarely has work been more enjoyable. 18-hour Sudoku days in complete peace and relaxation. Marvellous. This book is the result. I really hope you enjoy it. Let me know.

HOW THIS BOOK WORKS

This book will take you from being a Sudoku lover to a complete Sudoku master. It will cover **everything** you need to know to be able to complete every Sudoku grid around.

To make life even more Sudoku intense, I've also included all the tips and tricks needed for solving what has become known as Killer Sudoku, puzzles which first became popular in Japan as a progression from classic Sudoku. In Killer Sudoku no numbers are given. Instead clues are in the form of dotted lines around various boxes with a sum total of the numbers within those boxes. If that sounds confusing, don't worry, you'll get to know and love them, just as I have.

The puzzles we've included are:

EXTREME CLASSIC SUDOKU
SQUIFFY SUDOKU
SUDOKU 16
KILLER SUDOKU

This is the complete book of all that's best about Sudoku. Not only that, I'll show you how to do it too.

Like hundreds of thousands of Sudoku addicts, I love extreme Sudoku. It's one of the very few activities in life where everything else fades away and I can lose myself in pure thought. Bliss.

We're going to cover every possible technique I can think of, or have come across, to solve extreme puzzles. These techniques will, I guarantee, give you the capability to solve every Sudoku in every book and newspaper you see (apart from the very few where you are expected to perform "trial and error" - a technique which most Sudokuists like myself think is pointless).

I've also completed two classic Sudokus from start to finish so that you can see how these puzzles typically progress. There is no definitive order in which to fill in a Sudoku but with extreme, the order does help tremendously. There may be more than one way to progress a Sudoku grid, but there will only be one correct solution for each puzzle.

When we work through a puzzle from start to finish, I will progress through a number of grids. Each grid will contain more and more of the numbers we've managed to complete.

I'm a strong believer in practice and I might ask you to complete some of the numbers yourself, so please keep your pencil and eraser handy at all times. Don't worry, I will tell you what to write in those boxes, and those numbers will then appear in the grid that follows, just to keep life as simple as possible.

So you can test yourself, we've included 175 classic Sudoku puzzles.

Then we move onto Squiffy Sudoku where our minigrids become slightly more misshapen.

HOW THIS BOOK WORKS

Sudoku 16 is classic Sudoku but with many more numbers. The rules are the same but the combinations are more extensive and, therefore, have the potential to be much more confusing.

I did warn you that this book is the ultimate for twisting your mind!

Finally, we come to Killer Sudoku. I find these puzzles a joy to behold. They require another level of skill entirely and your clarity of thought is taken to the limit. However, do not fear as I'll take you through all the techniques you'll need, along with the solutions to a couple of puzzles from start to finish.

As with *Master Sudoku*, every puzzle comes with a timing guide.

Please enjoy. I know you will. Then let me know what you want next. Email me at:

carolsudoku@johnmiles.org.uk

CLASSIC SUDOKU

WELCOME TO CLASSIC SUDOKU

Excellent. You're ready to move on to the very best classic Sudoku. Welcome to the world of extreme.

From this point you can go no further without the magical keys. Everything you have learned so far will prove to be nothing when you are faced with extreme - unless, of course, you can master the special techniques needed to slay the grid.

You can attempt to "slice and dice" and "slice and slot" (techniques covered in my previous book, *Master Sudoku*) numbers to your heart's content, but you won't progress with extreme until you take a giant leap of faith and practice what is written in the following pages.

In this section I'm going to take you through everything I know about classic Sudoku. We will waltz through "writing options" and "lone numbers", and I won't allow you to become bogged down with "triplets" and "quadruplets" and "sextuplets". Nothing will beat you now. All you need is a keen pair of eyes, a pencil and an eraser, and attention to detail. You'll soon understand why. Are you ready? Then let's begin.

WHERE DO YOU BEGIN?

As Julie Andrews once said "let's start at the very beginning, a very good place to start".

So let's start. Have a look at the Sudoku below. This is an example of an extreme classic Sudoku, although it is at the easier end of the puzzles which follow later in this book.

				2			1	
3			1			9		5
	6			9			2	4
		7					9	
8	3			4			6	1
	9					5		
6	2			5			7	
7		4			2			6
	1			3				

WHERE DO YOU BEGIN?

The absolute key to solving any classic Sudoku is to do things in order, avoiding as much complication and confusion as you possibly can. For instance, when you're writing options always do it in numerical order; when you're working through grids always do it in the same order; when you're erasing options always do it immediately (absolutely never wait until you've placed another number, as that way leads to madness). I'll point all this out as we go through the chapter, but for now we'll begin as we always do with any Sudoku grid – slicing and dicing.

Once you've spent a little time looking at which numbers have been provided and which are a little sparse on the grid, you can start to slice and dice in the traditional way. So, starting with number 1, slice and dice your way around the grid. Move onto number 2 and work your way through to number 9. To see some classic Sudoku action in absolute detail, you should follow the two examples I've given later in the book of how to solve a classic Sudoku, where I'll take you through every step from start to finish.

At this point, however, simply use a pure slice and dice technique – don't even begin to write any options into the boxes. Once you've been through the numbers from 1 to 9, try them all again. Why? Well, as you will know by now, the golden rule when you're solving Sudoku is to remember this:

EVERY TIME YOU PLACE A NUMBER, THE CLUES ON THE GRID MAY CHANGE COMPLETELY. ALWAYS CHECK, DOUBLE CHECK AND THEN CHECK AGAIN TO SEE IF A NEW CLUE HAS BEEN REVEALED.

Have a look at the grid and see how many numbers you can place using slicing and dicing. I managed to place four numbers in total. Have a go now. It is also possible to place another 5 numbers using "slicing and slotting" and "the only one that fits" techniques. However, in the next grid I've only placed the 4 numbers found by "slicing and dicing", just to keep things simple.

It may not be possible to place any numbers using slicing and dicing in an extreme classic Sudoku but have no fear, you will still be able to solve the grid. Usually though, the number of boxes you can complete at the very beginning is a measure of how difficult the solution is going to be. So be prepared to scream if you're getting no luck with slicing and dicing and settle down for a fairly lengthy session.

No matter how many numbers you can or cannot place, one thing is certain, you will reach a point where you can't move forward until you start to write your options into each box. So get your pencil ready.

My favorite pencil is a propelling pencil as it has a very fine point and an eraser. The fine point helps no end when you're writing lots of options into a single box. Thick pencils don't help at all.

If you've sliced and diced, let's start to write in some options.

WRITING OPTIONS

Look at the grid below. No more numbers can be filled in with certainty, and we definitely don't want to go down the road of trial and error. So what next? Well, now it's time to start to pencil in our options for each of the boxes.

				2			1	
3			1			9		5
	6			9			2	4
		7					9	
8	3			4			6	1
	9					5		
6	2			5			7	
7		4			2			6
	1			3				

Here is an important tip to keep your Sudoku as simple as possible. This is the first tip for writing options.

Tip One: **Write your options in numerical order.**

You'll understand why this is so important when you begin to solve classic Sudoku. You see, once you've written in all the options, the solution to the grid is found by trawling through these options trying to spot the clues. It's easy to recognize patterns in numbers when they are written in order but it's so much more difficult if they have been written randomly. Have a look at these two lines of numbers. I have deliberately repeated one "set" of numbers three times in each line. See how quickly you can spot that set of numbers in the first line where all the numbers in each set are written in numerical order. Then look at the second line where a different "set" has again been written randomly three times and see how long it takes you to spot the repeated set of numbers in that line. Try it now.

135 236 136 357 237 347 236 269 236

357 862 539 759 735 953 683 758 593

Which was easier? I've no doubt that you found it far simpler to spot the repeated numbers 236 in the top line as they popped up out of the sequence automatically. Your eyes recognized the pattern and your brain could take a little nap.

However, in the second line, the repeated numbers 359 were written in a different order each time and were far more difficult to recognize. This is because your brain had to perform an extra operation to re-order them before it could process the information and then work out which sequence had been repeated. That's a lot of extra work.

So in Sudoku always keep it simple.

Write your options in numerical order.

Now we come to **how** you write your options.

I'm sure you've already done many Sudokus in news-papers, books and magazines and sometimes become frustrated by the size of the grid itself. Occasionally they are so small they are physically difficult to solve, particularly because you can't fit in all your number options and the numbers start to spill over from one box to another. Confusion can reign and we really don't want that - extreme puzzles are difficult enough without unnecessary complications.

When you're writing in options, the figures should be smaller than those you'd write if you were placing a correct number. So in the grid that follows, your eyes will instantly recognize the difference between number options and correctly placed numbers simply because of their size.

Without meaning to sound like a teacher in detention, I would also advise that you write in options as neatly as you can. The reason? Simplicity.

Tip Two:
Neat and small numbers make for a faster solution.

It's also important to work with options in the same order around the grid. So starting with number 1, I find it best to work through bands of grids. I always start with the top left mini-grid and work across the top band, writing in my options as I go. Then I work through the middle band in the same way. Finally I work through the bottom band of mini-grids adding in options all the time. Once all my options for number 1 have been placed, I move onto number 2 and start in the top left corner again. I will repeat this for all the numbers in order up to and including number 9.

You may want to do it randomly, hopping around the grid completing options in any mini-grids that take your fancy. By all means do that, but I guarantee that it will take you longer and there's a much greater chance of making a mistake. In extreme Sudoku there is no room for error. I want to make you an awesome Sudoku master so try it my way to start with and see if this method suits you. I hope it does.

Tip Three:
Start with the top band of grids and work through bands of grids for each number in the same order each time.

Time to write our options.

WRITING OPTIONS

Starting with number 1, we're going to look at the top left mini-grid and then work our way across each band of grids in turn.

				2		6	1	
3		2	1			9		5
/	6	/		9			2	4
/		7		/	/		9	
8	3			4			6	1
/	9	6		/	/	5		
6	2	3		5	/	/	7	
7		4		/	2	/		6
	1			3				

So by slicing and dicing with number 1 we can see there are two boxes where that number might fit in the top left mini-grid. I've made small neat pencil marks in those boxes to make a note of these options. Number 1 has already been placed in the other mini-grids in that top band so we can move down to the middle band of mini-grids. Again, starting with the middle left mini-grid I've found two boxes where the number 1 might be placed and I've pencilled options into those boxes. Moving along the band, we find there are four options for number 1 in the central mini-grid.

Finally, we move down to the bottom band of mini-grids and complete our options there.

Note: If you ever find there is only one box in a mini-grid where you can place an option for a number it means that the number can be placed in the box immediately. It's a nice bonus when this happens but before you write the number in, just check to see that it's correct. The last thing you want to do in Sudoku is make an error early on in the solution, as when you eventually realize you've gone wrong, you'll just have to erase all your work and start again.

Slicing and slotting your options

Before we move on to write our options for number 2, you might be able to spot something vital in the number options we've already written. Have a close look at the options down the left hand stack of mini-grids.

				2		6	1	
3		2	1			9		5
	6			9			2	4
		7					9	
8	3			4			6	1
	9	6				5		
6	2	3		5			7	
7		4			2			6
	1			3				

You'll see that all the options for number 1 in the middle left mini-grid are in column 1 which means that we can use slicing and slotting to narrow our options. Remember how we've used slicing and slotting to determine numbers? Well, we use exactly the same principle when we're writing options.

Tip Four:
If in any mini-grid all the options fit into one row or column then use slicing and slotting across that band or stack of mini-grids to reduce the options.

In this instance, we know that the number 1 in column 1 must eventually be placed somewhere in the middle left mini-grid as all the options in that mini-grid appear in that column. Therefore, the number 1 cannot remain as an option in column 1 in any other mini-grid. So now we can remove the option for number 1 in (column 1, row3).

As you become more familiar with this technique you'll find you do this automatically. Try to think about this while you're writing options rather than having to look at them afterwards. As you start to add more and more options, slicing and slotting becomes much more difficult to spot on paper. Keep it simple.

So, returning to our grid, use your pencil to cross out the option in (column 1, row 3). Obviously if you were doing this at home you would merely "erase" the option but as we're working with a printed grid you'll have to cross out the option instead - sorry.

As luck would have it, there is now only one option for number 1 in the top left mini-grid. This isn't always the case. You will usually be left with a reduced number of options due to slicing and slotting (which is what you want), but you won't be able to place a number immediately. However, in this case we can, so now cross out the option in (column 3, row 3) and write the correct number into the box. Excellent work. Let's carry on with the other numbers.

45	457	5	3457	**2**	3457	**6**	**1**	37
3	47	**2**	**1**	67	467	**9**		**5**
5	**6**	**1**	357	**9**	357	37	**2**	**4**
1245	45	**7**	2356	16	1356	234	**9**	23
8	**3**	5	257	**4**	57	27	**6**	**1**
124	**9**	**6**	237	17	137	**5**	34	237
6	**2**	**3**	4	**5**	14	14	**7**	
7	5	**4**		1	**2**	13	35	**6**
5	**1**	5	467	**3**	467	24	45	2

Writing options for a difficult number

In this grid I've added all the options for the numbers 2 3 4 5 6 and 7. Notice how they are all written in the correct numerical order to make life easier.

Now I want to add the options for number 8. Number 8 is a difficult number in this Sudoku as it has only been given once. Sometimes you'll find that a number doesn't appear at all in the original grid. It is a real pain when this happens as you then have to write options for that number in every single unsolved box. Aagh!

Before we write our options for 8, take a look at the top right mini-grid. You can see that only three numbers are missing and they are 3 7 and 8. The options for 3 and 7 have already been written in and there is still one completely empty box. This means that number 8, the only missing number left from the mini-grid, must be the correct number for (column 8, row 2), so write it in now.

Only at this point should you begin to write in your options for 8 as they will be markedly reduced. If ever you come across a difficult number like this, always try to slice and dice again or find some other way to place it in a mini-grid **before** you write the options.

This saves you a lot of time and it could make a huge difference to the way in which the Sudoku clues then reveal themselves, making the whole grid much simpler to resolve.

Once you've done this, you would then obviously complete all options by writing in those for number 9 before moving on to the techniques given a little later in this section.

3					5	8	4	(12)
		2	3				7	(15)
6	7			1			3	(25)
4				2				(1358)
1				8				9
				3				7
	3			4		5	2	6
				5	3	7	9	(18)
(27)	5	8	9	(67)	(1267)	(13)	(1)	4

Completing options by counting from 1 to 9 in a row, column or mini-grid

Have a look at the grid. I want us to concentrate on both column 9 and row 9 so I've deliberately left out options from the rest of the grid to help us view it more clearly.

You can sometimes write down options for a row, column or mini-grid simply by counting from 1 to 9 as we did in earlier examples. Watch this.

Look at the bottom right mini-grid. The numbers missing are 1 3 and 8. We could resolve it by slicing and dicing but this time we're going to do it with options.

I've written in the options for the mini-grid using additional information given to us in the associated rows and columns. We can see that in one box, the only option is number 1. Therefore we can immediately place number 1 in (column 8, row 9). By crossing out options for 1 in the rest of the mini-grid, we reduce the options in the other two boxes to a single number. Now we complete the mini-grid. Do that in the circled boxes. Remember to then cross out all the options for those placed numbers in their rows and columns.

Once those numbers have been placed, we can study column 9 where there are four boxes still left to complete. The numbers missing are 1 2 3 and 5, so by checking across each row to reduce the options where possible in each box, we can write those options immediately. Now you can see that the only place where number 3 could be placed in column 9 is in row 4, so write in the number. You could have reached this conclusion by slicing and dicing, but once you have started to work with options, it's going to be quicker than continually going back to slicing and dicing as you have with easier Sudokus.

	4	**9**	2 4	**5**	**1**	2 4	4	**3**
3	**1**	3 4	2 4	2 3 4	2 3 4	**9**	4	2
3	3 4	**2**	**9**	3 4	**6**	1 4	4	1
8	2 3 4	3 4	2 4	**1**	**7**	2 3	**5**	**9**
2 3	**6**	3 4	2 4	2 4	**9**	2 3	**1**	2
1	**9**		**3**	2	2	2		**4**
2 3	2 3	3	**1**	2 3 4	2 3 4	**8**	**9**	
9	3	**7**	4	3 4	3 4	1	**2**	1
4	2	**1**	2	**9**	2		**3**	

Erasing options

Now this is where your page can begin to get messy. Some people prefer to cross out options as numbers begin to be filled in but I find that visually confusing, so I prefer to have eraser crumbs everywhere. It's neater and it helps. However, as this is a printed example, we'll have to refer to crossing out.

Look at the grid and study where the options are. We're going to place some numbers in the circled boxes. I've only entered the options for 1 2 and 3 around the grid so far. While I'm entering the options for number 4 some nice things start to happen. Look at the bottom right mini-grid where there are only two options for number 1. By slicing and dicing with the 4s, we can place a 4 in (column 7, row 8). Write it in now. That means we have to cross out the option for number 1 in that box because it isn't correct and cross out all the options for 4 along that row and column. Always make sure that when you place a number you immediately erase all options for that row, column and mini-grid. Don't wait until later or you'll be on the road to madness.

That then leaves us with only one box where a 1 can be placed in the bottom right mini-grid, so we can write number 1 in as well. With a 1 now placed in column 9, we immediately cross out all other number 1 options in that row, column and mini-grid. That leaves only one box where 1 can be placed in the top right mini-grid, so we can fill that in at (column 7, row 3).

Don't confuse this situation with *lone numbers*, which we'll study next. Lone numbers only work when you have completed all options for the numbers from 1 to 9. This method works as you go along because there is only one box available for that number – in the same way as slicing and dicing, this is how options can sometimes fix a number in a specific box.

ONCE ALL OPTIONS HAVE BEEN WRITTEN

All the tips which follow **only** work once you have written all the options for all the numbers. **Do not try** any of these before you have completed all the options or you will go wrong.

Remember that every time you place a number, the clues across the whole grid may change. With extreme Sudoku you sometimes find that once your clues change in what seems like a tiny way, the whole grid will then tumble before your mighty power. That's why your attention to detail is critically important.

Once you've placed a number you must **immediately** erase all the options for that number in the same row, column and mini-grid. Please don't wait to place another number before you erase the options or this will increase your risk of error and spoil the hard work you've put in so far.

Whenever I've been completely stuck on an extreme Sudoku, I have always found that it's because I haven't erased the options properly and at the right time. I've learned the hard way, so take this tip from a woman who's been through that particular pain barrier.

Another little tip is for those times when you've been working with a box which started out full of options, let's say with:

1 2 3 4   2 5 6   5 6 7
5 6 7   8   9

Then, due to numbers being solved in other parts of the grid, some of those options have been erased. This might leave you with a list of options written something like this:

1   4   5   7
6   8   9

Often it's easier to erase all the options in that box and then write them in again in one row, like this:

1 4 6   5 8   7 9

The only reason for this is to make the options easier for your eyes to compute as they are far less confusing on the page. It isn't essential but it might well improve your speed and accuracy.

459	4578	58	3457	**2**	3457	**6**	**1**	37
3	47	**2**	**1**	67	467	**9**	**8**	**5**
5	**6**	**1**	3578	**9**	3578	37	**2**	**4**
1245	45	**7**	23568	168	13568	2348	**9**	238
8	**3**	5	257	**4**	**9**	27	**6**	**1**
124	**9**	**6**	2378	178	378	**5**	34	2378
6	**2**	**3**	48	**5**	148	148	**7**	**9**
7	58	**4**	**9**	18	**2**	138	35	**6**
59	**1**	589	4678	**3**	4678	248	45	28

Lone numbers

Lone numbers are lovely but they can only be found once all the options for all the numbers have been entered onto the grid.

Lone numbers leap out at you from the page, almost begging to be your friend as they show the only possible number option for a particular box.

Have a look at the grid. In (column 1, row 3) you can see that the only option written into the box is for number 5. Before you erase the option and enter 5 as the right number in all its glory, you should check for accuracy. The best way to check that your lone number is correct is to count from 1 to 9 using numbers from that row, column and mini-grid. In the mini-grid we have 1 2 and 3. In the row we have 4 and 6. In the column we have 7 and 8, and then finally back to the row for number 9. So now we know that number 5 is correct for that box and we can write it in.

At this point, you must erase all the options for number 5 on its row, column and mini-grid. Do not go chasing round the grid for other lone numbers until you have erased these. If you do, you could easily make some simple mistakes.

Once you've erased the options, then look at (column 3, row 5) to find another lone numbered box for number 5. Again check it's correct by counting through along the row, column and mini-grid for the other numbers from 1 to 9. They are all there, so write in number 5 as the correct solution for the box.

You'll find by doing this that you have now exposed two more lone numbered boxes in (column 1, row 9) and (column 2, row 4). That's due to the one thing you must always remember in Sudoku – when you enter a number, the clues change.

Keep going through the lone number process until you've filled in all the boxes and no further lone numbers are available.

At this point, you can move on to use other techniques. However, lone numbers will crop up later in your solution so always keep your eye out for them.

3	19	19	67	67	5	8	4	2
5	48	2	3	9	48	6	7	1
6	7	4	248	1	248	9	3	5
4	689	7	56	2	69	1	568	3
1	26	3	4567	8	467	24	56	9
89	2689	569	456	3	1469	24	568	7
79	3	19	78	4	78	5	2	6
2	46	46	1	5	3	7	9	8
7	5	8	9	67	267	3	1	4

Looking for single options in a row or column

Looking for single options in a row or column is a very neat way of finding the correct place for a number.

First, choose a row or a column and then trawl through all the options along it to see if there is only one position for a particular number.

This technique sometimes gives up a number early on in a Sudoku solution but it becomes particularly important when options are being erased.

Have a look at Column 4. Only three numbers have been placed in the column. By studying the options in more detail, we can see that only one possible option exists for number 2, which is in (Column 4, Row 3). Great. We can now place number 2 and then, of course, immediately erase all other options for 2 in its row and mini-grid.

Similarly, looking along Row 6, the only box with an option for number 1 is (Column 6, Row 6), so you can write it in.

In exactly the same way, in the bottom left mini-grid, there is only one option for number 1 in (Column 3, Row 7) so write it in.

Handy tip isn't it? And perfect when slicing and dicing doesn't get you anywhere.

Twinning

Twinning lies at the heart of extreme Sudoku. It is a simple principle which states:

If two boxes in the same row, column or mini-grid have the same options of just two numbers, then those two numbers can only be placed in those boxes and the boxes are twinned.

Twins carry immense power in the world of Sudoku. They can take place along rows, columns or within a mini-grid and they have different implications depending on where they occur.

With the grid below, I can show you lots of different ways in which twins can effect a solution.

4	8	9	(357)	2	(357)	6	1	(37)
3	7	2	1	6	4	9	8	5
5	6	1	(378)	9	(378)	(37)	2	4
(12)	4	7	(23568)	(18)	(13568)	(238)	9	(38)
8	3	5	(27)	4	9	(27)	6	1
(12)	9	6	(2378)	(178)	(1378)	5	4	(378)
6	2	3	(48)	5	(18)	(18)	7	9
7	5	4	9	(18)	2	(18)	3	6
9	1	8	(67)	3	(67)	4	5	2

Twins in the same column

Have a look at column 5 where three boxes have yet to be completed. Now look closely at the boxes in (column 5, row 4) and (column 5, row 8). Those boxes hold the same number options of 1 and 8 and, so, we can say the boxes are twinned.

This means that the numbers 1 and 8 must eventually be placed in those two boxes, they can't be placed anywhere else in the column. You can prove this very easily to yourself by going through a bit of trial and error. Pencil number 1 into the first box and cross out the options for 1 down the column. You'll see that number 8 automatically fits into the second box. Now do it the other way round. Pencil number 8 into the first box and number 1 immediately goes into the second box. You see, whichever way round the numbers are eventually placed in the final and correct solution for those boxes (which we don't know yet), it means that 1 and 8 must fit into the twinned boxes and cannot possibly be placed anywhere else in the column.

Excellent. Now we've spotted these twins in column 5, we can erase all other options for numbers 1 and 8 in the same column. Once we've done that, (column 5, row 6) is left with a lone number option of 7. This is the correct number for the box so you can fill it in. And then, of course, erase all options for 7 in that row and mini-grid. You can see in this example how being able to spot twinned boxes can lead to a solution for another box, although this doesn't always happen.

Now look at column 7 to find another pair of twinned boxes in (Column 7, row 7) and (column 7, row 8). These share the same number options of 1 and 8. So now we know that those two numbers must end up in our twinned boxes we can work our way up the column crossing out options for numbers 1 and 8 as we go. Unfortunately we can't resolve any other boxes in this example but we can cross out an option for 8 in (column 7, row 4). Not to worry, even a simple reduction of one number option can make a huge difference in Sudoku a little later in the solution, particularly if the Sudoku grid is very difficult.

Twins in the same row

Look at row 7 in the same grid. Here you've probably spotted a pair of twins with number options 1 and 8 (again!). We know immediately that those numbers will eventually be correctly placed in our twinned boxes. This time our twins are positioned on the same row and because they occur in the same row, we can work our way along the row crossing out all other options for numbers 1 and 8. By crossing out these options in (column 4, row 7) we're left with a lone number of 4 so fill it in. In this example, by spotting our twinned boxes we've managed to resolve another box. Good work.

Looking around the grid you'll be able to spot three other pairs of twinned boxes which occur in the same rows, and another pair of twins in a further column. Search for them now. However, in all these cases these are the last two boxes to be completed in their particular rows or columns. This means that by spotting them we aren't able to progress the grid any further. Not to worry, ending up with a pair of twinned boxes to complete in any row, column or mini-grid acts as a nice check to see that you haven't made any mistakes so far. It's always a good sign. If you do see any twins in these circumstances, you're allowed a little Sudoku smile.

Twins in the same mini-grid
Looking at the same grid again, study the bottom center mini-grid. You'll find two pairs of twins. The first has the two number options for 6 and 7. The second pair of twins is for the numbers 1 and 8.

We could now go through that mini-grid to cross out all other options for those numbers. If you do that, you can quickly find the solution for (column 4, row 7) which is number 4. However, I have to admit we had already found that solution using the twinned boxes in our example on row 7.

Twins in the same row or column AND mini-grid
Look at the bottom left mini-grid. There are four boxes still left to complete.

1578	1568	2	3678	138	1678	9	4	3578
178	9	6	5	4	178	2	37	378
4578	58	3	278	9	78	1	57	6
9	7	1	48	6	458	3	2	45
6	4	5	1	2	3	7	8	9
2	3	8	49	7	459	6	15	145
3	16	9	467	5	1467	8	17	2
18	18	4	3789	138	2	5	6	137
158	2	7	368	138	168	4	9	13

ONCE ALL OPTIONS HAVE BEEN WRITTEN

In the bottom left mini-grid on row 8 there are two boxes with identical number options of 1 and 8. These boxes in (column 1, row 8) and (column 2, row 8) are twinned. Unusually they occur in the same mini-grid as well as on the same row. This makes them doubly powerful as you'll see.

Spotting our pair of twins means that we now know the numbers 1 and 8 will eventually be placed in those boxes although at the moment we don't know which number will fit into which box.

In this example, our twinned boxes are on the same row **and** in the same mini-grid, so let's take each of these instances in turn.

Because our twins occur on the same row, we can now cross out all other options for numbers 1 and 8 on the same row.

First of all go along the row crossing out all options for number 1 and then go along the same row crossing out all options for number 8. You'll find that by crossing out options 1 and 8 in (column 5, row 8) we're left with a lone number of 3. We can fill that solution in now, even though another option for 3 exists further along the row. Remember to immediately erase all other options for 3 along the same row, column and in its particular mini-grid.

This yields yet more lone numbers along the row. Fill in (column 9, row 8) with the number 7 and number 9 in (column 4, row 8).

So you can see by finding the twins we have resolved three further boxes along the row and started to drastically reduce options all around the grid.

Now we must not forget that, coincidentally, these twinned boxes also occur in the same mini-grid. Excellent. This is like Sudoku Christmas. In exactly the same way as we have for the row, we can now erase all other options for numbers 1 and 8 in the unresolved boxes in the bottom left mini-grid which leaves us with a lone number 6 in (column 2, row 7) and lone number 5 in (column 1, row 9). Beautiful.

Fill in the boxes and give yourself a pat on the back.

Twins. We love them.

Triplets

The opportunity for using triplets will often crop up as you progress through our extreme grids. As you become more used to options, triplets can sometimes provide the only breakthrough possible to complete the grid. Using triplets is very similar to twinning - it's just that the clues aren't quite as obvious.

Triplets are three boxes occurring in the same row, column or mini-grid, which share the same three numbers as options, **or** just a selection of those numbers as options. Those three boxes are triplets and the three numbers can only be placed in those boxes.

You need to get used to seeing how selections work.

3						8	4	125
			3			12569	7	125
6	7			1		29	3	25
4				2				3
1		3		8				9
				3				7
	3			4		5	2	6
				5	3	7	9	8
	5	8	9			3	1	4

Look at Column 9 in the grid. Here we have three different options in the top three boxes. It seems at first as though there is no relationship between them, but they are connected.

The three boxes share the same number options of 1 2 and 5. Have a look more closely. In (column 9, row 1) all three of the number options 1 2 and 5 are given. In (column 9, row 2) all three of the number options 1 2 and 5 are given. However, in (column 9, row 3) only two of the options are given which are 2 and 5. It doesn't matter.

Triplets only have to **share** some of the same three number options; they do not have to include **all** the numbers.

The number options in (column 7, row 3) are 2 and 9. This could not be included as a triplet in this case as 9 is not one of our shared option numbers, only 1 2 and 5.

Here's a little exercise for you.

Here are three sets of numbers. See if you can spot which ones are the triplets and why.

236 568 368 23 689 26

Work your way along the row and find three sets of numbers, which share the same three numbers but remember they do not have to include all of those numbers.

The triplets are:

236 568 368 **23** 689 **26**

They all share the same number options of 2 3 and 6 although they don't all include all of the numbers.

This is such an important principle I want you to try another little exercise. Spot the triplets in this sequence:

34 56 58 48 57 38 89

Although each set only contains two numbers, there are still triplets hidden within the line. None of the triplets in this case contain all of the three shared number options but they are triplets nonetheless.

The triplets are:

34 56 58 **48** 57 **38** 89

They share the number options of 3 4 and 8.

These were tricky to spot, so practice some more triplets spotting on a spare bit of paper. It'll be worth it, as you're about to see.

Let's go back to our grid. In any row, column or mini-grid, you're looking for three boxes, which share three of the same number options. Our triplets in column 9 fit the bill.

This means that those three numbers will have to eventually be placed within those three boxes.

You can spend a bit of time proving this to yourself by writing one of the numbers into one of the triplet boxes and then erasing the other options for that number. Then place a second number in a second triplet box, again erase the options, and you'll find that the third triplet box must contain the third number. Try it again using a different number. Whichever way you try it, you'll find that the three numbers will eventually end up in the triplet boxes. We can use this information to help us solve a grid.

Just as with twinning, those numbers (which in this case occur in both the same column **and** in the same mini-grid) cannot remain as options anywhere else in that column or mini-grid.

Remember, if triplets all occur in the same row but not the same mini-grid then they only affect that row.

If triplets all occur in the same column but not the same mini-grid, then they only affect that column.

If triplets all occur in the same mini-grid on different rows or columns then they only affect that mini-grid.

If, however, the triplets all occur in the same row (or column) and the same mini-grid then they affect both the row (or column) and the mini-grid as well, as they do in this case.

So now we can delete the option numbers 1 2 and 5 in all other boxes in that mini-grid and column.

As it happens, they are the last three unresolved boxes in column 9 so we can't progress any further in the column. However, erasing those same three number options in the other boxes in the same mini-grid means that we are left with lone number 9 to place in (Column 7, Row 3). Now we must erase number option 9 in the same row, column and mini-grid to give us lone number 6 in (Column 7, Row 2). Clever stuff eh?

Two boxes resolved correctly simply by spotting our triplets.

125678	15678	256	23678	(138)	1678	9	4	3578
14678	9	46	5	1348	14678	2	37	378
24578	578	3	2478	9	478	1	57	6
579	57	1	489	6	4589	3	2	4579
5679	4	56	1	2	3	57	8	579
259	3	8	49	7	459	6	159	1459
3	16	9	467	5	1467	8	17	2
1458	158	45	3789	(138)	2	457	6	13579
14568	2	7	3689	(138)	1689	45	1359	1359

Look at column 5 in the grid above to see that we have a set of triplets with number options 1 3 and 8. This time all the boxes contain all of the numbers 1 3 and 8, so the triplets are easy to spot.

This time the triplets occur in different mini-grids so we can only use them to affect the column in which they are contained.

We now know that the numbers 1 3 and 8 will eventually end up in these boxes so we can work our way down the column.

Cross out all other options for 1 3 and 8 in all the other unresolved boxes in the column. This gives us a lone number 4 to place in (column 5, row 2). Excellent. Now erase all options for number 4 in its row and mini-grid to complete the exercise.

Quadruplets

Only when you are on the edge of a Sudoku cliff will you ever need to resort to using quadruplets, but they are interesting as they use exactly the same technique as twins and triplets except they use four number options in four boxes and the clues become increasingly more difficult to spot.

Quadruplets are four boxes occurring in the same row, column or mini-grid, with the same four numbers as options **or** a selection of those numbers as options. The four numbers will eventually be placed in those boxes and will not occur anywhere else within the particular row, column or mini-grid in question.

I want you to run through a couple of quadruplet spotting exercises.

Here is a list of number options. Try to spot the quadruplets.

1259 2569 2589 125 125 1269 1259

In this example, the quadruplets are pretty easy to spot. By the way, notice just how important it is to have written your number options in numerical order. If you hadn't, this exercise would be extraordinarily more difficult.

1259 2569 2589 **125** **125** 1269 **1259**

The quadruplets share the number options of 1 2 5 and 9 although they don't all contain all of the numbers. They don't have to, they only have to contain some of those number options, but they cannot contain any other number options other than the shared four.

Try this sequence of number options now to see if you can spot the quadruplets this time. Again, watch out for quadruplet boxes which don't contain all of the numbers.

24 256 4568 579 456 246 356 678 5689

The quadruplets in this case share the number options 2 4 5 and 6. They are as follows.

24 **256** 4568 579 **456** **246** 356 678 5689

Well done if you got it. It's not that easy to do and does require a lot of concentration.

Over the page you will find a nice grid. Look down column 6. In the circled boxes you'll see option combinations of the same four numbers 1 6 7 and 8. In three of those boxes only some of the numbers appear but, as we know by now, it doesn't matter. As long as they are made up of the same four numbers they are still quadruplets.

Just as with twins and triplets, the four number options shared by our quadruplets will eventually end up being placed in those four boxes and so they cannot occur anywhere else in the column.

This now allows us to erase all other options for 1 6 7 and 8 in that same column. When we do that, we're left with a lone number 4 in (column 6, row 7). Fill it in and erase the options for number 4 in that row, column and mini-grid. It's now easy to see a lone

178	158	2	3678	138	1678	9	4	3578
178	9	6	5	4	178	2	37	378
478	58	3	278	9	78	1	57	6
9	7	1	48	6	458	3	2	45
6	4	5	1	2	3	7	8	9
2	3	8	49	7	459	6	15	145
3	6	9	47	5	147	8	17	2
18	18	4	3789	138	2	5	6	137
5	2	7	368	138	168	4	9	13

number 5 in (column 6, row 4). Fill it in and erase the options for 5 in that row, column and mini-grid. Finally we have another lone number 9 in (column 6, row 6). Place it in and erase the options for 9 in that row, column and mini-grid.

So there you have it. In what seemed like an impossible and chaotic situation, we've managed to solve three boxes by spotting quadruplets.

Quadruplets. Worth studying particularly for our most difficult Sudokus.

Other combinations

You'll be relieved to hear that number option combinations such as quintuplets, sextuplets, septuplets and so on hardly ever occur but I'm showing this exercise to you to demonstrate how, in Sudoku, the number combinations can become increasingly more difficult to work with. You'll find this is particularly the case when you eventually start to try Sudoku 16 later in the book.

2578	23579	23679	4678	48	4567	14567	14567	457
57	157	167	3	9	4567	2	8	457
578	4	67	678	2	1	567	9	3
6	23	238	1	7	34	9	245	2458
9	137	1378	5	348	2	3478	47	6
4	237	5	89	6	39	378	27	1
1	8	79	2	5	4679	467	3	479
3	6	4	79	1	8	57	257	2579
257	2579	279	4679	34	34679	14678	1467	4789

Have a look at row 1 in this grid. No numbers have yet been placed in the row and this situation is typical of a time when you may have to look for multiple boxes with number options, such as sextuplets.

ONCE ALL OPTIONS HAVE BEEN WRITTEN

Sextuplets, as the name suggests, are six boxes occurring in the same row, column or mini-grid, with the same six numbers as options OR a selection of those numbers as options. The six number options will eventually be placed in those six boxes and will not occur anywhere else within the particular row, column or mini-grid in question.

On row 1 you can see six boxes circled for the number options of 1 4 5 6 7 and 8. These are sextuplets. Take a few minutes to study the different combinations of options which all fit into this pattern. None of these boxes contain all the number options but they do share the six numbers. Most importantly, they don't contain any number options other than those given.

We know that the six numbers, 1 4 5 6 7 and 8 will eventually fit into the sextuplet boxes and, therefore, can't be placed anywhere else along row 1.

Using this information, we can work along that same row erasing all these number options in the other boxes.

When you do this, you'll find a lone number 2 in (column 1, row 1). Fill it in and erase the other number options for 2 in the same row, column and mini-grid. And there we have sanity from chaos.

Brilliant!

SUMMARY

Slice and dice as many numbers as you can. If you can slice and slot or use any other basic technique to find numbers within the grid, do so now but **don't** write in any options just yet.

Write in your options

- Write your options in numerical order.
- Neat and small numbers make for a faster solution.
- Start with the top band of grids. Work through bands of grids for each number in the same order each time.
- Slice and slot options where you can.
- Fill in difficult numbers immediately if you're able.

After you've filled in all options

- Check for lone numbers
- Check for single options for particular numbers in each row, column and mini-grid.
- Look out for twinned boxes and delete options in the appropriate row, column and mini-grid.
- Look out for triplets or quadruplets or combinations of higher numbers, these can sometimes provide the big breakthroughs.

CRITICALLY IMPORTANT

Always remember that as soon as you have placed a number, you must immediately erase the other options for that number in the row, column and mini-grid. Also remember that as soon as a number has been placed or an option deleted, the whole basis of the Sudoku clues may have changed so it's worth going through the list of checks again, starting with lone numbers.

TWO CLASSIC PUZZLES FROM START TO FINISH

I want to take you through a couple of classic Sudoku from start to finish so that you can see how all the techniques you've studied in the previous section can be used together to solve every classic Sudoku in this book.

The grid we're going to work on here is puzzle 180 from my first book *Master Sudoku*. This is a difficult puzzle so hang on to your hat. Let's begin

You might want to copy the puzzle at this point and follow my instructions on your own grid with your pencil and eraser.

Look at the summary of how to solve a classic Sudoku on the previous page. Following that list of instructions we start by using some basic techniques to find as

						9	4	
	9		5					
		3		9		1		6
		1		6		3	2	
	4		1		3		8	
	3	8		7		6		
3		9		5		8		
					2		6	
	2	7						

many numbers as possible in the grid **without** writing any options. Start with number 1 and then work through to number 9, writing in the numbers as you go.

The first number we are able to place, using slicing and dicing, is number 2 in (column 9, row 7). After this, we can return to the top right mini-grid to slice and dice another number 2 into (column 7, row 2). Write those numbers in now.

Working our way through all the numbers in order you'll find it impossible to place any more numbers using our basic techniques. It's at this point that we need to start to write in our number options in strict numerical order beginning with number 1.

12	1	2	23	123	1	**9**	**4**	3
14	**9**	4	**5**	134	14	**2**	3	3
24		**3**	24	**9**	4	**1**		**6**
		1	4	**6**	4	**3**	**2**	(4)
2	**4**	2	**1**	2	**3**		**8**	
2	**3**	**8**	24	**7**	4	**6**	1	(14)
3	1	**9**	(4)	**5**	(14)	**8**	1	**2**
(14)	1	(4)	3	13	**2**	(4)	**6**	13
(14)	**2**	**7**	3	13	1	(4)	13	13

We can slice and dice our options for number 1 all the way around the grid, starting with the top band of mini-grids and continuing in bands down to the bottom. Once all those options have been entered, go back up to the top and do it all again with number 2 and then number 3.

While you're entering options for number 4, you'll find that in the middle right mini-grid we can only slice and dice into column 9. This is good as it means, looking down the right hand stack of mini-grids, we can now slice and slot our number 4 options for the bottom right mini-grid into just column 7, which reduces our options.

In the previous grid, look at the bottom band of mini-grids where the bottom left and the bottom right mini-grids can only take options for number 4 in rows 8 and 9. This means that only the bottom center mini-grid can hold options for number 4 on row 7. In this way we can now slice and slot all number 4 options for this mini-grid onto row 7.

125678	15678	(256)	23678	1238	1678	**9**	**4**	3578
14678	**9**	46	**5**	(1348)	14678	**2**	37	378
24578	578	**3**	(2478)	**9**	478	**1**	57	**6**
579	57	**1**	489	**6**	4589	**3**	**2**	4579
25679	**4**	256	**1**	(2)	**3**	57	**8**	579
(259)	**3**	**8**	249	**7**	459	**6**	159	1459
3	16	**9**	467	**5**	1467	**8**	17	**2**
1458	158	45	3789	138	**2**	457	**6**	13579
14568	**2**	**7**	3689	138	1689	45	1359	1359

Now we can write our options for number 5, then 6 7 and 8.

Finally enter the number options for 9.

The grid above contains all the correct options. Take some time to study it.

Now we have written all the options for all the numbers into the grid we should start by looking for lone numbers.

First of all, we find a lovely lone number 2 in the very center of the Sudoku in (column 5, row 5). Fill it in now and erase or cross out all the number 2 options in that row, column and mini-grid.

It isn't possible to place any more lone numbers so let's move onto the next technique, which is our search for single options.

This means trawling through each row in turn to look for single options. A single option is a situation where only one box in a row holds an option for a particular number; say 3, even if the option for number 3 is combined with other options in the same box. If we find such a box and it's the only place where number 3 has an option in a particular row, then it will give us an immediate answer.

Look at (column 1, row 6) to find a single option for number 2 in that row. This has changed from the original grid since we entered lone number 2 in the very center and erased its options. It demonstrates just how important it is to keep analyzing the grid as the clues keep on changing.

So, finding this single option for number 2 we can now enter the number and then erase all options for 2 in its row, column and mini-grid.

I can't find any further single options in the rows so it's time to check in the columns. In column 3 there is now a single option for number 2 in (column 3, row 1). Fill it in and erase all other number 2 options in its row, column and mini-grid. This is coming along nicely now.

Next we can spot a single option for 2 again in column 4. This time it's in (column 4, row 3). Fill it in and erase all the appropriate options. Notice how looking for single options is a little like slicing and dicing except you're doing it with options instead. It's often quite difficult to slice and dice once options have been entered as the patterns on the page become jumbled.

Continuing through our columns we find a single option for number 4 in (column 5, row 2). Put it in and erase the appropriate options for number 4.

15678	15678	**2**	3678	138	1678	**9**	**4**	3578
1678	**9**	6	**5**	**4**	1678	**2**	37	378
4578	578	**3**	**2**	**9**	78	**1**	57	**6**
579	57	**1**	489	**6**	4589	**3**	**2**	4579
5679	**4**	56	**1**	**2**	**3**	57	**8**	579
2	**3**	**8**	49	**7**	459	**6**	159	1459
3	16	**9**	467	**5**	1467	**8**	17	**2**
1458	158	45	3789	138	**2**	457	**6**	13579
14568	**2**	**7**	3689	138	1689	45	1359	1359

Now we have revealed a lone number in (column 3, row 2). Whenever you find a lone number always go to it straight away. It's crying out to be filled in and its number options deleted in its row, column and mini-grid. Do it now.

This leaves a lone number 5 in (column 3, row 5). Fill it in and erase the options in the usual way. Finally complete column 3 with number 4 in (column 3, row 8). Erase the appropriate options. Excellent.

Now let's tackle row 5 and show it off in all its glory. We have a lone number 7 in (column 7, row 5) and then a lone number 9 in (column 9, row 5). After deleting all the relevant number options for 7 and 9, we can complete row 5 with a lone number 6 in (column 1, row 5). Hooray!

1578	158	2	3678	138	1678	9	4	3578
178	9	6	5	4	178	2	37	378
4578	58	3	2	9	78	1	57	6
9	7	1	48	6	458	3	2	45
6	4	5	1	2	3	7	8	9
2	3	8	49	7	459	6	15	145
3	16	9	467	5	1467	8	17	2
158	158	4	3789	138	2	5	6	1357
158	2	7	3689	138	1689	45	1359	135

Let's do a bit of tidying up now and complete the middle left mini-grid entering 7 into (column 2, row 4) and lone number 9 into (column 1, row 4). Take a breather. You're doing well.

It's easy to complete column 7 with lone number 5 in (column 7, row 8) and then number 4 in (column 7, row 9). Fill them in and delete the appropriate number options immediately.

Now look at the bottom right mini-grid in more detail to see that we only have one box left with an option for number 9. Write number 9 into (column 8, row 9) now and delete its options where you find them along the row, column and mini-grid.

1578	158	2	3678	138	1678	9	4	3578
178	9	6	5	4	178	2	37	378
4578	58	3	2	9	78	1	57	6
9	7	1	48	6	458	3	2	45
6	4	5	1	2	3	7	8	9
2	3	8	49	7	459	6	15	145
3	16	9	467	5	1467	8	17	2
18	18	4	3789	138	2	5	6	137
158	2	7	368	138	168	4	9	13

There are no more lone numbers which we can immediately fill in, but I can spot a pair of twinned boxes in the bottom left mini-grid. Look at the twins with number options 1 8. They are doubly powerful as they are in both the same mini-grid and the same row. Let's start to use them.

Looking at the mini-grid first of all, we can now use the twins to delete all other options for 1 and 8 in that same mini-grid. Doing that gives us a lone number 6 in (column 2, row 7). Fill it in and delete the relevant options. We are also given a lone number 5 in (column 1, row 9). Excellent.

Now looking at row 8 where the twins are also positioned, we can delete all options for numbers 1 and 8 in that row as well. This immediately gives us a lone number 3 in (column 5, row 8). Fill it in and delete the relevant options for number 3. This is followed quickly by lone number 7 in (column 9, row 8) and lone number 9 in (column 4, row 8) as well. Fill in these correct numbers and then delete their relevant options in their row, column and mini-grid.

It's quite a simple process to now complete the bottom right mini-grid with a lone number 1 in (column 8, row 7) and then lone number 3 in (column 9, row 9).

From this point on we have a wealth of lone numbers to fill in. Now every time I ask you to fill in a number I am going to assume you know you must then cross or erase all options for that number in its row, column and mini-grid.

Let's finish off column 8 with a lone number 5 in

178	158	2	3678	18	1678	9	4	58
178	9	6	5	4	178	2	37	8
478	58	3	2	9	78	1	57	6
9	7	1	48	6	458	3	2	45
6	4	5	1	2	3	7	8	9
2	3	8	4	7	459	6	5	145
3	6	9	47	5	47	8	1	2
18	18	4	9	3	2	5	6	7
5	2	7	68	18	168	4	9	3

(column 8, row 6), lone number 7 in (column 8, row 3) and lone number 3 in (column 8, row 2). All done. Let's move onto column 9.

Fill in lone number 8 in (column 9, row 2), lone number 5 in (column 9, row 1), lone number 4 in (column 9, row 4) and finish it off with lone number 1 in (column 9, row 6). Lovely.

Now all we need is a quick hike along row 4 with lone number 8 in (column 4, row 4) and finally number 5 in (column 6, row 4).

Moving down to row 6 place lone number 4 in (column 4, row 6) and lone number 9 in (column 6, row 4). Good work.

(178)	(18)	2	(367)	(18)	(1678)	9	4	5
(17)	9	6	5	4	(17)	2	3	8
(48)	(58)	3	2	9	(8)	1	7	6
9	7	1	8	6	5	3	2	4
6	4	5	1	2	3	7	8	9
2	3	8	4	7	9	6	5	1
3	6	9	(7)	5	(47)	8	1	2
(18)	(18)	4	9	3	2	5	6	7
5	2	7	(6)	(18)	(168)	4	9	3

It's now a simple process of filling in lone numbers. Just like before I will assume you will delete all options for the number you've placed in its relevant row, column and mini-grid.

We're on the home straight now. In column 4 fill in:
Lone number 7 in (column 4, row 7),
Lone number 6 in (column 4, row 9) and finally
Lone number 3 in (column 4, row 1). Hooray!

Now we'll move over to column 6 with:
Lone number 4 in (column 6, row 7),
Lone number 8 in (column 6, row 3)
Lone number 1 in (column 6, row 9)
Lone number 7 in (column 6, row 2) and
Lone number 6 in (column 6, row 1) completes column 6.

(178)	(18)	2	3	(1)	6	9	4	5
(1)	9	6	5	4	7	2	3	8
(4)	(5)	3	2	9	8	1	7	6
9	7	1	8	6	5	3	2	4
6	4	5	1	2	3	7	8	9
2	3	8	4	7	9	6	5	1
3	6	9	7	5	4	8	1	2
(18)	(18)	4	9	3	2	5	6	7
5	2	7	6	(8)	1	4	9	3

Let's finish off the grid starting with:
Lone number 1 in (column 5, row 1)
Lone number 8 in (column 2, row 1)
Lone number 7 in (column 1, row 1)
Lone number 1 in (column 1, row 2)
Lone number 4 in (column 1, row 3)
Lone number 5 in (column 2, row 3)
Lone number 8 in (column 1, row 8)
Lone number 1 in (column 2, row 8) and finally
Lone number 8 in (column 5, row 9).

7	8	2	3	1	6	9	4	5
1	9	6	5	4	7	2	3	8
4	5	3	2	9	8	1	7	6
9	7	1	8	6	5	3	2	4
6	4	5	1	2	3	7	8	9
2	3	8	4	7	9	6	5	1
3	6	9	7	5	4	8	1	2
8	1	4	9	3	2	5	6	7
5	2	7	6	8	1	4	9	3

That's it. Our first extreme puzzle together. Please work through the next example of a puzzle I've analyzed from start to finish as it is much more difficult to process than this one and it will really help you to solve all 175 classic Sudokus I've included in this book.

Well done and good luck!

			3	9		2	8	
	4			2	1		9	3
6				7		9		
9			5		2			6
		5		6				1
1	8		2	5			3	
	6	4		1	8			

Second puzzle from start to finish

You may recognize this grid as the most extreme and difficult puzzle I gave you in the original *Master Sudoku* book – it is puzzle 200. The average time to complete this puzzle is between one and two hours and I've been inundated with emails about it, most of them from Sudokuers who couldn't crack it. It is a devilish puzzle so I thought this would be a good opportunity to explain "how to do puzzle 200". Here goes.

You might want to copy out the puzzle at this point and follow my instructions on your own grid with your own pencil and eraser.

Look at the summary of how to solve a classic Sudoku. Following that list of instructions we start by using some basic techniques to find as many numbers as possible in the grid **without** writing any options. Start with number 1 and then work through to number 9, writing in the numbers as we go.

Slice and dice number 1 into (column 4, row 4).

Slicing and dicing along the bottom band of mini-grids, you will see that number 3 will have to be eventually placed on row 9 of the bottom center mini-grid. Therefore, by using slicing and slotting across the bottom band we find number 3 fits nicely into (column 1, row 8) of the bottom left mini-grid.

2578	239	23679	4678	48	4567	14567	14567	457
57	157	167	3	9	4567	2	8	457
578	4	67	678	2	1	567	9	3
6	23	238	1	7	34	9	245	2458
9	137	1378	5	348	2	3478	47	6
4	237	5	89	6	39	378	27	1
1	8	79	2	5	4679	467	3	479
3	6	4	79	1	8	57	257	2579
257	2579	279	4679	34	34679	14678	1467	4789

Now slice and dice number 4 into (column 1, row 6).

You can try simple techniques for all the numbers again, just in case you get lucky. In this grid, however, we can get no further. We can't enter any more numbers.

Time to move on to writing options in strict numerical order, beginning with number 1.

Slicing and dicing options across the top band of mini-grids immediately shows that the options for number 1 in the top right mini-grid can only be placed in row 1. Using this information we can slice and slot our options for number 1 into row 2 of the top left mini-grid. Carry on as normal for the rest of the grid.

Move onto number 2 and write in the options. Then do the same for numbers 3 4 and 5.

When you start to slice and dice options for number 5 into the bottom band of mini-grids, you'll find all the options in the bottom left mini-grid are in row 9. Therefore, you can slice and slot the number 5 options of the bottom right mini-grid onto row 8. Remember we should always reduce our options wherever we possibly can. Now continue with options for number 6.

Number 7 is an example of a difficult number as only one number 7 was given in the original puzzle and it isn't possible to fill in any more. So get your pencil sharpened and complete your options for number 7.

When writing options for number 8 down the left stack of mini-grids it becomes obvious that all the options in the middle left mini-grid are in column 3.

This allows us to slice and slot our number 8 options into just column 1 of the top left mini-grid, again reducing our options.

Finally enter in the number options for 9. The grid on page 66 contains all the correct options. Take some time to study it.

Now we have written all the options for all the numbers into the grid we should start by looking for lone numbers. A simple scan of the grid will show you that there aren't any lone numbers at the moment.

Let's move onto the next technique after writing all the options which is our search for single options. Next we have to trawl through each row in turn to look for single options. This is a situation when only one box in a row holds an option for a particular number, say 3, even if the option for number 3 is combined with other options in the same box. If we find such a box, and it's the only place where number 3 has an option in a particular row, then it would give us an immediate answer. Unfortunately it isn't possible to find any single options in any of the rows here.

Next trawl through each column looking for single options. Again, there aren't any in this grid.

Finally trawl through each mini-grid. Frustratingly that doesn't help either. **I told you this puzzle was hard!**

Notice how you should always look for the easier and more obvious options first, like lone numbers, before you progress to the more complicated stuff. Keep it easy at all times if you can. If it isn't possible because the grid is too difficult, then be prepared for a battle.

Our next technique is a search for twinned boxes. Look for them in every row, column and mini-grid.

On the bottom band of mini-grids you might spot two boxes with the same options of 7 9 in (column 3, row 7) and (column 4, row 8). Your heart might have taken a little leap but your hopes will be dashed on the Sudoku rocks. These boxes are **not** twins as they are not on the same row, in the same column or in the same mini-grid. Boo! No twins anywhere.

OK, this is not for the faint-hearted. Let's move onto triplets. Looking for triplets is significantly more difficult than looking for twins as the three boxes only have to **share** the number options and not contain all three number options in each box. If you're in any doubt, check the section about triplets again. The only set of triplets in the whole grid are in column 5. The number options in the triplets are 3 4 8. The box in (column 5, row 1) only contains 4 8 and (column 5, row 9) only contains 3, 4 but together with (column 5, row 5), the three boxes make a set of triplets. Great? No. Because they are only in the same column and not in the same mini-grid we can only use these triplets to cross out the number options for 3 4 8 in that column. However, they are the last three boxes in the column so we have no other boxes to play with. Stalemate - again!

We've tried lone numbers, single options, twins and triplets and still nothing has budged.

At this point I would normally check all my options again to see if I've made a mistake but I know with this puzzle that I haven't so we have no choice but to look for quadruplets!

2578	2357 9	2367 9	467 8	48	456 7	145 67	145 67	457
57	157	167	3	9	4567	2	8	457
578	4	67	678	2	1	567	9	3
6	23	238	1	7	34	9	245	2458
9	137	1378	5	348	2	3478	47	6
4	237	5	89	6	39	378	27	1
1	8	79	2	5	4679	467	3	479
3	6	4	79	1	8	57	257	2579
257	2579	279	4679	34	3467 9	1467 8	1467	4789

Quadruplets give us our big breakthrough. Look at the top left mini-grid to find quadruplets of 1 5 6 7 in the four circled boxes. Notice they don't all contain all the four numbers but they do contain combinations of them. That's good.

Also look at column 8 – (column 8, row 4), (column 8, row 5), (column 8, row 6) and (column 8, row 8) all share the number options of 2 4 5 7, even though none of the quadruplet boxes contain all the numbers. You can see how important it is to practice quadruplet spotting now! You could now probably begin by using these quadruplets to cross out other options for numbers and complete the puzzle that way.

At this point, though, I want you to have a look at a set of sextuplets with number options 1 4 5 6 7 8 which are all on row 1. Please see the "Other Combinations" example on page 49 for a full explanation.

Please note that now we have found more than one set of numbers, there will be more than one way to begin solving this Sudoku from here. What follows is just one of those ways.

First of all, let's do the work on row 1 with our sextuplets (which are circled). On row 1 we can cross out all the options for numbers 1 4 5 6 7 8 in the boxes other than our sextuplets. Pencil over those options now to reveal a lone number 2 in (column 1, row 1). Now immediately erase (or cross out) all options for number 2 in that row, column and mini-grid. We can't go any further so let's move onto our first set of quadruplets in the top left mini-grid.

The number options for these quadruplets are 1 5 6 7. Crossing out these number options around this mini-grid gives us a lone number 8 in (column 1, row 3). Now erase options for 8 along that row, column and in the mini-grid.

Notice that we have now revealed a pair of twins in column 1. Even though they are the last two unresolved boxes in that column and we can't use them to give us any further clues, it is comforting to see them there. They are a sign that we haven't yet made a mistake.

We have also revealed a pair of twins with number options 6 7 on row 3. Excellent. Crossing out all options for 6 and 7 in the other boxes on row 3 gives us lone number 5 in (column 7, row 3). Fill it in now and erase all options for 5 in that row, column and mini-grid immediately.

We're doing well. The quadruplet breakthrough has opened up the grid to us. Now all we need is accuracy.

2	39	39	4678	48	4567	1467	1467	47
57	157	167	3	9	4567	2	8	47
8	4	67	67	2	1	5	9	3
6	23	238	1	7	34	9	245	2458
9	137	1378	5	348	2	3478	47	6
4	237	5	89	6	39	378	27	1
1	8	79	2	5	4679	467	3	479
3	6	4	79	1	8	7	257	2579
57	2579	279	4679	34	34679	14678	1467	4789

Hooray! I've found a lone number 7 in (column 7, row 8). Fill it in and erase all options for 7 in that row, column and mini-grid. This is really significant as only one number 7 was given in the original puzzle, finding another will have a big effect.

Sure enough it does have a huge effect as lone numbers now come streaming into play.

Fill in lone number 9 in (column 4, row 8) and then erase the options for 9 in the row, column and mini-grid. Next we have lone number 8 in (column 4, row 6). Fill in the box and erase the appropriate options.

Lone number 3 is found in (column 7, row 6). Fill it in and erase its options.

Lone number 9 is now in (column 6, row 6). Fill it in and erase all the number 9 options in its row, column and mini-grid.

Excellent. That was a great run of numbers. There are no more lone numbers for the time being so let's try to spot some twins.

2	39	39	467	48	4567	146	1467	47
57	157	167	3	9	4567	2	8	47
8	4	67	67	2	1	5	9	3
6	23	238	1	7	34	9	245	2458
9	137	1378	5	34	2	48	47	6
4	27	5	8	6	9	3	27	1
1	8	79	2	5	467	46	3	49
3	6	4	9	1	8	7	25	25
57	2579	279	467	34	3467	1468	146	489

Look for the twinned boxes of number options 6 7 on row 3. There are twinned boxes of number options 2 7 on row 6.

There are also twinned boxes of number options 3 4 in the center mini-grid. None of these twins, however, are useful. We can't work with them to reduce any options in any other boxes as they are the last two boxes in their rows or mini-grid. However, it is reassuring to see them as it indicates we haven't yet made a mistake.

There are also twins of numbers 2 5 on row 8 which are both in the bottom right mini-grid. Sadly, in this particular case we aren't able to reduce any further options around the grid or along the row. Not to worry, we have one pair of twins left to analyze and they are for number options 4 7 in column 9.

At last we can move forward. The power of the twins allows us to erase all options for 4 and 7 in the other boxes in the column. Also, because the twins are in the same mini-grid, we can now erase all options for 4 and 7 in the other boxes in the top right mini-grid.

Doing this gives us a lone number 9 in (column 9, row 7). Fill it in and erase all other options for 9 in that row, column and mini-grid.

Again we have a run of lone numbers. I'm going to list them now. Fill them in as you work your way down this list and erase the options for those numbers in their row, column and mini-grid as you go along.

Lone number 7 in (column 3, row7).
Lone number 8 in (column 9, row 9).

Lone number 6 in (column 3, row 3).
Complete row 3 with lone number 7 in (column 4, row 3).
Lone number 1 in (column 3, row 2).

2	39	39	46	48	456	16	16	47
57	57	1	3	9	456	2	8	47
8	4	6	7	2	1	5	9	3
6	23	238	1	7	34	9	245	25
9	137	38	5	34	2	48	47	6
4	27	5	8	6	9	3	27	1
1	8	7	2	5	46	46	3	9
3	6	4	9	1	8	7	25	25
57	259	29	46	34	3467	146	146	8

Look at the grid now. See how we're left with two sets of twins in the top left mini-grid, the top right mini-grid and another two sets of twins in column 9. These are all signs that we haven't yet made an error. Good.

For the time being we've run out of lone numbers so let's look for useful twins again.

We have twins of number options 1 6 on row 1, so we can cross out all options for 1 and 6 in the other boxes on the row. Do that now and place the following numbers. Don't forget to erase the appropriate options as you go.

Lone number 4 in (column 4, row 1).
Lone number 8 in (column 5, row 1).
Lone number 5 in (column 6, row 1).
Lone number 7 in (column 9, row 1).
Lone number 6 in (column 6, row 2).
Lone number 4 in (column 9, row 2).
Lone number 6 in (column 4, row 9).
Lone number 4 in (column 6, row 7).
Lone number 3 in (column 6, row 4).
Lone number 7 in (column 6, row 9).
Lone number 4 in (column 5, row 5).
Lone number 3 in (column 5, row 9).
Lone number 6 in (column 7, row 7).

2	39	39	4	8	5	1	16	7
57	57	1	3	9	6	2	8	4
8	4	6	7	2	1	5	9	3
6	2	28	1	7	3	9	245	25
9	137	38	5	4	2	8	7	6
4	27	5	8	6	9	3	27	1
1	8	7	2	5	4	6	3	9
3	6	4	9	1	8	7	25	25
5	259	29	6	3	7	14	14	8

From now on we are simply working with lone numbers. Always remember to erase the options for those numbers in the same row, column or mini-grid as you work.

Now enter the following:
Lone number 1 in (column 7, row 1).
Lone number 6 in (column 8, row 1).
Lone number 4 in (column 7, row 9).
Lone number 1 in (column 8, row 9).
Lone number 8 in (column 7, row 5).
Lone number 7 in (column 8, row 5).
Lone number 2 in (column 2, row 4).
Lone number 8 in (column 3, row 4).
Lone number 3 in (column 3, row 5).
Lone number 5 in (column 9, row 4).
Lone number 4 in (column 8, row 4).

2	39	9	4	8	5	1	6	7
57	57	1	3	9	6	2	8	4
8	4	6	7	2	1	5	9	3
6	2	8	1	7	3	9	4	5
9	1	3	5	4	2	8	7	6
4	7	5	8	6	9	3	2	1
1	8	7	2	5	4	6	3	9
3	6	4	9	1	8	7	25	2
5	59	29	6	3	7	4	1	8

Again, we can simply work our way through lone numbers.

Lone number 9 in (column 3, row 1).
Lone number 3 in (column 2, row 1).
Lone number 1 in (column 2, row 5).
Lone number 7 in (column 2, row 6).
Lone number 2 in (column 8, row 6).
Lone number 2 in (column 9, row 8).
Lone number 5 in (column 8, row 8).
Lone number 5 in (column 1, row 9).
Lone number 7 in (column 1, row 2).
Lone number 5 in (column 2, row 2).
Lone number 9 in (column 2, row 9).
Lone number 2 in (column 3, row 9).

2	3	9	4	8	5	1	6	7
7	5	1	3	9	6	2	8	4
8	4	6	7	2	1	5	9	3
6	2	8	1	7	3	9	4	5
9	1	3	5	4	2	8	7	6
4	7	5	8	6	9	3	2	1
1	8	7	2	5	4	6	3	9
3	6	4	9	1	8	7	5	2
5	9	2	6	3	7	4	1	8

If you followed all that, you could now become a Sudoku classic master. I hope it helped.

1

		6	2		4	9		
				6				
		3	8	7	9	2		
	3	5		9		7	1	
	9						8	
	1	8		2		6	9	
		7	5	1	2	8		
				4				
		2	7		3	1		

Time: ____ Score: ____

Scoring: Less than 12 minutes = 15 points; 12–20 minutes = 10 points; over 20 minutes = 5 points

2

		9						
4							9	
	2	5	4	9	3			
7					9	1		
3			6			8		
	6			1		3		
5	7					2		8
		4	2			7		
		6		7	1		4	

Time: ______ Score: ______

Scoring: Less than 12 minutes = 15 points;
12–20 minutes = 10 points; over 20 minutes = 5 points

3

	6			4			2	
1		2				4		5
	1						7	
2		6	5	3	9	1		4
	4	9	8		2	7	5	
		7	9	6	4	2		
6				7				8

Time: Score:

Scoring: Less than 12 minutes = 15 points;
12–20 minutes = 10 points; over 20 minutes = 5 points

4

			7	1		6		
9				2	8		3	7
	1			4		9	8	5
			1		7			
5	6	4		9			1	
8	4		9	7				1
		2		8	5			

Time: Score:

Scoring: Less than 12 minutes = 15 points;
12–20 minutes = 10 points; over 20 minutes = 5 points

5

8		4				1		3
	7	9				2	5	
			5		1			
	8	7				5	4	
6			4		3			1
	4	1				3	2	
			1		6			
	1	6				9	8	
5		2				6		4

Time:

Score:

Scoring: Less than 12 minutes = 15 points;
12–20 minutes = 10 points; over 20 minutes = 5 points

6

						4		3
			3	8				
	1			4	9	8	5	
4		6	8			7	1	
		7	4		5			
8		9	7			5	3	
	6			3	8	2	7	
			2	7				
						3		1

Time: ______ Score: ______

Scoring: Less than 12 minutes = 15 points;
12–20 minutes = 10 points; over 20 minutes = 5 points

7

							9	
6				1			3	5
1					9	2		6
	7	2		8		5		
			9		1			
		1		4		6	8	
2		9	8					3
3	8			9				7
	6							

Time: Score:

Scoring: Less than 12 minutes = 15 points;
12–20 minutes = 10 points; over 20 minutes = 5 points

8

	6							5
			6			7	4	
		3	8	7			2	
	5			3		9		
7			5		2			1
		2		9			7	
	8			2	6	1		
	1	6			4			
2							8	

Time: ______ Score: ______

Scoring: Less than 12 minutes = 15 points;
12–20 minutes = 10 points; over 20 minutes = 5 points

9

6					4			
		1					3	
	3	9		2				7
				4	2		7	
		3	1				2	9
7			6		9	5	1	
					5			
	6		2	1	8			
		8		6				

Time: Score:

Scoring: Less than 12 minutes = 15 points;
12–20 minutes = 10 points; over 20 minutes = 5 points

10

	9				5			
			8					
2				1	4	5		
	4					9		8
	2	5	7			4		
	8			5			2	
1				8				
			1	3	9			2
		2				7		

Time: ____________ Score: ____________

Scoring: Less than 12 minutes = 15 points; 12–20 minutes = 10 points; over 20 minutes = 5 points

11

		2				1		
			2			9		
		6			3	5	2	8
		8	5	3		2		
6	1				7			
			4		1		8	
	6				8	3		9
5	3	4		6				
	8			1				

Time: Score:

Scoring: Less than 12 minutes = 15 points;
12–20 minutes = 10 points; over 20 minutes = 5 points

12

			8					
6			4	5				
	4					5		
1		2	9	3				
		4			1		5	
					8		2	4
4	3			8	2			
2		7				9		
	8	1			3		6	

Time:

Score:

Scoring: Less than 12 minutes = 15 points;
12–20 minutes = 10 points; over 20 minutes = 5 points

13

					6		8	9
			7	1	8	6	4	
		6		4			1	8
		8	6		2	7		
	4	9		8				3
		4		7				6
	9	1	5					
	8		3		9	4		

Time: ______ Score: ______

Scoring: Less than 12 minutes = 15 points;
12–20 minutes = 10 points; over 20 minutes = 5 points

14

2								9
	4	9				1	6	
1		8		7		4		2
			4	8	5			
		1	7		2	8		
			1	6	9			
3		5		1		2		6
	1	2				3	4	
4								5

Time: Score:

Scoring: Less than 12 minutes = 15 points;
12–20 minutes = 10 points; over 20 minutes = 5 points

15

	4				7			
					3			7
	6		5	4	2	9		
							5	2
	1	6	2	8	4	7	9	
7	2							
		3	4	9	6		7	
2			7					
			3				1	

Time: Score:

Scoring: Less than 12 minutes = 15 points;
12–20 minutes = 10 points; over 20 minutes = 5 points

16

			5					
1					2		6	3
	2		1	7				5
9			3			2		1
	3						8	
5		8			4			9
2				6	3		5	
6	8		4					2
					9			

Time: Score:

Scoring: Less than 12 minutes = 15 points;
12–20 minutes = 10 points; over 20 minutes = 5 points

17

		5					4	
					1		7	3
		6		9	3	1		5
2	3							
6		7	3		8	5		2
							3	6
7		4	2	3		9		
8	5		1					
	2					3		

Time: ________ Score: ________

Scoring: Less than 12 minutes = 15 points;
12–20 minutes = 10 points; over 20 minutes = 5 points

18

						8		7
			1	4	7		2	
		6					4	
		2			4	3		6
		3		5		1		8
	4			3	5		1	
		9	4			2		5
	8			2	6		3	

Time:

Score:

Scoring: Less than 12 minutes = 15 points;
12–20 minutes = 10 points; over 20 minutes = 5 points

19

		8	3		6	7		
	1						8	
		6	5	1	8	9		
	8			2			7	
2		4				1		9
	6			5			2	
		2	7	3	9	5		
	9						6	
		7	8		2	4		

Time: Score:

Scoring: Less than 12 minutes = 15 points;
12–20 minutes = 10 points; over 20 minutes = 5 points

20

2		5		4	3		6	8
					6	1	2	
9							5	7
		2	3		9	8		
7	1							2
	5	1	7					
8	7		5	6		3		1

Time: ______ Score: ______

Scoring: Less than 12 minutes = 15 points;
12–20 minutes = 10 points; over 20 minutes = 5 points

21

							5	9
		4		7				8
9			6			7	1	
5		8	7			3		
					3	5		
1		2	8			9		
8			4			1	7	
		7		1				4
							9	3

Time: ______ Score: ______

Scoring: Less than 12 minutes = 15 points;
12–20 minutes = 10 points; over 20 minutes = 5 points

22

1				8	3			
	8		7					
	4	3						
	7		3	1				2
		6			8			9
8		4			2		7	
			2	5		1		
					7	5	2	
5			4					8

Time: Score:

Scoring: Less than 12 minutes = 15 points;
12–20 minutes = 10 points; over 20 minutes = 5 points

23

				2				
		9	5	4	7	1		
	9						7	
7		8	3		5	4		6
	7	1	6		9	2	3	
3			2	5	1			9
	6			7			8	

Time: Score:

Scoring: Less than 12 minutes = 15 points;
12–20 minutes = 10 points; over 20 minutes = 5 points

24

		3				5		
	2	5				4	7	
				1				
	7	1	2		4	3	5	
		4	5		6	1		
		6	8		1	7		
	4		3		9		6	
	8	2	7		5	9	3	

Time:

Score:

Scoring: Less than 12 minutes = 15 points;
12–20 minutes = 10 points; over 20 minutes = 5 points

25

		4	5					
2			6			3		7
	9			8	1			4
6							4	3
			8	4				
5							8	1
	2			7	3			5
4			9			7		2
		9	4					

Time: Score:

Scoring: Less than 12 minutes = 15 points;
12–20 minutes = 10 points; over 20 minutes = 5 points

26

		1					4	
		9		6				1
8	3		5					9
		6	2		4			
	9					4		3
			3				2	
				8			9	
9					6	2	3	8
	8	7		3			5	

Time:

Score:

Scoring: Less than 12 minutes = 15 points;
12–20 minutes = 10 points; over 20 minutes = 5 points

27

							5	
	6		7	3	5			4
		3	9					
		8	3	5			9	
	3				2		1	
5					6	3	4	
	4				7	1		
6		1		4			8	
	8		5					

Time: Score:

Scoring: Less than 12 minutes = 15 points;
12–20 minutes = 10 points; over 20 minutes = 5 points

28

		5				7		
7	2						1	3
			5		8			
2			6		5			7
5	8			9			4	6
1			8		7			5
			4		9			
4	3						7	9
		9				2		

Time: [ ] Score: [ ]

Scoring: Less than 12 minutes = 15 points;
12–20 minutes = 10 points; over 20 minutes = 5 points

29

7		5				9		1
	4	8				6	7	
	6			2			9	
2		4				1		7
8	3						4	2
	7		8	3	5		2	
		6	2		7	3		
				4				

Time: Score:

Scoring: Less than 12 minutes = 15 points;
12–20 minutes = 10 points; over 20 minutes = 5 points

30

	7	4				1	8	
					3	2		7
							4	5
				9			5	
2					7			
7	5	6						
9			6					3
6			1					4
	3	5	2	4				

Time:

Score:

Scoring: Less than 12 minutes = 15 points;
12–20 minutes = 10 points; over 20 minutes = 5 points

31

	7							
			8	2	7			6
	6			4	3		7	
8	2	1	4					3
		6				7		
9					5	1	6	8
	9		3	6			2	
4			7	9	2			
							3	

Time: ______ Score: ______

Scoring: Less than 12 minutes = 15 points;
12–20 minutes = 10 points; over 20 minutes = 5 points

32

					5	2		
7				4				5
	8			1	2		7	
	3					8		
	4	5		3		6	9	
		6					5	
	2		6	9			4	
9				5				8
		1	2					

Time: Score:

Scoring: Less than 12 minutes = 15 points; 12–20 minutes = 10 points; over 20 minutes = 5 points

33

9								
	8		6			3	9	
	5	7			9	1		
		5			4			3
	6	1	3		8	4	5	
2			9			6		
		4	8			5	3	
	7	9			3		6	
								7

Time:

Score:

Scoring: Less than 12 minutes = 15 points;
12–20 minutes = 10 points; over 20 minutes = 5 points

34

		5						
						7	8	
	8				6	4	9	
3			4		7	8		
		4	8					
8	7	6		3	9			
6			5	2				4
5			6			3		
	2	9	1		3			

Time: ______ Score: ______

Scoring: Less than 12 minutes = 15 points; 12–20 minutes = 10 points; over 20 minutes = 5 points

35

					9			5
	1	2				8		
	5				8			
				7				6
			9			5	3	
6		7				9		1
	8			3	6		5	
				9		1		3
1			5		4		6	

Time:

Score:

Scoring: Less than 12 minutes = 15 points;
12–20 minutes = 10 points; over 20 minutes = 5 points

36

	4						6	
			4	1	5			2
		9				8	7	
		7			6		1	9
		2		9		6		5
			2		8			
	3		6	4				8
		1		5	9		3	

Time: Score:

Scoring: Less than 12 minutes = 15 points;
12–20 minutes = 10 points; over 20 minutes = 5 points

37

						6		
			1				5	2
				2	9	3		7
	9				7			6
		8		1			3	
		3	5			4		
6		2			5		7	
	8			7		1		3
	3	4	2				6	

Time: Score:

Scoring: Less than 12 minutes = 15 points;
12–20 minutes = 10 points; over 20 minutes = 5 points

38

5			7		9			1
		4				3		
	4		8		6		1	
		7	5		1	8		
		8				5		
	7						6	
	8	3	1		5	4	9	
2			4		7			8

Time:

Score:

Scoring: Less than 12 minutes = 15 points;
12–20 minutes = 10 points; over 20 minutes = 5 points

39

7			5		8			4
4		5	2		3	6		9
5	2		1		4		3	8
1	7		6		5		9	2
6		1	4		2	8		3
8			7		6			5

Time:

Score:

Scoring: Less than 12 minutes = 15 points;
12–20 minutes = 10 points; over 20 minutes = 5 points

40

						5		
					1			3
	7	4		9			1	6
		1	5			3		4
	9				8		7	
		2	7			1		9
	8	5		6			2	1
					3			7
						9		

Time:

Score:

Scoring: Less than 12 minutes = 15 points;
12–20 minutes = 10 points; over 20 minutes = 5 points

41

				3				
	3			6	9	1		
		7	5		1		6	
7		2		4		3		
	1		2		6		5	
		4		7		2		1
	7		8		3	6		
		1	6	5			7	
				1				

Time: Score:

Scoring: Less than 12 minutes = 15 points;
12–20 minutes = 10 points; over 20 minutes = 5 points

42

	9						3	
		7				6		
3			4		1			7
	1		2		3		8	
	4		7		6		1	
	7		8		5		4	
8			3		2			4
		2				8		
	6						5	

Time: Score:

Scoring: Less than 12 minutes = 15 points;
12–20 minutes = 10 points; over 20 minutes = 5 points

43

				4		6	9	1
6	2			7	3			8
	1				7	4		
3				1			8	5
	7				8	3		
1	6			3	2			4
				5		9	7	2

Time: ______ Score: ______

Scoring: Less than 12 minutes = 15 points;
12–20 minutes = 10 points; over 20 minutes = 5 points

44

					2		1	
	3		1			6		8
						4		
	9				8		5	
					3		6	
5			6	7		8		1
	6	2			7			3
4			2	3				
	7				6	2		

Time: Score:

Scoring: Less than 12 minutes = 15 points;
12–20 minutes = 10 points; over 20 minutes = 5 points

45

2					9			
		8				1		
	7		5		1	3		
	9		7	5			3	2
						7	1	
	6		4	1			5	9
	8		2		4	5		
		7				9		
1					6			

Time: Score:

Scoring: Less than 12 minutes = 15 points;
12–20 minutes = 10 points; over 20 minutes = 5 points

46

					8		6	2
		1		3	2		8	4
					4	9		
		2			6		5	
	5	9	8	7	1	4		
			6		5			3
	3	5		8				
	1	6				2		

Time: Score:

Scoring: Less than 12 minutes = 15 points;
12–20 minutes = 10 points; over 20 minutes = 5 points

47

						6		
		4	1					9
9			6	4		3	7	
		3	4	2				8
		9				5		
6				5	1	9		
	9	6		8	4			2
2					5	4		
		7						

Time:

Score:

Scoring: Less than 12 minutes = 15 points;
12–20 minutes = 10 points; over 20 minutes = 5 points

48

			1	2	9	8		
		6			5	2		
	9			8		5	7	
	4		6					
	6	2					1	
	1	7	9					4
			7		4			8
						1	9	

Time: ______ Score: ______

Scoring: Less than 12 minutes = 15 points;
12–20 minutes = 10 points; over 20 minutes = 5 points

49

			2		7			
		2	6	3	8	1		
	3			4			6	
1	8		3		2		4	5
	9	5				7	2	
2	7		4		5		8	1
	1			2			7	
		8	7	6	1	2		
			9		3			

Time: Score:

Scoring: Less than 12 minutes = 15 points;
12–20 minutes = 10 points; over 20 minutes = 5 points

50

							6	
			3			2		
					7		9	3
	1				5			
				2	1		7	5
		5	4	8		1	3	
	6				8		1	4
1		9		6	3	5		
		3		1		6		

Time: Score:

Scoring: Less than 12 minutes = 15 points;
12–20 minutes = 10 points; over 20 minutes = 5 points

51

	8		9		3		5	
		5		4		7		
8	4		1		5		6	7
	5	6				2	1	
7	3		2		9		8	4
		7		5		3		
	2		8		6		7	

Time: Score:

Scoring: Less than 12 minutes = 15 points;
12–20 minutes = 10 points; over 20 minutes = 5 points

52

						5		8
	6		5	9		4		
5		8	4					
2	9		8	7				4
			2		6			
8				4	5		2	3
					4	2		7
		1		2	3		4	
6		4						

Time: ______ Score: ______

Scoring: Less than 12 minutes = 15 points;
12–20 minutes = 10 points; over 20 minutes = 5 points

53

	2			3				1
			5			6	2	
			7	4			3	
	3		8	1				
		5			7	4		9
	8				4	1	7	
5				2				
			6		3			4
		3						

Time: Score:

Scoring: Less than 12 minutes = 15 points;
12–20 minutes = 10 points; over 20 minutes = 5 points

54

	8							
		1					4	5
5			1	2				
6				8		4		2
8					3	7		
3				7		1		6
2			6	9				
		9					6	3
	7							

Time: ________ Score: ________

Scoring: Less than 12 minutes = 15 points; 12–20 minutes = 10 points; over 20 minutes = 5 points

55

								3
5				1		7		
3	7				6			2
4	5			2	7		6	
	3	7	9					
1	9			6	8		3	
8	4				5			1
7				9		4		
								6

Time: Score:

Scoring: Less than 12 minutes = 15 points;
12–20 minutes = 10 points; over 20 minutes = 5 points

56

				2		8		6
3			9					
2	5						7	
5		3						7
	2		6		7			
1		6						3
4	1						5	
8			7					
				1		2		4

Time: Score:

Scoring: Less than 12 minutes = 15 points;
12–20 minutes = 10 points; over 20 minutes = 5 points

57

				1				
	1		8		3			2
	5	8			4			
		1		9		4		3
	9						8	
7		4		5		9		
			6			2	4	
5			2		1		3	
				4				

Time: Score:

Scoring: Less than 12 minutes = 15 points;
12–20 minutes = 10 points; over 20 minutes = 5 points

58

			7		6		2	8
		4	8		1	9		3
1				6		3		4
			9		4			
4		9		7				2
9		6	2		5	1		
5	3		4		8			

Time: ______ Score: ______

Scoring: Less than 12 minutes = 15 points;
12–20 minutes = 10 points; over 20 minutes = 5 points

59

	6						7	
3			9			4		
		5		3				
	4			2				3
		3	5		7			
				6		7	2	
	2				5			
9					4			6
			7				1	

Time: Score:

Scoring: Less than 12 minutes = 15 points;
12–20 minutes = 10 points; over 20 minutes = 5 points

60

7								
	3			1	2	7		
	2		6				5	
		2	1				9	
4		7		8			2	
					5	8		
1	5			2	9			
		6				5	8	
		8		6				3

Time: Score:

Scoring: Less than 12 minutes = 15 points;
12–20 minutes = 10 points; over 20 minutes = 5 points

61

3			2		6			7
4		9		3		6		8
		4	6		1	2		
1								6
	7	2				3	4	
		7				9		
	4		9		7		6	
		6	1		2	8		

Time: Score:

Scoring: Less than 16 minutes = 15 points;
16–35 minutes = 10 points; over 35 minutes = 5 points

62

6			3		2		9	
4		2		6				7
	5	8	6			9		3
					3	7		8
	6	4	8			2		1
8		7		3				9
9			4		8		3	

Time: Score:

Scoring: Less than 16 minutes = 15 points;
16–35 minutes = 10 points; over 35 minutes = 5 points

63

			3	1			5	
				6				
8		7			9			1
2					5		1	4
		9	8		1	3		
1	7		4					2
7			5			8		9
				8				
	2			9	3			

Time: Score:

Scoring: Less than 16 minutes = 15 points;
16–35 minutes = 10 points; over 35 minutes = 5 points

64

		9						
	6			8	9			
						9	3	8
1			3				8	4
9		8	4		5	6		3
2	4				7			1
5	8	7						
			2	5			7	
						4		

Time: Score:

Scoring: Less than 16 minutes = 15 points;
16–35 minutes = 10 points; over 35 minutes = 5 points

65

7			2		9			5
	6		3		7		4	
	9		5		2		8	
	1		4		3		7	
	4			9			3	
		3				8		
8	2						1	4
4			9		8			7

Time: Score:

Scoring: Less than 16 minutes = 15 points;
16–35 minutes = 10 points; over 35 minutes = 5 points

66

				5	3		2	
			8				5	4
				6				7
	6				2			
9		2					6	
1			4					9
						9		2
4	1			7				
	8	6			1	4		

Time: Score:

Scoring: Less than 16 minutes = 15 points;
16–35 minutes = 10 points; over 35 minutes = 5 points

67

					7		8	5
						9		7
			6	2				
7					3	5		6
	6		8		2		9	
2		9	7					3
				3	6			
3		7						
1	2		9					

Time: ______ Score: ______

Scoring: Less than 16 minutes = 15 points;
16–35 minutes = 10 points; over 35 minutes = 5 points

68

			4					
7	3		8		5			
		6				3	4	5
6		5	2					4
	8						1	
1					4	5		7
9	4	1				6		
			9		7		5	2
					1			

Time: Score:

Scoring: Less than 16 minutes = 15 points;
16–35 minutes = 10 points; over 35 minutes = 5 points

69

			1		5			
9	1	5	6		2	3	4	8
		2	5		7	6		
4		6				8		7
8								2
	8			3			6	
5	9	7				1	8	3

Time: Score:

Scoring: Less than 16 minutes = 15 points;
16–35 minutes = 10 points; over 35 minutes = 5 points

70

					7			
9					1			8
		4				1		2
		9		1	2	3		5
			6		3			
6		1	5	4		8		
2		5				4		
7			3					6
			9					

Time: Score:

Scoring: Less than 16 minutes = 15 points;
16–35 minutes = 10 points; over 35 minutes = 5 points

71

					5			
	9		7			4		2
3	1			2				
1	7				3		8	6
					1	3		
6	2				7		9	1
7	5			3				
	3		1			9		8
					8			

Time: Score:

Scoring: Less than 16 minutes = 15 points;
16–35 minutes = 10 points; over 35 minutes = 5 points

72

					5			
				7	2			6
	8		3				7	1
	2			3		9		4
9	7						6	2
1		6		9			5	
6	9				3		4	
7			9	2				
			4					

Time: Score:

Scoring: Less than 16 minutes = 15 points;
16–35 minutes = 10 points; over 35 minutes = 5 points

73

		9						
			7	8	5			
8						5	4	
	1				7			9
	7				8		1	
	2		3	1		7		8
		5			3	2	6	
		3		6		8		5
			5		4		3	

Time: Score:

Scoring: Less than 16 minutes = 15 points;
16–35 minutes = 10 points; over 35 minutes = 5 points

74

	3						8	
		6				5		
				7				
	8						6	
			5		9			
2		4	1		8	7		3
		1				9		
8			9		1			2
3		9				6		1

Time: ____ Score: ____

Scoring: Less than 16 minutes = 15 points; 16–35 minutes = 10 points; over 35 minutes = 5 points

75

6								1
		7				4		
	2		1		5		7	
		9	4		6	7		
	6						9	
			3		8			
	3			8			5	
		6		1		9		
4	8			2			1	7

Time: Score:

Scoring: Less than 16 minutes = 15 points;
16–35 minutes = 10 points; over 35 minutes = 5 points

76

		1			7		2	
								3
3				5		9		
	1							4
		8	6	7		5		
4		5		1				
	4		9	8				7
1		3			2			
8	5		1			4		

Time: Score:

Scoring: Less than 16 minutes = 15 points;
16–35 minutes = 10 points; over 35 minutes = 5 points

77

	1				3	9		
2			6					
			9		5		8	
	2	8						7
					1			8
1		3		6				5
6							1	
		2				7		
			3	2	6			

Time: Score:

Scoring: Less than 16 minutes = 15 points;
16–35 minutes = 10 points; over 35 minutes = 5 points

78

		1	5					8
			7	8		2	9	
7					6		8	1
6			4	5	8			3
9	4		1					2
	3	6		9	4			
4					3	6		

Time: Score:

Scoring: Less than 16 minutes = 15 points;
16–35 minutes = 10 points; over 35 minutes = 5 points

79

		7				6		
		4	8		6	2		
5	2						4	9
4			2		3			7
				9				
3			7		8			5
2	5						9	6
		1	9		5	3		
		3				5		

Time: Score:

Scoring: Less than 16 minutes = 15 points;
16–35 minutes = 10 points; over 35 minutes = 5 points

80

					7			6
	2					9		
					8	1	5	
1				2	3	7	6	
6	9						8	3
	3	5	8	6				2
	1	4	6					
		9					4	
8			7					

Time: Score:

Scoring: Less than 16 minutes = 15 points;
16–35 minutes = 10 points; over 35 minutes = 5 points

81

7		1		3		6		
9	6				7	2		1
		8	6				3	
		9	8	2	4	7		
	7				1	9		
4		7	9				2	6
		2		4		5		9

Time: Score:

Scoring: Less than 16 minutes = 15 points;
16–35 minutes = 10 points; over 35 minutes = 5 points

82

	1							
		2	8				9	
			9		4	7		8
9			3		7	6		
4								3
		6	4		2			7
2		4	5		3			
	6				1	2		
							8	

Time: Score:

Scoring: Less than 16 minutes = 15 points;
16–35 minutes = 10 points; over 35 minutes = 5 points

83

					1			9
	5		2	7				
1			6					
4		8			9			7
	6						9	
		7				2	5	
	7		3		5			
8		5		1			4	
	9				8	1		

Time: Score:

Scoring: Less than 16 minutes = 15 points;
16–35 minutes = 10 points; over 35 minutes = 5 points

84

				6				3
		1			3		8	
	3	9			2	5	1	
			7			6	3	
7						9		8
	9	5						2
		7	6	1				
	2	6	8					
1				9	5			

Time: Score:

Scoring: Less than 16 minutes = 15 points; 16–35 minutes = 10 points; over 35 minutes = 5 points

85

						9		
			7				3	5
2	4				5		7	
8				6	9			4
	2		5					
6				4	2			9
9	6				4		8	
			8				9	7
						3		

Time: 　　　　Score:

Scoring: Less than 16 minutes = 15 points;
16–35 minutes = 10 points; over 35 minutes = 5 points

86

							1	
8			4		2			
	5			9		6		
		8			6	7		9
		2					6	5
		9			4	2		3
	6			7		8		
4			9		5			
							5	

Time: ______ Score: ______

Scoring: Less than 16 minutes = 15 points;
16–35 minutes = 10 points; over 35 minutes = 5 points

87

6								
	9		4				7	
1					7	4		9
		9		3			1	7
8	3		9					
		7		6			9	4
3					2	6		8
	2		6				3	
7								

Time: Score:

Scoring: Less than 16 minutes = 15 points;
16–35 minutes = 10 points; over 35 minutes = 5 points

88

3		9	8					
	1				4			
			9		2			
	6		4			1	3	
		7	6					
	2			1	5	6		4
	7			9				5
		4	5		7		1	
								9

Time: Score:

*Scoring: Less than 16 minutes = 15 points;
16–35 minutes = 10 points; over 35 minutes = 5 points*

89

	9	2		7	1			
	5		9			8	7	
6	1			2				4
	7						3	
8				3			1	6
	4	9			3		6	
			4	8		5	9	

Time: Score:

Scoring: Less than 16 minutes = 15 points;
16–35 minutes = 10 points; over 35 minutes = 5 points

90

			5					
5			4					9
	8	4	2	6				
	3	7	9					
		2				9		
					5	1	4	
				4	2	8	3	
7					9			1
					1			

Time: ______ Score: ______

Scoring: Less than 16 minutes = 15 points;
16–35 minutes = 10 points; over 35 minutes = 5 points

91

							4	
			6					7
1	8	5		2				
		3		6				
	5		9		1	8		
2		8		4			9	
	2		8		4	1		
	7	1		5		4		
			1			3		

Time: Score:

Scoring: Less than 16 minutes = 15 points;
16–35 minutes = 10 points; over 35 minutes = 5 points

92

								2
			6		7			
				8		3		
	3				1	2	5	
		9				1		7
	7		5		8		6	
		4	8	3				1
			2		4		7	
1				9		6		

Time: Score:

Scoring: Less than 16 minutes = 15 points;
16–35 minutes = 10 points; over 35 minutes = 5 points

93

		6		3	5	9	1	
	7		2		1	5		
		1	8				5	
	9				7			1
		5	3				7	
	8		1		6	7		
		7		5	2	6	3	

Time: ______ Score: ______

Scoring: Less than 16 minutes = 15 points;
16–35 minutes = 10 points; over 35 minutes = 5 points

94

		3		2		1	6	
4		1						7
	8				1			2
	4				5	6		
1	7		4					9
			9	1				
9							8	6
				5	6	2		
		2		8			4	

Time:

Score:

Scoring: Less than 16 minutes = 15 points;
16–35 minutes = 10 points; over 35 minutes = 5 points

95

	1						7	
4								1
			7		3			
		1	5		7	2		
		5		4		9		
			3	2	6			
6		8	2		1	4		5
7		9				3		6

Time: Score:

Scoring: Less than 16 minutes = 15 points;
16–35 minutes = 10 points; over 35 minutes = 5 points

96

								8
				5		4		1
		9	4		8			2
4		8	6					
	6	3	8		2	1	5	
					7	6		4
8			1		3	9		
3		4		8				
7								

Time: Score:

Scoring: Less than 16 minutes = 15 points;
16–35 minutes = 10 points; over 35 minutes = 5 points

97

			7	2	9			
	1		3		6		8	
		8	2		7	1		
7								4
		6		5		9		
6								5
	5		8		4		9	
	7	4		1		8	2	

Time: Score:

Scoring: Less than 16 minutes = 15 points;
16–35 minutes = 10 points; over 35 minutes = 5 points

98

			8	4	7	2		
6			9			3		7
	1		7				6	3
7			6		2			5
5	3				8		7	
8		4			3			1
		9	1	7	4			

Time: ______ Score: ______

Scoring: Less than 16 minutes = 15 points;
16–35 minutes = 10 points; over 35 minutes = 5 points

99

	7	2	1	8		6		
	4				9		5	
		9			5	3		
6	3		7				2	
		4		3			1	
		1	8		3		4	
				7		1	3	
				4				

Time: Score:

Scoring: Less than 16 minutes = 15 points;
16–35 minutes = 10 points; over 35 minutes = 5 points

100

						3		
		5	6					2
	6						5	8
	1				7	4		5
					3			
			5	9		2	8	1
7			4		6			
		3			9		2	4
	4	6	2		8		7	

Time: Score:

Scoring: Less than 16 minutes = 15 points;
16–35 minutes = 10 points; over 35 minutes = 5 points

101

6								
			9			4	1	
			4		2	8		6
		6					5	7
2			6	3	7			8
4	7					1		
7		1	2		8			
	6	2			4			
								5

Time: ____ Score: ____

Scoring: Less than 16 minutes = 15 points;
16–35 minutes = 10 points; over 35 minutes = 5 points

102

			7		2			
7			4		3			1
		2				5		
	2	8				1	7	
		6	8		5	3		
	7	9		4		8	5	
				3				
	3		5		8		2	
			9		7			

Time: Score:

Scoring: Less than 16 minutes = 15 points;
16–35 minutes = 10 points; over 35 minutes = 5 points

103

						9		
		5		3				
	8		5	6			2	
		3				1	7	
	2	6			1		4	
				9				5
6			1					4
		2	7	4				3
					8	7	9	

Time: ____ Score: ____

Scoring: Less than 16 minutes = 15 points;
16–35 minutes = 10 points; over 35 minutes = 5 points

104

						1		
			4		6			8
	8			7	5			6
		6			1		4	2
	4		3		8		5	
5	3		2			8		
4			7	9			1	
9			5		4			
		7						

Time: Score:

Scoring: Less than 16 minutes = 15 points;
16–35 minutes = 10 points; over 35 minutes = 5 points

105

6				1			3	
5	1		9					
		8				4		1
					9			2
9	8		3			7		
					1			9
		1				2		7
8	7		5					
3				2			5	

Time: Score:

Scoring: Less than 16 minutes = 15 points;
16–35 minutes = 10 points; over 35 minutes = 5 points

106

				3		8		2
			4	1				
3		2					6	
	1	9		5	3			4
6		3				2		7
2			9	6		1	5	
	7					4		6
				9	4			
4		1		8				

Time: Score:

Scoring: Less than 16 minutes = 15 points;
16–35 minutes = 10 points; over 35 minutes = 5 points

107

		1				5		
				2				
		5	1	8	7	2		
		2	6		4	1		
				9				
3			8		1			4
9			7		3			2
6	4						9	5
	1						4	

Time: Score:

Scoring: Less than 16 minutes = 15 points;
16–35 minutes = 10 points; over 35 minutes = 5 points

108

			3					
		1					2	3
		7	1			5		4
	4		6		3		8	7
		8		5		2		
3	7		8		9		4	
9		3			1	4		
4	1					7		
					4			

Time: Score:

Scoring: Less than 16 minutes = 15 points;
16–35 minutes = 10 points; over 35 minutes = 5 points

109

	7		6			4	8	5
	2	4	5					
	8	6			9	5		2
	9		2		5	1		
	5	2			3	7		4
	6	7	3					
	1		9			2	4	3

Time: 　　　　 Score:

Scoring: Less than 16 minutes = 15 points;
16–35 minutes = 10 points; over 35 minutes = 5 points

110

	9		2		4		3	
		5				2		
			5	6	8			
		1	4		2	6		
	7	3	6		1	9	8	
		8	7		9	1		
	8	7				3	4	
3								9
	6						1	

Time: ______ Score: ______

Scoring: Less than 16 minutes = 15 points;
16–35 minutes = 10 points; over 35 minutes = 5 points

111

7			5		6			2
				3				
		5				4		
		6	8		7	1		
9		3		2		5		8
1	6		7		8		3	4
4								6
	8		4		9		1	

Time: Score:

Scoring: Less than 16 minutes = 15 points;
16–35 minutes = 10 points; over 35 minutes = 5 points

112

				2	1			
			8			7		
				6			2	4
	5				3	1		8
9		4				3		
3			9			4	6	2
	9		3	1	4			
		2			6			
		5	2		8			3

Time: Score:

Scoring: Less than 16 minutes = 15 points;
16–35 minutes = 10 points; over 35 minutes = 5 points

113

8	3						4	2
4	6						1	7
			4		8			
		6	1		3	4		
	4		2		9		7	
		8	7	9	6	5		
5		9				7		6

Time: ______ Score: ______

Scoring: Less than 16 minutes = 15 points;
16–35 minutes = 10 points; over 35 minutes = 5 points

114

							5	
	4	3	7				8	
6					1	3		
2					3			4
	3		8		4		2	
8			5					3
		6	1					8
	7				8	1	3	
	2							

Time: ______ Score: ______

Scoring: Less than 16 minutes = 15 points;
16–35 minutes = 10 points; over 35 minutes = 5 points

115

				9	2			1
			1		8			
2						3	9	
		9					3	6
5			3		1			8
		3					2	4
8						4	6	
			5		3			
				4	9			3

Time: Score:

Scoring: Less than 16 minutes = 15 points;
16–35 minutes = 10 points; over 35 minutes = 5 points

116

						5		
	9						3	
2	7		1					4
		9		2				
6	5	2	4		7			
1				5		2		
	1	6		3	2			
		4		8		7	2	
			6	4		9		

Time: ______ Score: ______

Scoring: Less than 16 minutes = 15 points;
16–35 minutes = 10 points; over 35 minutes = 5 points

117

			2					
			1	7		3		
					6	2	9	
1	5							
	7			8		5	3	
		2					6	8
	8	3		2				
		5		6	7			3
					1		2	

Time: Score:

Scoring: Less than 16 minutes = 15 points;
16–35 minutes = 10 points; over 35 minutes = 5 points

118

			5	3				9
					9	3		
					1	4	7	
		5				2	9	
8	4		1					3
	2			4				6
	7	3			2			
	1	2	7	9				
				1				

Time: ____ Score: ____

Scoring: Less than 16 minutes = 15 points;
16–35 minutes = 10 points; over 35 minutes = 5 points

119

	1	8	2					6
		6		8	9		1	2
6					4	2		9
					7	6	3	
1					8	5		4
		5		1	2		9	3
	2	4	9					8

Time: Score:

Scoring: Less than 16 minutes = 15 points;
16–35 minutes = 10 points; over 35 minutes = 5 points

120

								2
	6						7	
8		2			4			
7	2		5			3		
1			6					
		5		7	3			
6	9		8			7		
	1	8			7		3	
		3		6	9	2		

Time: Score:

Scoring: Less than 16 minutes = 15 points;
16–35 minutes = 10 points; over 35 minutes = 5 points

121

			3		5	4	9	
	2			1	7			8
3		8		9				4
						1		
2		6		4				7
	9			3	1			2
			9		6	7	3	

Time: Score:

Scoring: Less than 16 minutes = 15 points;
16–35 minutes = 10 points; over 35 minutes = 5 points

122

			7	6		5		
		8	5	1	9		3	
			1			4		
2			8			6	5	
		1		9	6	8	2	
	9		2			3		
1	5	3						
6	8			5				

Time: Score:

Scoring: Less than 16 minutes = 15 points;
16–35 minutes = 10 points; over 35 minutes = 5 points

123

	9	8				3	6	
2	5						7	4
7			9		3			6
5								9
	2		8		5		3	
	6			1			4	
	7	9	5		8	2	1	
			4		2			

Time: ______ Score: ______

Scoring: Less than 16 minutes = 15 points;
16–35 minutes = 10 points; over 35 minutes = 5 points

124

					6			
9	6					1	8	
2	1			5			9	4
	5			6				9
		3		4		8		
8				3			5	
5	4			8			7	1
	3	2					6	8
			9					

Time:

Score:

Scoring: Less than 16 minutes = 15 points;
16–35 minutes = 10 points; over 35 minutes = 5 points

125

		4			9		5	
	6	1	7	3				
		9		2		3		8
4	5		8		3		1	2
2		3		9		5		
				6	4	7	8	
	7		9			2		

Time: Score:

Scoring: Less than 16 minutes = 15 points;
16–35 minutes = 10 points; over 35 minutes = 5 points

126

						9		
	7	3			5	8		
	8						7	3
	1	6		3			5	
9	5		2		7			
				1				
4					8		9	
				2	4	1	8	
		7		6				

Time: Score:

Scoring: Less than 20 minutes = 15 points; 20–45 minutes = 10 points; over 45 minutes = 5 points

127

								8
5						4		
		2		6	5		3	9
2	9		3		7			
1	3						9	7
			1		8		2	6
6	1		8	2		9		
		3						5
4								

Time: Score:

Scoring: Less than 20 minutes = 15 points;
20–45 minutes = 10 points; over 45 minutes = 5 points

128

			9				1	
					4	7		
			2				9	3
					1	5		2
	1	9	8		5	4	7	
5		6	3					
1	4				3			
		8	7					
	5				2			

Time:

Score:

Scoring: Less than 20 minutes = 15 points;
20–45 minutes = 10 points; over 45 minutes = 5 points

129

					3			
	4		6					2
		6			1	4		9
4		7					8	
1	9	5	4					
6		2					3	
		8			4	2		6
	7		9					3
					5			

Time:

Score:

Scoring: Less than 20 minutes = 15 points;
20–45 minutes = 10 points; over 45 minutes = 5 points

130

		8				7		
				1				
6	3						8	5
		4	2		3	8		
	8	6				1	7	
	9	5	6		7	3	1	
3	1		4		8		6	2

Time:

Score:

Scoring: Less than 20 minutes = 15 points;
20–45 minutes = 10 points; over 45 minutes = 5 points

131

	5				6			
6							5	8
	9		7		8			
		5	4		7	2		1
		2	3		1	9		5
	1		8		2			
5							7	9
	4				5			

Time: Score:

Scoring: Less than 20 minutes = 15 points;
20–45 minutes = 10 points; over 45 minutes = 5 points

132

			3		8			
	4						7	
1								9
	2		6		5		9	
	7			8			5	
4	1						2	6
2				6				3
		4				2		
7		6	2		4	9		1

Time: ______ Score: ______

Scoring: Less than 20 minutes = 15 points;
20–45 minutes = 10 points; over 45 minutes = 5 points

133

3								
5			2				8	
8			6	4		2	5	
		4		8				
		8	1		4	9		
				9		4		
	9	3		2	1			7
	5				6			3
								1

Time: Score:

Scoring: Less than 20 minutes = 15 points;
20–45 minutes = 10 points; over 45 minutes = 5 points

134

7								
			8				2	3
1		4	3		5	9		
	6	2						1
		1	5		2	6		
3						7	4	
		5	7		3	2		8
6	3				8			
								5

Time: ______ Score: ______

Scoring: Less than 20 minutes = 15 points;
20–45 minutes = 10 points; over 45 minutes = 5 points

135

			7			9		
3				2		8		
8	7			3			2	4
		6	5					
7		8				5	6	
					9			7
5	8			1	2			
		9				3		
4		2		9		7	5	

Time: Score:

Scoring: Less than 20 minutes = 15 points;
20–45 minutes = 10 points; over 45 minutes = 5 points

136

					9	7	5	
2								4
	5			6				1
			3		4			6
		8	7			2		
	3			1	2			
1				4				
8	9		2			5		
	4	7					9	

Time: Score:

Scoring: Less than 20 minutes = 15 points;
20–45 minutes = 10 points; over 45 minutes = 5 points

137

								1
	8					5	6	
				7	1	3	8	
9		4			7	2		
		7	6			4		
	6			3				
8				6	3			
3			5				9	
4	5	2			8			

Time: Score:

Scoring: Less than 20 minutes = 15 points;
20–45 minutes = 10 points; over 45 minutes = 5 points

138

								4
4				2	8	7		5
5		8			9		1	
				5		2		
6		5				4		7
		1		9				
	6		3			1		9
2		3	9	1				6
1								

Time: Score:

Scoring: Less than 20 minutes = 15 points;
20–45 minutes = 10 points; over 45 minutes = 5 points

139

7					8			1
	6	3						9
				4		8		3
	9	8		3	4		2	
	7	6		1	5		3	
				8		7		6
	8	5						2
1					2			4

Time: Score:

Scoring: Less than 20 minutes = 15 points;
20–45 minutes = 10 points; over 45 minutes = 5 points

140

						3		
8							5	9
			9	1	2			4
2		3	8					6
7	8			6			1	3
9					1	4		2
6			7	2	4			
4	9							5
		8						

Time:

Score:

Scoring: Less than 20 minutes = 15 points;
20–45 minutes = 10 points; over 45 minutes = 5 points

141

3						9		
		1	3				4	
				4	1			3
	3	4				7		
	9	5	6	2		8		
				7			9	
5				9	2		8	
				1	6			
		2						5

Time: | Score:

Scoring: Less than 20 minutes = 15 points; 20–45 minutes = 10 points; over 45 minutes = 5 points

142

				8		4		
			5					
		7					1	6
	5			2	8		3	7
9			3					
			9			8	6	
4					2	1		
		3	6		5			2
		2	8				4	

Time: 　　　Score:

Scoring: Less than 20 minutes = 15 points;
20–45 minutes = 10 points; over 45 minutes = 5 points

143

					4			1
1			2			3		
			7	6		2	4	
	1					7	9	
	6				2			
	5					4	2	
			8	4		6	5	
3			1			8		
					5			4

Time: [ ] Score: [ ]

Scoring: Less than 20 minutes = 15 points;
20–45 minutes = 10 points; over 45 minutes = 5 points

144

				7		6		
			4	5		9		
			2		6		3	
	8	4		1	7			9
7	5		6					
		6	8				4	5
1	4							6
		3			2			
			7		8	5		

Time: ______ Score: ______

Scoring: Less than 20 minutes = 15 points; 20–45 minutes = 10 points; over 45 minutes = 5 points

145

					4			2
		1		7				5
	7		8			1		
		4	2			5		9
	9					8		
7							2	
		3	9	5				8
					3		6	
2	1		7			4		

Time: ________ Score: ________

Scoring: Less than 20 minutes = 15 points;
20–45 minutes = 10 points; over 45 minutes = 5 points

146

	2		3		4		5	
		4				8		
9		5		6		7		4
4			7		6			1
		8				9		
5			9		2			8
7		6		1		2		9
		9				6		
	8		6		9		1	

Time: Score:

Scoring: Less than 20 minutes = 15 points;
20–45 minutes = 10 points; over 45 minutes = 5 points

147

		9		7		3		
5			3	8	1			6
1								7
	5		4		8		3	
4								8
	9		2		7		5	
9								5
8			1	4	6			9
		7		9		1		

Time: ______ Score: ______

Scoring: Less than 20 minutes = 15 points;
20–45 minutes = 10 points; over 45 minutes = 5 points

148

		2		8		7		
	3						2	
		3				8		
		7				6		
5	1		7		3		9	4
	5			9			7	
		9	1		5	3		
3			6		2			8

Time: Score:

Scoring: Less than 20 minutes = 15 points;
20–45 minutes = 10 points; over 45 minutes = 5 points

149

							5	
			2		9			7
	9	6		1		2		
6			4	9	1			5
	4		8		3			
1			6	2	7			4
	5	1		4		7		
			7		8			1
							9	

Time: Score:

Scoring: Less than 20 minutes = 15 points;
20–45 minutes = 10 points; over 45 minutes = 5 points

150

			8	9	6			
	2	6				7	4	
	4		6		1		5	
7								2
3								8
		4	1		3	6		
	3						2	
		2	4	8	7	3		

Time: Score:

Scoring: Less than 20 minutes = 15 points;
20–45 minutes = 10 points; over 45 minutes = 5 points

151

	1		8		9		2	4
4	2	6					3	
	4			9			5	2
1		9		2				
	5			8			1	6
2	6	1					9	
	9		6		3		4	1

Time: ______ Score: ______

Scoring: Less than 25 minutes = 15 points;
25–55 minutes = 10 points; over 55 minutes = 5 points

152

			2	7	4	1		
			6	9		8	7	
	4			6	7		9	
	2				8	4	3	
9						6	1	
2	1	4						
3		8		2	5			
	9	5	1					

Time: ________ Score: ________

Scoring: Less than 25 minutes = 15 points;
25–55 minutes = 10 points; over 55 minutes = 5 points

153

	9							5
2		6				1		
				2			9	
			4					
1	4	9				8		
6	5	3			9			
	8		1	6			3	
		1	9	7				8
9			3	8			2	

Time: Score:

Scoring: Less than 25 minutes = 15 points;
25–55 minutes = 10 points; over 55 minutes = 5 points

154

				1		2	9	
								4
6		5	4					7
	1		3	8				
8					7			5
		6			9	8		
9			2			7		
4					8			
	6	1		9		4		

Time: Score:

Scoring: Less than 25 minutes = 15 points;
25–55 minutes = 10 points; over 55 minutes = 5 points

155

				9		5		1
					4			2
	9	6	8					
	7			2	6			
	2		9				5	7
	4			8	5			
	1	2	3					
					9			3
				4		2		6

Time: ____ Score: ____

Scoring: Less than 25 minutes = 15 points;
25–55 minutes = 10 points; over 55 minutes = 5 points

156

	5					2	4	
9	7	1			5			8
2		3		6				5
			5		9			
5				1		4		3
4			1			3	9	7
	1	8					2	

Time: Score:

Scoring: Less than 25 minutes = 15 points;
25–55 minutes = 10 points; over 55 minutes = 5 points

157

		9	6		8	2		
	2		5		9		6	
	7		2		5		9	
		2				7		
4	1						3	2
2								5
	4	1				3	7	
3	9	7				1	2	8

Time: Score:

Scoring: Less than 25 minutes = 15 points;
25–55 minutes = 10 points; over 55 minutes = 5 points

158

		1	8		9	4		
	9						6	
	6	7	5		1	9	3	
		9		3		5		
	7						4	
1	5		7		4		9	3
			6		7			
7	8						1	9
			4		8			

Time: Score:

Scoring: Less than 25 minutes = 15 points;
25–55 minutes = 10 points; over 55 minutes = 5 points

159

					7			5
	6					2	8	
2		7		5				
	1		2	9	5			
			1				3	
	8		7	3	4			
8		2		7				
	9					6	7	
					9			4

Time:

Score:

Scoring: Less than 25 minutes = 15 points;
25–55 minutes = 10 points; over 55 minutes = 5 points

160

	1					4	6	
			3	4		1		5
		2		9		6		3
		3	6		5			7
				3				
	7	6	9					
	5							6
		4	7	2			5	9

Time: Score:

*Scoring: Less than 25 minutes = 15 points;
25–55 minutes = 10 points; over 55 minutes = 5 points*

161

	7						5	
				3				
		2	6		7	1		
3		9	5		2	7		1
8		5				9		3
		7				5		
7			3	4	6			9
		3	8	7	9	6		

Time: Score:

Scoring: Less than 25 minutes = 15 points;
25–55 minutes = 10 points; over 55 minutes = 5 points

162

		9			3	5	8	
7	8					9	3	2
	3			5				
5		6	3		7	2		8
				2			4	
8	5	7					9	3
	2	3	6			8		

Time:

Score:

Scoring: Less than 25 minutes = 15 points;
25–55 minutes = 10 points; over 55 minutes = 5 points

163

				6				
		1	3		7	8		
		7	6		9	4		
		8		5		2		
	3		7		8		1	
		2				9		
5								4
4	9	6	2		5	1	8	7

Time:

Score:

Scoring: Less than 25 minutes = 15 points;
25–55 minutes = 10 points; over 55 minutes = 5 points

164

							4	8
					7	6		
	1	6	5		3			
4		7	2					
	2	1	7	8			6	
6		8	9					
	7	9	1		5			
					9	5		
							2	9

Time:

Score:

Scoring: Less than 25 minutes = 15 points;
25–55 minutes = 10 points; over 55 minutes = 5 points

165

			1	8	4			
6	2		5		7		8	4
2		1				5		8
	9			6			4	
3		4				6		9
7	1		4		8		3	5
			3	7	1			

Time: Score:

Scoring: Less than 25 minutes = 15 points;
25–55 minutes = 10 points; over 55 minutes = 5 points

166

		5	3					8
4						5		
	7		4				9	
	9		6	8				
5	6				3			
		7			2	6		9
9			7					2
				1	4	9		
		4		3			1	

Time: Score:

Scoring: Less than 25 minutes = 15 points;
25–55 minutes = 10 points; over 55 minutes = 5 points

167

		7						4
4		9			3			
	8	5		9				
		4		8			6	
1			7		6	2		
5	9			2				
					7	6	2	9
			8			7		
			6	3			5	

Time: Score:

Scoring: Less than 25 minutes = 15 points;
25–55 minutes = 10 points; over 55 minutes = 5 points

168

		9				6		
				5	7			8
	1	5	8				2	
				1	5		9	
7	5		2		9		4	1
	9		7	8				
	2				8	1	6	
3			5	6				
		1				3		

Time: ______ Score: ______

Scoring: Less than 25 minutes = 15 points; 25–55 minutes = 10 points; over 55 minutes = 5 points

169

			2	8	4			
4			7		5			6
		6				9		
		9	4		7	1		
	1			2			4	
8			3		1			4
5								3
	2						5	

Time: ______ Score: ______

Scoring: Less than 25 minutes = 15 points;
25–55 minutes = 10 points; over 55 minutes = 5 points

170

							4	5
		4	6	9		3		
1							6	
		7	4		2			
4	1	6	7					
		9	3		1			
5							3	
		2	5	4		9		
							2	6

Time: ______ Score: ______

Scoring: Less than 25 minutes = 15 points;
25–55 minutes = 10 points; over 55 minutes = 5 points

171

3								7
		9				8	5	
			5	8	7	1	3	
		6		5	1			
4								1
			2	9		7		
	8	3	6	7	2			
	6	7				9		
2								6

Time: Score:

Scoring: Less than 25 minutes = 15 points;
25–55 minutes = 10 points; over 55 minutes = 5 points

172

		5		6				
		4			9			
		7		4	1	8		5
8		9					6	
5		1				9		8
	6					4		3
2		3	6	9		5		
			1			6		
				3		7		

Time: ______ Score: ______

Scoring: Less than 25 minutes = 15 points;
25–55 minutes = 10 points; over 55 minutes = 5 points

173

1								9
		5	6	2	9	4		
9		7				1		8
		2	9		8	7		
	2			1			4	
	4		2		7		6	
6			5		3			7

Time: Score:

Scoring: Less than 25 minutes = 15 points;
25–55 minutes = 10 points; over 55 minutes = 5 points

174

					3			2
				5	4	9		
1		9						4
		8			1		7	
3	5						9	6
	6		3			2		
6						8		9
		7	6	8				
5			9					

Time: Score:

Scoring: Less than 25 minutes = 15 points;
25–55 minutes = 10 points; over 55 minutes = 5 points

175

					4	8		9
			9	1	2		6	7
	4	5			1	9		
		6				3	8	
	3	9			8	5		
			2	5	6		9	4
					7	2		3

Time: Score:

Scoring: Less than 25 minutes = 15 points;
25–55 minutes = 10 points; over 55 minutes = 5 points

SQUIFFY SUDOKU

SQUIFFY RULES

Have a look at this slightly comical Sudoku. I call these grids Squiffy Sudoku because it's sometimes how a classic puzzle looks when you've come home from a night on the town!

Squiffy Sudoku is not the most complicated grid around but it is amusing simply because of its shape.

This time the mini-grids are strangely shaped. However, they always contain 9 boxes and the rules are exactly the same as before.

Each row must contain the numbers 1 through to 9.

Each column must contain the numbers 1 through to 9.

Each squiffy mini-grid must contain the numbers 1 through to 9.

This grid is the first Squiffy Sudoku (puzzle 176) in the puzzles we give you in this section. Here are a few tips on how to solve it.

First of all, choose a mini-grid and then try to slice and dice a number into it. I've circled some boxes where numbers can be immediately placed. Try to complete them.

Work your way through mini-grids in turn and then look at rows and columns.

			4			2		
9		6		4				3
		○						9
		7		○	1		2	
6	○	5					7	
	2		7		5		○	
		8	9				5	
			○			9	○	1
2				7			6	

			4			2		
9		6		4				3
		2						9
		7		9	1		2	
6	9	5					7	
	2		7		5		9	
		8	9				5	
		○	5			9	3	1
2		○		7			6	

Analyzing rows and columns in turn is the key to solving a Squiffy Sudoku. You have to work your way across a row or down a column carefully studying which numbers are missing and which are already included in the misshapen mini-grids that cross over the row or column in question. Here's an example.

Have a look at the grid now and study column 3. We know that the numbers 1 3 4 and 9 are missing but where do they go?

We know that number 9 can't go in row 1 as it already exists in that squiffy mini-grid. Number 9 can't go in row 6 for the same reason. Nor can it be placed in row 8 as a number 9 already exists in that row. Therefore, number 9 must be placed in row 9 of column 3. Fill it in now.

Now look at (column 3, row 8). The missing numbers in column 3 are 1 3 and 4. However, 1 and 3 have already been placed in row 8 so the number to be filled in on row 8 in column 3 is the only number now possible which is number 4. Fill it in.

We can't go any further but we can start to look at column 8 and a couple of other squiffy mini-grids using the traditional Sudoku rules of slicing and dicing.

It isn't as simple to do Squiffy Sudoku in the traditional order of a classic extreme puzzle. Somehow the clues manage to jump around the grid a lot more.

I hope you like these puzzles. They're very nice with a cup of tea and a biscuit!

176

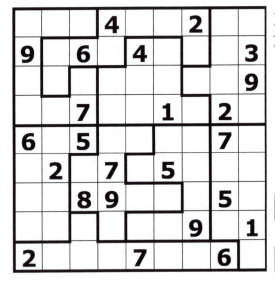

			4			2		
9		6		4				3
								9
		7			1		2	
6		5					7	
	2		7		5			
		8	9				5	
						9		1
2				7			6	

Scoring:
Less than 20 mins = 15 points
20–35 mins = 10 points
over 35 mins = 5 points

Time:

Score:

177

								8
	1		6	5		9		
		3		4				
			9	8			3	
					4			1
	2		4		6			
7			8				1	
5							9	7
			1	9			2	

Scoring:
Less than 20 mins = 15 points
20–35 mins = 10 points
over 35 mins = 5 points

Time:

Score:

178

Scoring:
Less than 20 mins = 15 points
20–35 mins = 10 points
over 35 mins = 5 points

	9	3					2	
4					1			
7					2	8		5
1		8					6	
			3		9			4
	3					5		7
			6					
		7	2			1		9
2							3	

Time:

Score:

179

Scoring:
Less than 20 mins = 15 points
20–35 mins = 10 points
over 35 mins = 5 points

7	4		9					2
				1				
	5				7			9
		2		4	9	6		
						2		
			1		6			3
3	7		6				9	
	8					5		
	9	7		2				

Time:

Score:

180

4			6				2	
7		2						
		4			5	8		
		3	2			1		
3		5				4		1
5		6						
				2				9
	6			1	3		5	
8			3					4

Scoring:
Less than 20 mins = 15 points
20–35 mins = 10 points
over 35 mins = 5 points

Time:

Score:

181

		5	3	6				
		6				3		
9							1	
5			6				4	2
	3						2	
6		4	9					8
	1	8		4				5
1					5		7	
4			5		6			

Scoring:
Less than 20 mins = 15 points
20–35 mins = 10 points
over 35 mins = 5 points

Time:

Score:

182

Scoring:
Less than 20 mins = 15 points
20–35 mins = 10 points
over 35 mins = 5 points

	5				7	3		
	4				2		5	9
9								
2		5		6				
6			2			7		
				5			4	
		7		8	9	6		
								3
4		8	1					6

Time:

Score:

183

Scoring:
Less than 20 mins = 15 points
20–35 mins = 10 points
over 35 mins = 5 points

5							4	
7						3	2	
		6	7					
	4				6	7		
		1					9	
	5						6	
	8	2		7	1			
1			8		3			
	6					9		5

Time:

Score:

184

			8	3			6	
	7				9			8
	4	9	3			1		
1			6					7
2	9			1				5
						7		
			5				2	
	8			7			3	
	2				6			

Scoring:
Less than 20 mins = 15 points
20–35 mins = 10 points
over 35 mins = 5 points

Time:

Score:

185

	9			2		8	3	
			8			6		
		3					9	6
7	1			4			5	
8					2			
		4	1	3		5		
6							7	
		1	6	8				2
	4					7		

Scoring:
Less than 20 mins = 15 points
20–35 mins = 10 points
over 35 mins = 5 points

Time:

Score:

186

Scoring:
Less than 20 mins = 15 points
20–35 mins = 10 points
over 35 mins = 5 points

		3	6		5	4		
						2		8
	7					3	1	
4		6						
7			3		8			4
	8	1						
	6			9	3		5	1
		2			9			
			1				4	9

Time:

Score:

187

Scoring:
Less than 20 mins = 15 points
20–35 mins = 10 points
over 35 mins = 5 points

3								2
6					3	1		4
1				7	8		9	3
		3			4		7	
						6		
8	1						5	
					5			
7	6				9	4	1	

Time:

Score:

188

7			9			6		
					3		1	
		8	6		2			
	7						4	
5	4		1			3		
				6	8		9	7
		4	7				2	
8	2		3					
		1		5				

Scoring:
Less than 20 mins = 15 points
20–35 mins = 10 points
over 35 mins = 5 points

Time:

Score:

189

						4		5
3		9			7			
				1			9	
1			5		4			
	3		6	2		1		
	7	8						
				8				2
		1				9		6
	2						7	

Scoring:
Less than 20 mins = 15 points
20–35 mins = 10 points
over 35 mins = 5 points

Time:

Score:

190

Scoring:
Less than 20 mins = 15 points
20–35 mins = 10 points
over 35 mins = 5 points

	4		1					3
			8	2		7		
	5	6		7	9			
						8	2	
1								
	7				2			5
9							7	
	8		7		6			1
3		5					8	

Time:

Score:

191

Scoring:
Less than 20 mins = 15 points
20–35 mins = 10 points
over 35 mins = 5 points

		2		4		1		3
		8					9	
7				6				
		7					8	5
	2		8		3			
			3				1	
		9			7			
		6			2	3		
4			6				5	2

Time:

Score:

192

				1				
2		1						8
			4	3			7	
8			2					
		6						
7	2			8		6		4
					1			5
	6							
	9				6	1		2

Scoring:
Less than 20 mins = 15 points
20–35 mins = 10 points
over 35 mins = 5 points

Time:

Score:

193

8					3			
5			8	2			1	9
	3						7	
2		6						5
9			7					8
4		5						2
	8	7			2		5	
			6			3		7

Scoring:
Less than 20 mins = 15 points
20–35 mins = 10 points
over 35 mins = 5 points

Time:

Score:

194

Scoring:
Less than 20 mins = 15 points
20–35 mins = 10 points
over 35 mins = 5 points

9					6			
	4						1	
			4	7		6	3	
		8			1			
			2					8
1	3	9						
							6	2
		2		9				
		5						4

Time:

Score:

195

Scoring:
Less than 20 mins = 15 points
20–35 mins = 10 points
over 35 mins = 5 points

				8				
5			7			3		4
		4			2		3	
		1		5			6	
2			3	6		7		
					9			
6					3	8		
			2				7	
	4		1					2

Time:

Score:

196

		3			4		2	
		5					6	9
1						2		
3							8	
	2		4			6		3
9				8		7		
							7	
	4							
				3			1	7

Scoring:
Less than 20 mins = 15 points
20–35 mins = 10 points
over 35 mins = 5 points

Time:

Score:

197

2	5			4				
			2	7		5		6
	6							8
		7		6		1		
							5	
		6			4			
	9	1				7		
3		4		2			9	
					1	3	4	

Scoring:
Less than 20 mins = 15 points
20–35 mins = 10 points
over 35 mins = 5 points

Time:

Score:

198

Scoring:
Less than 20 mins = 15 points
20–35 mins = 10 points
over 35 mins = 5 points

4	7	9	1		2			
					4	3		7
	9	4	6					
				2		8	1	
								8
		8	3			2		4
3	2			4		6		
		6						1

Time:

Score:

199

Scoring:
Less than 20 mins = 15 points
20–35 mins = 10 points
over 35 mins = 5 points

		2			9		1	
6	9						4	
						6		
		8		4			3	
8			3					
	6	1						8
				3				9
1		5			2			

Time:

Score:

200

7		5			3			
		7			8		4	
9			3					7
2	4							
	8	3			9			
		9				2		8
		2			7			6
			6					
						8	6	9

Scoring:
Less than 20 mins = 15 points
20–35 mins = 10 points
over 35 mins = 5 points

Time:

Score:

SUDOKU 16

SUDOKU 16 RULES

	11		6	16			8	10			9	1		12	
4		9				13	1	5	8				3		2
	13			4	5					15	1			11	
16						10	7	4	14						5
3		16		5		7			4		2		10		1
		13				11			6				5		
	10		1	14	6	9			15	13	5	4		8	
2	15		7									3		6	16
8	4		16									9		7	14
	14		2	8	9	3			11	6	4	5		16	
		6				15			9				12		
13		10		12		2			7		16		11		6
14						16	6	11	10						3
	12			7	4					1	14			2	
6		1				12	14	7	5				8		11
	5		11	9			10	6			3	13		15	

Just as Squiffy Sudoku is lovely with a cup of tea and a biscuit, Sudoku 16 is the perfect extreme Sudoku for those who have a whole afternoon to spare. Expect some of the following 25 puzzles to take you a number of hours to complete.

It might also be useful to enlarge the puzzle. Copy it onto a piece of paper with larger squares than we have been able to print in this book as you will need to write in options and these can become very complicated due to the sheer scale of the exercise.

Sudoku 16 follows the same rules as classic Sudoku 9 except that there are 16 rows, 16 columns and 16 mini-grids.

Therefore, each row, column and mini-grid needs to hold the numbers from 1 through to 16.

All the tips and tricks used to solve extreme classic Sudoku can be used in just the same way here.

However, be very careful. When you're writing options, it's so easy to write an option for "12" and mistake it for options for the numbers "1" and "2". You really do have to check constantly for simple errors. One way of getting around this is to circle an option for a two-digit number, say number "12", like this (12). In this way, it's much easier to distinguish between single and two-digit numbers. You really don't want to waste hours of work just by misreading an option.

I always start Sudoku 16 in the traditional manner. Try to complete as many numbers as possible by slicing and dicing or completing rows, columns and mini-grids with just 3 or 4 missing numbers. It is usually possible to make some kind of contribution to the final solution in this way. Then the really tough work begins. Start to write numerical options in all boxes using slicing and slotting wherever you can. Above all else, remember to erase your options once you've filled in a number. In Sudoku 16 you can go wrong so easily and I don't want you taking your frustrations out on your loved ones and then blaming me!

Sharpen your pencils, settle down and enjoy!

201

	11		6	16			8	10			9	1		12	
4		9				13	1	5	8				3		2
	13			4	5					15	1			11	
16						10	7	4	14						5
3		16		5		7			4		2		10		1
		13				11			6				5		
	10		1	14	6	9			15	13	5	4		8	
2	15		7									3		6	16
8	4		16									9		7	14
	14		2	8	9	3			11	6	4	5		16	
		6				15			9				12		
13		10		12		2			7		16		11		6
14						16	6	11	10						3
	12			7	4					1	14			2	
6		1				12	14	7	5				8		11
	5		11	9			10	6			3	13		15	

Time: Score:

Scoring: Less than 60 minutes = 15 points;
60–80 minutes = 10 points; over 80 minutes = 5 points

202

		3	10	2	16					7	1	14	5		
	7					15			10					1	
13			11	8			14	4			15	12			2
14		8			11		1	13		5			6		4
3		11			4		12	6		10			14		9
1			12	13			9	14			3	5			10
	10					3			16					11	
		14	4	1	8					15	5	7	13		
		2	15	11	3					12	4	16	9		
	9					1			13					7	
11			8	14			15	10			2	1			5
4		6			9		16	11		3			12		15
2		16			13		10	3		1			15		8
12			14	15			3	7			16	6			13
	8					14			6					12	
		13	7	16	6					11	8	9	4		

Time:

Score:

Scoring: Less than 60 minutes = 15 points;
60–80 minutes = 10 points; over 80 minutes = 5 points

203

	1		10		11	9	4	14	13	5		2		6	
2	15				7	13			6	9				16	8
			9	8							15	7			
5		12	7			16	15	8	3			9	4		14
		11			12					15			9		
16	5			15	6					13	10			1	11
14	12		8									3		7	2
6			13				5	2				10			15
7			15				11	1				4			10
11	6		16									5		8	12
12	14			10	4					11	9			13	7
		13			15					10			16		
15		8	6			3	7	9	11			16	14		1
			12	16							6	8			
9	16				2	12			5	8				10	6
	11		1		13	6	8	10	14	3		12		15	

Time:

Score:

Scoring: Less than 60 minutes = 15 points;
60–80 minutes = 10 points; over 80 minutes = 5 points

204

		14	16	15		5			6		8	4	3		
				4	3	13			5	9	15				
8		3		6		11			4		13		1		10
5															16
6	10	4					9	8					2	3	1
	13				4	12			3	7				15	
14	5	1			13		16	11		15			6	4	12
				8		14			13		10				
				12		16			10		3				
1	9	6			11		4	15		16			13	14	7
	4				1	10			2	14				12	
11	15	2					5	12					8	16	3
10															9
9		8		16		1			7		4		11		6
				2	10	3			16	5	14				
		15	2	9		6			12		11	3	16		

Time:

Score:

Scoring: Less than 60 minutes = 15 points;
60–80 minutes = 10 points; over 80 minutes = 5 points

SUDOKU 16 PUZZLES

205

	16		10		5	8	15	7	13	6		9		3	
15	7				1	3			16	5				14	13
			9	13							14	7			
8		3	13			7	2	15	1			5	10		6
		7			13					1			11		
13	2			16	7					10	8			5	1
14	10		6									8		12	2
4			5				12	3				16			15
10			7				3	9				15			11
2	1		12									4		6	7
3	5			7	15					11	4			10	9
		4			11					12			2		
16		15	14			13	1	8	7			11	9		10
			2	10							6	12			
9	6				2	16			11	14				15	3
	12		8		3	5	14	16	10	9		1		7	

Time:

Score:

Scoring: Less than 60 minutes = 15 points;
60–80 minutes = 10 points; over 80 minutes = 5 points

206

	6					13	11	1	2					12	
		1	2	5	9					8	15	11	10		
		3			15	10	6	9	5	4			8		
		7			1	2	5	14	12	16			13		
		5	16	13							9	7	2		
	1		14	11			3	13			2	6		16	
	12		11	4		9			3		6	10		5	
	11		7	2		5			16		3	12		4	
	13		10	15			16	7			4	5		2	
		15	6	12							11	3	9		
		16			11	7	10	12	9	1			6		
		9			3	6	12	5	11	7			16		
		10	4	8	2					13	16	15	7		
	14					4	13	10	15					6	

Time:

Score:

Scoring: Less than 60 minutes = 15 points;
60–80 minutes = 10 points; over 80 minutes = 5 points

207

	2	15			14	9			11	13			4	10	
14	1					13	12	7	6					9	3
12			16	8			5	1			3	13			2
		6			16					14			7		
		1			11					16			13		
11			13	14			8	6			7	3			4
3	12					1	6	4	13					5	15
	5	8			13	4			2	12			11	1	
	15	14			6	3			16	10			9	11	
1	4					11	10	5	9					8	14
2			9	7			16	12			4	6			5
		3			12					15			1		
		13			9					11			15		
15			2	5			11	9			6	16			1
9	7					6	2	13	8					3	10
	16	5			10	15			3	7			2	4	

Time: Score:

Scoring: Less than 60 minutes = 15 points;
60–80 minutes = 10 points; over 80 minutes = 5 points

208

	12		16	10			8	11			6	9		3	
3		6				2	1	4	7				8		16
	8			11	13					14	1			2	
15						12	4	10	5						1
6		2		1		11			9		8		12		13
		4				3			6				10		
	11		9	5	7	13			16	10	4	3		8	
8	10		3									16		6	15
11	5		8									10		12	6
	6		15	13	11	8			14	1	9	4		7	
		7				4			15				16		
12		13		6		15			11		10		5		9
5						6	2	9	3						4
	3			4	15					2	12			16	
1		11				14	3	16	4				13		10
	4		6	9			13	7			5	1		14	

Time:

Score:

Scoring: Less than 60 minutes = 15 points;
60–80 minutes = 10 points; over 80 minutes = 5 points

209

	13	9			5	12			6	15			2	11	
4	14					10	2	3	16					12	8
2			6	11			14	8			9	3			16
		8			9					2			15		
		3			14					11			8		
9			7	2			10	15			12	13			11
6	1					13	11	16	3					10	15
	2	11			12	3			14	6			1	9	
	11	14			3	8			13	1			6	2	
1	10					6	4	2	11					7	9
3			4	9			7	6			14	5			10
		6			11					7			13		
		4			10					3			14		
14			13	3			6	4			16	8			7
15	5					7	12	1	2					3	13
	6	12			13	15			5	14			4	1	

Time: Score:

Scoring: Less than 60 minutes = 15 points;
60–80 minutes = 10 points; over 80 minutes = 5 points

210

2							7	1							13
	14	13	8	5	11	15			3	7	4	16	9	1	
	9					8			2					3	
	10		16	13		9			5		12	6		7	
	16		2	9		4			12		8	1		15	
	11					16			15					9	
	6	4	10	1	13	5			11	9	3	7	8	12	
15							12	7							11
1							3	4							9
	3	16	13	2	12	11			6	10	5	8	14	4	
	15					14			13					5	
	5		4	15		7			9		11	12		6	
	12		3	6		2			7		15	9		11	
	2					10			4					14	
	13	14	9	3	4	1			16	11	6	2	10	8	
5							8	14							16

Time:

Score:

Scoring: Less than 60 minutes = 15 points;
60–80 minutes = 10 points; over 80 minutes = 5 points

211

	3		9		8	12	10	13	7	11		15		6	
6	16				13	7			9	8				1	2
			12	1							6	9			
4		11	7			6	15	5	1			12	14		10
		10			4					15			1		
9	14			3	10					1	16			15	5
15	1		16									4		13	14
13			2				8	14				3			16
16			13				14	12				8			3
10	4		8									16		2	6
11	2			13	5					4	15			7	12
		6			7					10			5		
7		4	6			15	5	2	16			14	8		11
			3	16							4	7			
2	15				6	3			14	5				12	9
	9		11		1	8	4	10	6	7		13		16	

Time:

Score:

Scoring: Less than 60 minutes = 15 points;
60–80 minutes = 10 points; over 80 minutes = 5 points

212

		10	4	15	2		14	9		8	6	1	13		
	8	5			3		7	1		11			4	6	
	13				12	4			5	7				2	
	7				5	16			3	9				14	
	15	2	5	11			10	13			1	6	7	16	
			1	7			3	14			10	12			
	4	11			14	6			15	5			2	8	
	9	1			16	2			14	12			8	13	
			15	13			11	10			16	9			
	6	3	16	9			5	8			2	11	12	4	
	5				15	14			13	3				10	
	12				7	9			4	1				15	
	2	14			11		13	15		10			1	3	
		15	3	6	4		2	5		14	12	8	11		

Time:

Score:

Scoring: Less than 60 minutes = 15 points; 60–80 minutes = 10 points; over 80 minutes = 5 points

213

11					3	7	15	2	9	13					10
		8			2					6			14		
	7			5	14		9	10		8	11			12	
				11		4			7		12				
		16	10	8		5			12		6	4	1		
12	14	6				11			1				7	3	8
8			7	1	4					16	13	10			2
9		3					14	8					15		6
3		7					10	14					9		13
15			14	16	5					11	9	6			7
16	2	9				8			5				11	1	4
		13	4	12		1			8		15	14	16		
				7		9			13		14				
	11			4	13		16	3		9	1			8	
		15			11					4			13		
7					1	10	6	11	15	5					16

Time:

Score:

Scoring: Less than 60 minutes = 15 points;
60–80 minutes = 10 points; over 80 minutes = 5 points

214

		8	13	2	6					5	11	16	7		
		1			12					7			3		
7	3	5			15	8	11	14	4	9			12	6	10
14							13	10							8
8							10	1							15
12	9	15			4	14	6	8	7	10			5	2	11
		4			16					6			14		
		7	2	12	9					11	13	6	4		
		3	8	11	14					1	6	10	15		
		13			5					14			2		
5	10	14			2	6	1	9	12	8			13	4	16
11							7	15							5
3							2	11							12
6	4	2			8	10	9	16	5	3			11	15	13
		11			7					13			10		
		10	15	3	1					12	14	7	6		

Time:

Score:

Scoring: Less than 60 minutes = 15 points;
60–80 minutes = 10 points; over 80 minutes = 5 points

215

		11	9	12	1					10	14	4	7		
	5					16			8					14	
14			16	6			3	13			11	8			2
1		10			14		15	4		16			12		13
2		6			9		8	7		14			3		10
5			1	2			14	8			3	15			11
	10					12			1					7	
		3	12	7	11					5	13	14	16		
		1	4	3	12					2	7	6	11		
	8					10			5					13	
12			5	15			6	16			1	10			3
10		7			2		1	9		8			14		15
7		5			4		13	6		9			2		1
4			14	16			2	5			8	3			7
	6					11			2					5	
		2	10	14	5					3	4	9	6		

Time: Score:

Scoring: Less than 70 minutes = 15 points;
70–90 minutes = 10 points; over 90 minutes = 5 points

216

2		14			7		3	5		12			8		13
		8	9	11	16					10	15	3	1		
5	15					12	1	2	8					14	4
	16					6			9					2	
	13					3			5					12	
1	8					13	16	6	2					3	10
		15	2	12	6					7	4	13	14		
16		6			2		8	12		13			15		11
8		3			13		15	14		4			12		9
		9	1	8	11					5	3	2	16		
12	6					2	9	10	13					7	14
	2					7			12					15	
	10					11			3					16	
7	9					10	5	11	15					6	1
		16	5	14	4					2	7	12	13		
11		4			12		13	9		16			3		15

Time:

Score:

Scoring: Less than 70 minutes = 15 points;
70–90 minutes = 10 points; over 90 minutes = 5 points

217

	3		1		2	8	14	11	7	10		4		12	
12	15				13	5			8	14				7	10
			7	12							4	16			
10		8	14			6	7	9	1			15	2		13
		11			15					2			12		
9	4			13	8					3	10			16	11
1	8		6									7		10	4
3			10				1	15				5			9
8			2				10	13				3			12
16	13		4									8		2	15
14	7			2	4					1	5			9	16
		5			3					4			7		
11		10	9			3	12	7	5			13	16		2
			16	5							13	11			
15	1				16	13			3	9				5	6
	2		12		1	11	8	4	10	6		14		15	

Time: Score:

Scoring: Less than 70 minutes = 15 points;
70–90 minutes = 10 points; over 90 minutes = 5 points

218

		7	6	12	11					8	4	1	10		
	10	9			7	5	14	1	3	12			2	6	
5	3	14			4					13			9	11	15
15							10	2							13
3							12	14							1
2	13	16											7	3	6
	5					14	6	16	13					4	
	6		15	11		3			12		9	10		16	
	8		3	16		4			6		13	11		2	
	16					9	8	15	10					7	
1	9	6											13	14	10
14							11	8							12
13							2	4							8
6	7	1			8					9			12	13	16
	15	2			14	1	9	3	8	6			4	10	
		4	8	7	10					5	15	2	6		

Time:

Score:

Scoring: Less than 70 minutes = 15 points;
70–90 minutes = 10 points; over 90 minutes = 5 points

SUDOKU 16 PUZZLES

219

	3					2			10					5	
9		15			16		6	4		12			8		2
	11		7	10							15	6		3	
		5			12	15			8	3			1		
		1			9	7			16	15			3		
	13		5	8							4	15		7	
14			11	4			16	2			7	1			6
	12					11			3					4	
	4					9			7					13	
1			10	7			14	12			5	4			3
	15		8	3							2	12		14	
		7			2	1			6	8			16		
		4			3	16			13	5			2		
	14		13	15							1	9		6	
3		6			1		2	9		10			5		7
	8					14			11					15	

Time: Score:

Scoring: Less than 70 minutes = 15 points;
70–90 minutes = 10 points; over 90 minutes = 5 points

220

	2		11		5	10	13	12	4	6		8		7	
10	8				14	9			7	11				16	15
			5	3							2	14			
14		13	9			1	16	15	5			4	10		2
		12			13					16			7		
2	10			16	12					8	5			13	9
4	11		16									15		1	12
7			15				5	1				3			14
6			12				4	9				7			3
16	7		8									10		14	6
9	5			2	1					4	3			11	16
		3			6					7			4		
8		2	7			15	10	3	14			12	13		11
			3	1							12	6			
11	9				4	8			2	15				3	10
	4		13		2	3	11	8	6	10		1		5	

Time:

Score:

Scoring: Less than 70 minutes = 15 points;
70–90 minutes = 10 points; over 90 minutes = 5 points

221

12		10			13		6	4		14			7		16
		13	16	5	14					12	1	4	15		
4	11					9	1	10	15					14	13
	2					15			13					1	
	1					11			12					2	
2	16					6	3	11	1					9	8
		15	12	16	5					10	8	6	13		
3		9			10		14	16		6			12		4
14		1			6		7	3		8			9		11
		6	11	4	16					2	12	3	8		
8	12					1	13	15	14					4	6
	5					8			16					7	
	9					13			6					10	
1	4					5	15	7	3					12	2
		7	14	10	2					16	15	9	1		
15		2			1		11	12		4			6		5

Time:

Score:

Scoring: Less than 80 minutes = 15 points;
80–100 minutes = 10 points; over 100 minutes = 5 points

222

		4	11	12	6		5	2		13	8	15	9		
	5	7			3		1	15		12			16	6	
	6				4	10			1	16				13	
	9				11	15			14	7				3	
	11	10	5	13			7	4			2	9	6	1	
			16	4			3	13			5	11			
	4	6			1	14			3	10			8	12	
	16	3			5	4			11	1			14	8	
			10	1			6	8			16	12			
	13	15	9	14			8	6			12	2	7	16	
	1				2	9			13	5				15	
	3				13	12			6	2				11	
	10	5			8		2	14		11			4	9	
		14	13	6	9		4	7		8	3	16	10		

Time:

Score:

Scoring: Less than 80 minutes = 15 points;
80–100 minutes = 10 points; over 100 minutes = 5 points

SUDOKU 16 PUZZLES

223

	3	6	16	11							14	4	13	2	
9			15			7	1	2	4			10			5
7			1			3			12			9			15
13	10	14				6			5				1	3	16
15				7							4				14
					1	8			3	9					
	1	12	13		11		9	16		15		5	8	10	
	11					5			8					12	
	16					4			9					15	
	14	15	10		3		7	12		5		2	4	16	
					5	1			13	8					
2				6							15				12
16	13	7				2			11				14	8	1
12			3			13			1			11			7
8			14			10	11	3	2			13			4
	2	9	11	4							7	16	10	6	

Time:

Score:

Scoring: Less than 80 minutes = 15 points;
80–100 minutes = 10 points; over 100 minutes = 5 points

224

13							2	5							16
	7	16	8	9	1	14			6	4	2	3	5	13	
	5					7			16					4	
	14		11	5		3			7		1	2		9	
	12		10	4		1			9		15	6		5	
	8					13			12					1	
	6	13	14	8	10	9			4	16	3	11	12	2	
2							6	8							10
6							1	4							15
	1	5	16	7	2	4			3	15	14	10	11	12	
	9					11			1					8	
	10		15	6		8			11		12	14		3	
	3		7	13		5			15		9	1		11	
	4					10			2					7	
	16	12	9	14	8	2			5	1	13	15	10	6	
10							12	7							2

Time:

Score:

Scoring: Less than 120 minutes = 15 points;
120–240 minutes = 10 points; over 240 minutes = 5 points

SUDOKU 16 PUZZLES

225

1		16	13				6	4				5	12		9
		2				8	15	12	13				1		
4	9		15			3			16			11		8	14
10		3		16		12			2		9		7		6
			14									2			
					6	2			11	10					
	15	8	16		1					9		4	11	14	
12	6						10	13						1	8
11	7						1	6						16	12
	12	14	3		10					15		1	9	7	
					8	9			10	2					
			6									13			
15		6		10		5			9		7		8		2
14	13		1			16			5			7		12	3
		4				15	3	10	14				6		
7		5	9				12	8				14	4		15

Time:

Score:

Scoring: Less than 120 minutes = 15 points;
120–240 minutes = 10 points; over 240 minutes = 5 points

KILLER SUDOKU

KILLER RULES

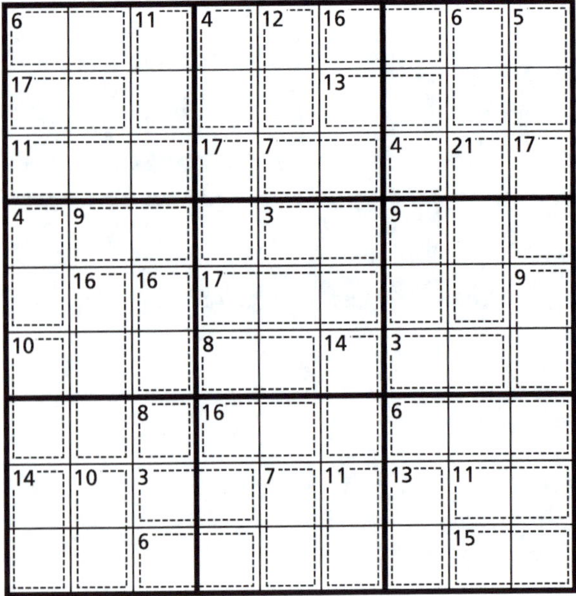

Killer Sudoku is known as Samunamupure in Japan. It is a fabulous version of a classic Sudoku where none of the numbers are printed in the grid to begin with.

However, a dotted line is put around a number of boxes and the sum total of the numbers within that dotted line is given.

Look at the grid opposite. This is a Killer Sudoku. The basic rules are exactly the same as for classic Sudoku.

In every row, column and mini-grid, you must have each of the numbers 1 2 3 4 5 6 7 8 and 9.

In Killer, you cannot repeat any number within a dotted line.

The same techniques of "slicing and dicing", "slicing and slotting" and "finding missing numbers" still apply.

The beauty of Killer is that it will stretch your levels of logic to take them to a higher level.

The problem with Killer is getting started.

Be confident, be brave and you'll manage it. Onward Sudoku soldier!

HOW TO DO KILLER

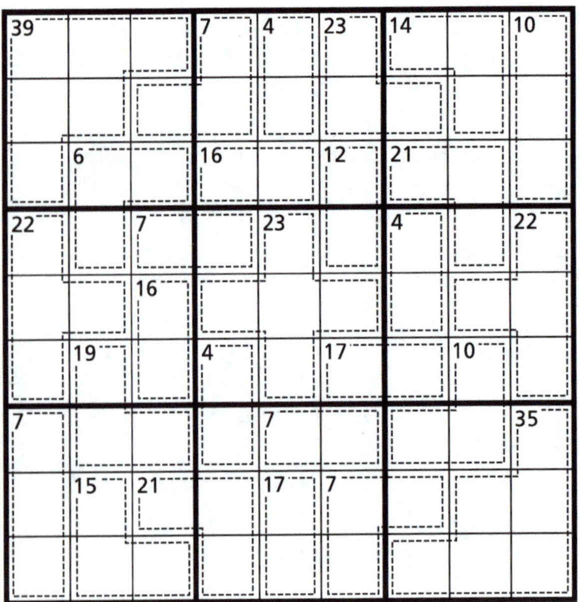

Introduction

Have a little look at this Killer Sudoku. Some of the dotted lines contain 2 boxes with small sum totals of 4 or 7. Others have 3 boxes with sum totals ranging from 6 to 21. One contains as many as 6 boxes with a massive total of 39. Aagh!

Notice how dotted lines with the same sum totals can hold different numbers of boxes. Look at row 7 to find a dotted line with a sum total of 7 containing two boxes. Now look at column 1 to find another dotted line with a sum total of 7, this time containing three boxes.

Sometimes our dotted lines contain boxes within a column or a row and sometimes they are more strangely shaped passing through a number of different mini-grids. The dotted lines are set in many and varied ways. It's your job to solve them.

Let's just say that at first glance Killer seems confusing. It can be very complicated, but just as with classic 9 x 9 Sudoku, there are some simple techniques you can learn to help you master the Killer.

Get a nice cuppa and snuggle up because it's time for a bit of brainpower.

6		11	4	12	16		6	5
17					13			
11			17	7		4	21	17
4	9			3		9		
	16	16	17					9
10			8		14	3		
		8	16			6		
14	10	3		7	11	13	11	
		6					15	

Single boxes

The very first thing you should do with every Killer Sudoku is look for dotted lines containing a single box.

In this grid you'll find a single box within a dotted line in (column 7, row 3) with the sum total of 4 written in the corner. Obviously if the dotted line only contains one box and the sum total of that one box is 4, then the number contained in that box must be 4. Doh!

Write it in and be grateful. As the Killers become more fiendishly difficult these single boxes will disappear from our starting grid.

Another single box has been given in (column 3, row 7). Write it in immediately and smile.

Two single boxes give us a good start.

However, be warned. Single boxes don't always appear within a Killer. They're only put in if the puzzle master is being nice!

It's now time to do a bit of adding up within dotted lines.

6		11	4	12	16		6	5
17					13			
11			17	7		4	21	17
4	9			3		9		
	16	16	17					9
10			8		14	3		
		8	16			6		
14	10	3		7	11	13	11	
		6					15	

Adding up the numbers

The grid above is one of the more gentle Killers. Have a look around the grid and you'll see that it doesn't have any dotted lines containing more than 3 boxes, and all the totals lie somewhere between 3 and 21. This is a nice way to begin to approach Killer.

The absolute key to cracking these puzzles is to think about what combination of numbers can fit into each dotted line.

Take the example of the dotted line along row 8 containing two boxes and a sum total of 3.

Which combination of numbers could possibly fit into

those boxes? In other words, which two numbers between 1 and 9 add up to a total of 3?

Only the numbers 1 and 2 could be used to add up to a total of 3 in this situation.

$$1 + 2 = 3$$

Notice that at the moment we aren't sure into which individual box the numbers 1 and 2 will eventually be placed. Don't worry; they are very useful even like this.

Write in the options for 1 2 just as you would for twins in a classic Sudoku. There are two further examples of a dotted line around two boxes with a sum total of 3. I've circled the boxes so you can now fill them in with exactly the same options.

6		11	4	12	16		6	5
17					13			
11			17	7		4	21	17
4	9			3 1 2	1 2	9		
	16	16	17					9
10			8		14	3 1 2	1 2	
		8	16			6		
14	10	3 1 2	1 2	7	11	13	11	
		6					15	

In exactly the same way I've circled sets of dotted lines where they contain two boxes and a sum total of 17 (next page). Think about which two numbers between 1 and 9 could fit into those boxes to give a total of 17.

As we aren't allowed to repeat any number within a dotted line (this is very very important), there is only one possible combination. This is a combination of numbers 8 and 9.

$$8 + 9 = 17$$

Write the number options for 8 and 9 within all the dotted lines with a sum total of 17.

Now look at row 7, which has a dotted line with three boxes and a sum total of 6. Which numbers could fit into these boxes to give this total? Again, there is only one possible combination of numbers and that is numbers 1 2 and 3.

$$1 + 2 + 3 = 6$$

Excellent. I think we're getting the hang of this.

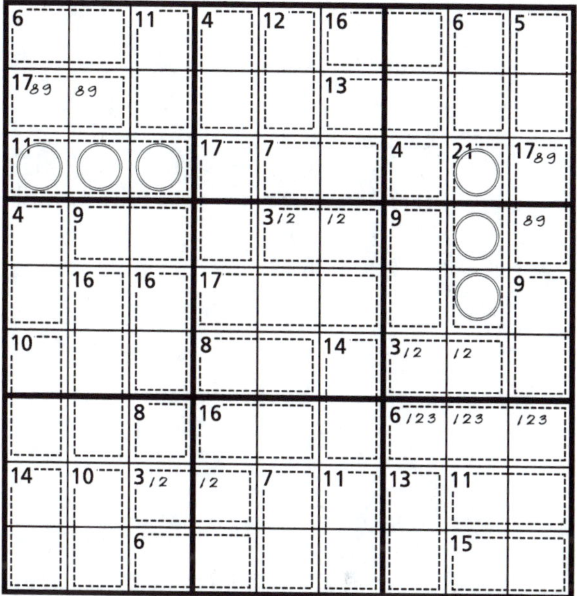

Next we'll look at a slightly more complicated dotted line in column 8. This dotted line holds three boxes and has a sum total of 21. So which numbers could possibly fit into those boxes?

Now, we start to see lots of different possibilities. The numbers could be any of the following combinations

4 8 9 (4 + 8 + 9 = 21)
5 7 9 (5 + 7 + 9 = 21)
6 7 8 (6 + 7 + 8 = 21)

We'll see how to write these multi-options into the grid later but for now I just want to demonstrate how dotted lines can sometimes be filled with a guaranteed combination of numbers (I call them the classic combinations) and sometimes it can be much more difficult.

Finally, look at the dotted line on row 3, which contains three boxes and a sum total of 11. With such a low total you would imagine that it isn't going to be too complicated, but as is typical of Killer Sudoku, it's much more difficult than it first appears. The 5 possible combinations are as follows

1 2 8 (1 + 2 + 8 = 11)
1 3 7 (1 + 3 + 7 = 11)
1 4 6 (1 + 4 + 6 = 11)
2 3 6 (2 + 3 + 6 = 11)
2 4 5 (2 + 4 + 5 = 11)

It's important to note that you shouldn't be frightened of the larger sum totals, which might appear in a grid. They can be just as friendly as the very small targets. Larger sum totals do not mean an added layer of difficulty.

Look at the table of number combinations for dotted lines on the following pages to help you out.

Number combinations

To make life a little easier I've printed out all of the possible options for dotted lines with two or three boxes and different sum totals.

I've also given shorter tables for dotted lines containing four, five and six boxes. Following on, I've combined all the situations where there is only one possible combination of numbers (the guaranteed classic combinations) into one invaluable table for you to keep handy. Have a look at these tables now.

Hope you like them.

Two box combinations

Sum total				
3	1 2			
4	1 3			
5	1 4	2 3		
6	1 5	2 4		
7	1 6	2 5	3 4	
8	1 7	2 6	3 5	
9	1 8	2 7	3 6	4 5
10	1 9	2 8	3 7	4 6
11	2 9	3 8	4 7	5 6
12	3 9	4 8	5 7	
13	4 9	5 8	6 7	
14	5 9	6 8		
15	6 9	7 8		
16	7 9			
17	8 9			

Three box combinations

Sum total								
6	123							
7	124							
8	125	134						
9	126	135	234					
10	127	136	145	235				
11	128	137	146	236	245			
12	129	138	147	156	237	246	345	
13	139	148	157	238	247	256	346	
14	149	158	167	239	248	257	347	356
15	159	168	249	258	267	348	357	456
16	169	178	259	268	349	358	367	457
17	179	269	278	359	368	458	467	
18	189	279	369	378	459	468	567	
19	289	379	469	478	568			
20	389	479	569	578				
21	489	579	678					
22	589	679						
23	689							
24	789							

Four box combinations

Sum total					
10	1234				
11	1235				
12	1236	1245			
13	1237	1246	1345		
14	1238	1247	1256	1346	2345
26	2789	3689	4589	4679	5678
27	3789	4689	5679		
28	4789	5689			
29	5789				
30	6789				

Five box combinations

Sum total	
15	12345
16	12346
34	46789
35	56789

Six box combinations

Sum total		
21	123456	
22	123457	
23	123458	123467
37	256789	346789
38	356789	
39	456789	

Classic combinations of numbers

In Killer Sudoku you will most often see dotted lines, which contain 2 3 4 or 5 boxes. Sometimes they might contain 6 boxes or more but very rarely.

Let's have a look at some classic situations where you are absolutely guaranteed to be able to write down the only options which could possibly be placed within a dotted line with a specific sum total. This is because with certain situations there is only one possible combination of numbers which could be added to achieve the sum total.

We've already seen the lists of number options for dotted lines with different numbers of boxes and their sum totals.

Now, to make life simpler, I've put together a grid containing only the classic and guaranteed combinations. By all means, copy this and keep it handy whenever you're attempting a Killer. Here it is.

Two box classic combinations

3	1 2
4	1 3
16	7 9
17	8 9

Three box classic combinations

6	1 2 3
7	1 2 4
23	6 8 9
24	7 8 9

Four box classic combinations

10	1 2 3 4
11	1 2 3 5
29	5 7 8 9
30	6 7 8 9

Five box classic combinations

15	1 2 3 4 5
16	1 2 3 4 6
34	4 6 7 8 9
35	5 6 7 8 9

Six box classic combinations

21	1 2 3 4 5 6
22	1 2 3 4 5 7
38	3 5 6 7 8 9
39	4 5 6 7 8 9

Filling in classic combinations

One of the first things you should do with any Killer Sudoku is fill in all the classic combinations where you can be absolutely sure what your options are in each box.

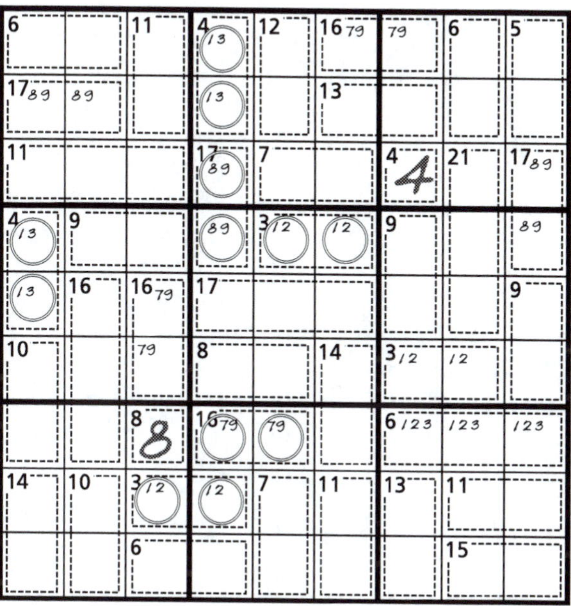

Have a look at this grid. None of the dotted lines contain more than three numbers and quite a few of them contain classic combinations. I've filled in the dotted lines containing classic combinations so that we can start to use them as twins and triplets in the traditional way to reduce our options.

Have a look at row 4. We have a pair of twins in the dotted line with a sum total of 3; this is a classic combination as it can only be filled with the number options for 1 and 2 as shown. This means we can cross out all other number options for 1 and 2 in row 4. You'll see that in (column 1, row 4) I've already written in the classic combination options for numbers 1 and 3 to satisfy the dotted line with the sum total of 4. This means that now we can delete the number option 1 giving us a definite lone number 3 for that box. Write it in.

Of course, now we can delete all number options for 3 in that row, column and mini-grid in exactly the same way as we do in classic Sudoku.

When you place a number in Killer Sudoku you cross out all options for that in its row, column, mini-grid **and** dotted line. You can delete that number option in all boxes within its dotted line even if those boxes don't fit into its row, column or mini-grid. I'll show this in more detail later on.

For now, this deletion gives us a lone number 1 in (column 1, row 5). Fill it in now.

We're starting to build up a good base of definite numbers in the grid.

In exactly the same way we have a pair of twinned number options for 1 and 3 at the top of column 4. We can, therefore, delete all other options for numbers 1 and 3 in that column and mini-grid giving us a definite lone number 2 in (column 4, row 8) Fill it in and then delete all other options for 2 in that row, column, dotted line and mini-grid. Do this to find a lone number 1 in (column 3, row 8). Fill it in and delete options in the usual way, not forgetting to also delete options within its dotted line (although in this case, no further options exist).

Again in column 4, we have a pair of twins for number options 8 and 9. By deleting all other options for 8 and 9 in that column, you will quickly find a lone number 7 in (column 4, row 7) and then a lone number 9 in (column 5, row 7). Hooray! We love it.

Slicing and slotting with twins

Look at the middle band of mini-grids where we have one pair of twins for number options 1 and 2 on row 4, and another pair of twins with the same number options 1 and 2 on row 6.

By slicing and slotting using the normal rules of Sudoku we know that both numbers 1 and 2 have to fit onto row 5 in the middle left mini-grid.

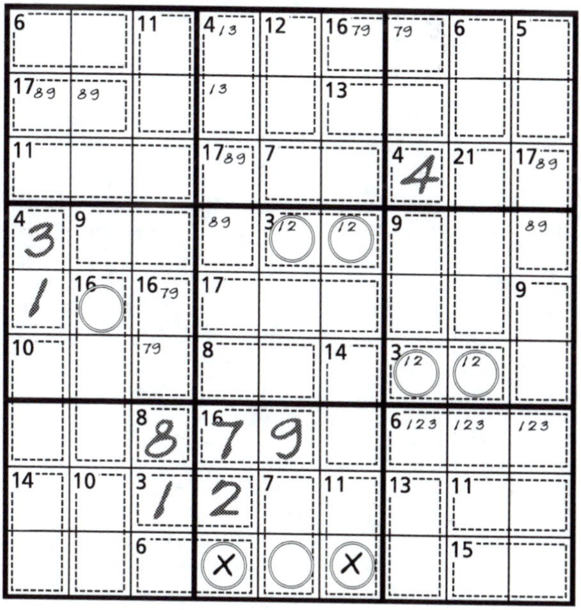

As luck would have it, we have already placed the number 1 in (column 1, row 5). We also know that number 2 cannot be placed in (column 3, row 5) as that is part of a pair of twins. Therefore, we can happily slice and slot number 2 into (column 2, row 5). Excellent work.

Now have a look at the bottom band of mini-grids. Let's try to place a number 1 into the bottom center mini-grid. We already have a number 1 placed in row 8, and we have triplets in row 7 in the bottom right mini-grid. Therefore, we know that number 1 in the bottom center mini-grid must be placed on row 9.

Now let's look at the columns. We have a pair of twins with number option 1 at the top of column 4, so that rules out (column 4, row 9).

Time to look at the dotted lines along row 9. If we placed number 1 into (column 6, row 9) it would mean that to make up a total of 11 for that dotted line, we would have to write a number 10 in the other box. Obviously we can't do that in Sudoku so (column 6, row 9) is wrong for number 1. We can now place number 1 into the only remaining box with an option which is (column 5, row 9) with confidence.

6		11	4 13	12	16 79	79	6	5
17 89	89		13		13			
11			17 89	7		4 4	21	17 89
4 3	9		89	3 12	12	9		89
1	16 2	16 79	17					9
10		79	8		14	3 12	12	
		8 8	16 7	9		6 123	123	123
14	10	3 1	2	7	11	13	11	
		6					15	

Using twins

Let's try to place the correct options for the dotted line with sum total of 8 given on row 6 in the central mini-grid. The possible options are (look at the number combination table to check):

17 26 35

We already know that the correct number options on row 5 within this mini-grid are for numbers 1 and 2. Therefore, we can use this twinned pair to cut down our options within the mini-grid.

This means that we can forget about number options 1 and 7 for our dotted line with a sum total of 8 as we can't repeat an option for number 1 within the mini-grid.

We can also forget about the number options 2 and 6 as we can't repeat an option for number 2 within the mini-grid.

Therefore, we can write in the only number options remaining which are for numbers 3 and 5, giving us another powerful pair of twins on row 6.

It is now possible to look down column 4 where we have a pair of twins with number options 1 and 3. This means that we must delete our option for number 3 in (column 4, row 6) which leaves us with a lone number 5 for this box. Fill it in and then delete all options for 5 in that row, column, dotted line and mini-grid (if there are any).

Obviously now we have a lone number 3 in (column 5, row 6) so we can fill that in as well and then delete the relevant number 3 options elsewhere in the usual way (although this time none have yet been given).

Now look at the center mini-grid on the top band. We have a dotted line with a sum total of 7 containing two boxes, which are both within the mini-grid. The combinations for a sum total of 7 with two boxes are as follows:

1 6   2 5   3 4

We already know that the correct number options in column 4 within this mini-grid are for numbers 1 and 3. Therefore, we can use this twinned pair to cut down our options within the mini-grid.

This means that we can forget about number options 1 and 6 for our dotted line with a sum total of 7, as we can't repeat an option for number 1 within the mini-grid.

We can also forget about the number options 3 and 4, as we can't repeat an option for number 3 within the mini-grid. (We have also placed a 4 on row 3, which means we couldn't place a number 4 on the row again either.)

Therefore, we can write in the only number options remaining which are for numbers 2 and 5, giving us another powerful pair of twins on row 3.

This time, however, we can't resolve the numbers any further so let's try something else.

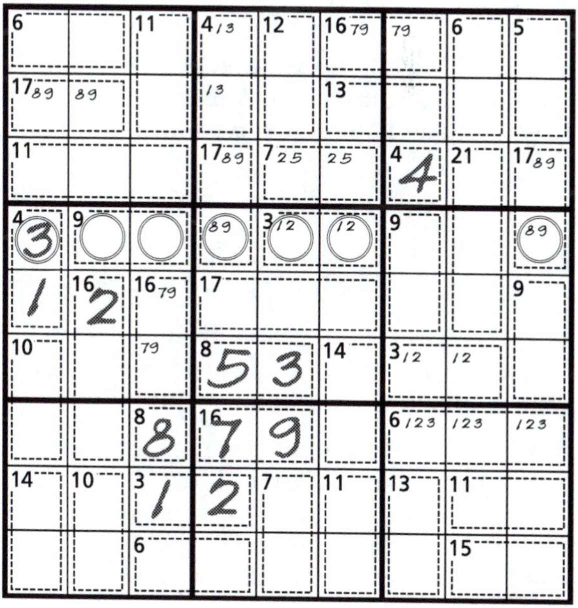

6		11	4 /3	12	16 79	79	6	5
17 89	89		/3		13			
11			17 89	7 25	25	4 4	21	17 89
4 3	9		89	3 /2	/2	9		89
1	16 2	16 79	17					9
10		79	8 5	3	14	3 /2	/2	
		8 8	16 7	9		6 /23	/23	/23
14	10	3 1	2	7	11	13	11	
		6					15	

Now we're going to study a **very important principle** and you must become clear about the logic of it.

In the same way as we've placed options within mini-grids in the previous pages, we're now going to try to place options in the middle left mini-grid using the two sets of twins on row 4.

Look at row 4 and you can see twins of number options 1 and 2 contained within the same dotted line.

Look closely and you will also see two boxes along the row, which contain number options 8 and 9. They are (column 4, row 4) and (column 9, row 4). These boxes are twins. This sometimes confuses Sudokuers as they start to believe that twins can only exist within dotted lines when you're playing Killer. This isn't true. The basic rules of Sudoku still apply.

Boxes are twinned in a row, column or a mini-grid if they contain the same two number options. They do not have to be held within the same dotted line.

So let's use this information to shorten our options for the dotted line with a sum total of 9 containing two boxes on row 4 of the middle left mini-grid. The possible combinations for a sum total of 9 with two boxes are:

1 8   2 7   3 6   4 5

However, thanks to the power of the two sets of twins on row 4 we can cross out the options for 1 2 8 and 9 on the row. (Numbers 1 and 2 have also, coincidentally, been placed in this mini-grid as well which would automatically delete those options.) This means that in our dotted line with sum total 9 we can cross off the potential number options of 1 8 and 2 7 from our list.

We also know that number 3 has been placed within this mini-grid so we can delete our options for 3 6. This leaves us with the only correct options for this dotted line of numbers 4 and 5. Write them in now.

Slicing and slotting with extra logic

You've probably noticed that we have started to get a lot of information about the numbers 1 and 2 around the grid so let's see if we can use that information to resolve any boxes. Have a look at the bottom left mini-grid where we have only managed to place two numbers and we don't have any twinned boxes.

6		11	4 13	12	16 79	79	6	5
17 89	89		13		13			
11			17 89	7 25	25	4 4	21	17 89
4 3	9 45	45	89	3 12	12	9		89
1	16 2	16 79	17					9
10		79	8 5	3	14	3 12	12	
		8 8	16 7	9		6 123	123	123
14	10	3 1	2	7	11	13	11	
○		6 ○					15	

By slicing and dicing with number 2 in column 2 and row 8 we can eliminate some of the boxes. We can also use our triplets on row 7 containing the numbers 1 2 and 3 to slice and slot away any options for number 2 on that row.

That leaves us with two boxes on row 9 which could hold the number 2. The box in (column 1, row 9) is contained within a dotted line with a sum total of 14. Now we need to do a bit of mental arithmetic and use an extra bit of logic.

At this point we always have to ask the question, if I place the number I am working with in this box, what must I then place in the other box (or boxes) within the same dotted line to make sure that I reach the sum total. Is it possible to place those other numbers correctly?

So if I placed number 2 in (column 1, row 9), what number must I place in (column 1, row 8) to make a sum total of 14 for the dotted line?

$$14 - 2 = 12$$

Obviously we can only place numbers between 1 and 9 in Sudoku. We cannot place a number 12. In this way, we can now eliminate the possibility of placing number 2 in (column 1 , row 9). This leaves just one option for number 2 in the bottom left mini-grid so write number 2 into (column 3, row 9).

You will often have to use this kind of logic in Killer but take your time and you should be fine. Make little notes on a scrap of paper if that helps. It's all allowed.

6		11	4 13	12	16 79	79	6	5
17 89	89		13		13			
11			17 89	7 25	25	4 4	21	17 89
4 3	9 45	45	89	3 12	12	9		89
1	16 2	16 79	17					9
10 ○	○	79	8 5	3	14	3 12	12	
○	○	8 8	16 7	9		6 123	123	123
14	10	3 1	2	7	11	13	11	
		6 2	4				15	

Extra logic in mini-grids

We're going to try to complete the middle left mini-grid where we have two empty boxes. We've already managed to place numbers 1 2 and 3. We also have twins for number options 4 and 5 and a separate pair of twins with number options 7 and 9 which are all held within the same mini-grid.

That leaves us with two boxes and, by counting through from 1 to 9 in the mini-grid, two number options of 6 and 8. Is it possible to place the numbers firmly into their correct positions?

This is where we need a bit of extra logic with the information given to us by our dotted lines.

Notice that both empty boxes are contained within different dotted lines that overlap into the mini-grid in question.

In this situation it's simplest to attempt a very small amount of trial and error. So putting the number 6 into (column 2, row 6) we can see that we then have two numbers placed into the dotted line with a sum total of 16. Those numbers are 2 and 6. So if we have placed the number 6 correctly, what would the final number in that dotted line be?

$$16 - 2 - 6 = 8$$

Now if you write number 8 into that final box in (column 2, row 7) you can see that it is wrong. By placing it there you now have two lots of number 8 in the bottom left mini-grid and two lots of 8 on row 7, breaking all the rules of Sudoku. So the number 6 was placed incorrectly. Now we can safely place number 6 in the only potential box remaining which is in (column 1, row 6).

Not only that, we can now complete the dotted line with a sum total of 10 as:

$$10 - 6 = 4$$

So place the number 4 in (column 1, row 7). Excellent.

Going back to the mini-grid, we can place our only remaining option for number 8 in (column 2, row 6) and then by doing a bit of mental arithmetic for the dotted line with a sum total of 16:

$$16 - 2 - 8 = 6$$

We can place number 6 in (column 2, row 7).

Don't forget to erase all the other options for a number in its row, column, dotted line and mini-grid once you have placed it correctly. In this way, by erasing the options for number 8 in column 2 we can solve our twins with number options 8 and 9 on row 2.

You can see how you can use various pieces of information to get the correct answers but you must remember to do this carefully. It's easy to rush at a Killer and make a mistake.

Missing numbers in rows, columns and mini-grids

It's very easy to count through rows, columns or mini-grids to find a missing number in a Killer Sudoku. You use the same principles as in classic Sudoku but you'll find you're often helped by the number of twins and triplets positioned around the grid. Use all their powers to help you.

Look at column 4 in the grid overleaf. Let's find the missing number in (column 4, row 5) by counting through from 1 to 9. Number 1 is in the twin at the top of the column, number 2 has been placed, number 3 is in the top twin, number 4 has been placed and so has number 5. Number 6 isn't showing at the moment so this is probably our number. Let's carry on counting just to check we haven't made a mistake.

Number 7 has been placed and numbers 8 and 9 are locked into twins further up the column.

6		11	4 13	12	16 79	79	6	5
17 8	9		13		13			
11			17 89	7 25	25	4 4	21	17 89
4 3	9 45	45	89	3 12	12	9		89
1	16 2	16 79	17					9
10 6	8	79	8 5	3	14	3 12	12	
4	6	8 8	16 7	9		6 123	123	123
14	10	3 1	2	7	11	13	11	
		6 2	4				15	

So by counting through we find our missing number is 6. Pop it in.

Using the same technique on row 7 by counting through from 1 to 9 and using the triplets in the row, we find the missing number in (column 6, row 7) is number 5. Write it in.

Whenever you see a situation with just one missing number in a row, column or mini-grid, try to complete it if possible.

You'll find with Killer that once you have written in some firm numbers the rest of the Sudoku will fall into place.

WRITING OPTIONS

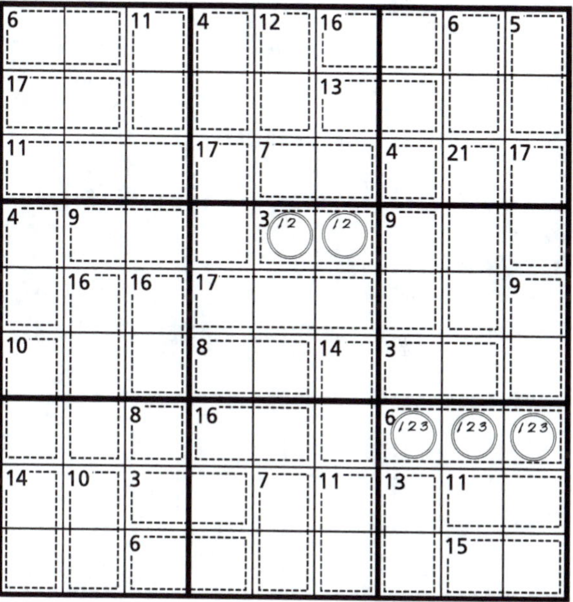

Writing simple options

I'm going to start with writing simple classic combinations of numbers where we can be absolutely sure of the number options, as they are the only ones which satisfy the sum total given in the dotted line.

WRITING OPTIONS

So referring to our grid and our table of classic combinations, we can start to place definite number options within some of the dotted lines.

When you write your options in Killer Sudoku you must be very clear about how you do it. Writing options neatly and in numerical order is vital for classic Sudoku but Killer Sudoku will test your option writing skills even further

You must always write your options together and in numerical order. I know you must think I sound like an old battleaxe sometimes but I'm only thinking of you and how to reduce your Sudoku frustration.

Let's look at a classic combination. On row 4, we have a dotted line with a sum total of 3 containing two boxes. We know that we can only have the classic combination of number options 1 and 2 within the dotted line. In this situation, you should write your options like this.

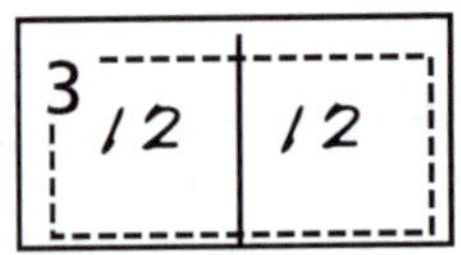

Do not loosely squiggle them around the box like this or you'll end up in serious Sudoku trouble.

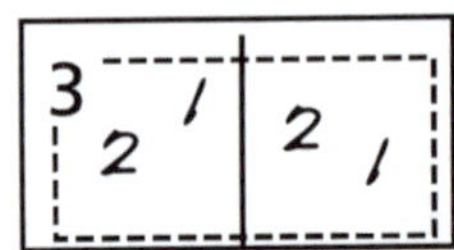

You'll see why the way in which you write your options is so important when we start to write multi-options in the next section. Writing options of all descriptions is something you will have to master in Killer Sudoku.

Going back to the grid we have another classic combination of options in the dotted line containing three boxes with a sum total of 6 on row 7. The options for numbers 1 2 and 3 are the only ones which could possibly fit the bill and these must be written together.

We can write them together like this because we are guaranteed that these are the correct and only number options for these three boxes and we do not have to consider alternatives.

Writing options becomes progressively more difficult when we look at some other boxes within dotted lines with trickier totals.

6		**11**	**4** 13	**12**	**16** 79	79	**6**	**5**
17 89	89		13		**13**			
11			**17** 89	**7**		**4**	**21**	**17** 89
4 13	**9**		89	**3** 12	12	**9**		89
13	**16**	**16** 79	**17**					**9**
10		79	**8**		**14**	**3** 12	12	
		8	**16** 79	79		**6** 123	123	123
14	**10**	**3** 12	12	**7**	**11**	**13**	**11**	
		6					**15**	

Writing multi-options

I've now filled in all the classic combinations of numbers. You must understand that the numbers which have been written, can be used as twins and triplets. We can do this, as these number options are the correct and guaranteed numbers for those boxes. They are classic combinations and have no alternatives.

Now we're going to fill in some dotted lines with multi-options. These will **not** be twins or triplets at this stage and this is why I can't stress enough, you must be extremely careful how you write them into the boxes on the grid.

Please note that this isn't necessarily the order in which I would attempt a puzzle. I'm writing in multi-options at this stage for the purposes of demonstration. I'll show you how to use them properly later on.

Let's start with the bottom right mini-grid and the dotted line with a sum total of 11 containing just two boxes. Here are the options for this situation.

2 9   3 8   4 7   5 6

We have already written triplets of numbers 1 2 and 3 into the same mini-grid so let's run through our options. We cannot have a combination of numbers 2 and 9 (because number option 2 is included in our triplets). We can't have a combination of 3 and 8 for the same reason (number option 3 is included in our triplets in the same mini-grid) so we are left with two possible sets of two number options, which are 4 7 and 5 6.

To write multi-options like this you must write each set of options on a different level or line within the box. If you don't you are almost sure to make an error.

Let's write these multi-options like this.

11 47 56	47 56

You absolutely must not write them like this with all of them in a line otherwise the Killer would win.

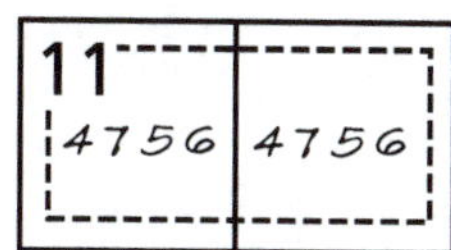

It's vital to remember that you cannot use these options as twins as we are not sure exactly which set of options is correct. Only if we can reduce them to one set of options can we use them as twins.

Now look at the top left mini-grid where there is a dotted line with a sum total of 6 on the top row. The combinations for this are as follows:

1 5   2 4

Now you could be forgiven for thinking that, because we have a pair of twins in column 1 with number options 1 and 3, we can cross out our options for numbers 1 and 5 in the dotted line of 6 leaving us with just number options 2 and 4 to write into this dotted line on row 1.

Wrong. The twins of number options 1 and 3 in column 1 only affect one box within the dotted line we're analyzing, which is in (column 1, row 1).

This is a critically important piece of logic to understand.

To appreciate it more fully, write both sets of options into the dotted line like this:

Now use the twins in column 1 to delete all options for numbers 1 and 3 in its column and mini-grid. This means we can only cross out the number option 1 in (column 1, row 1) but the number option 5 remains.

This number option 5 is now potentially a lone number so we can use it to cross out number option 5 in (column 2, row 1) to leave us with a potential lone number 1 in this box.

This will only be the correct placement of numbers **if** we eventually discover that this set of number options is the right one and that the alternative number options of 2 and 4 are wrong.

If you are ever in doubt about writing options, then write in all the options first of all. Then proceed to cross them out one by one.

Now look at the bottom right mini-grid where we want to fill in options for the dotted line with a sum total of 15 on row 9. There are only two possible sets of number options to satisfy this situation and they are

6 9   7 8

Write them in and then look up column 9 to find a powerful pair of twins with number options 8 and 9. This pair of twins means we can delete the number 8 from our 7 8 option in (column 9, row 9) and we can also delete number 9 from our 6 9 option in (column 9, row 9). Because we have now been left with lone numbers 6 and 7 for both potential options in (column 9, row 9) we can now delete those numbers in their appropriate set of options in (column 8, row 9).

This is good, but we still don't know for sure which set of numbers is correct. We'll have to wait for further information.

Always look for opportunities to reduce options particularly when you are dealing with multi-options. Remember as soon as one set of options has been completely eliminated from one box in a dotted line, you can then completely remove that set of options from all boxes in the dotted line as well. I'll show you how that happens next.

DELETING OPTIONS

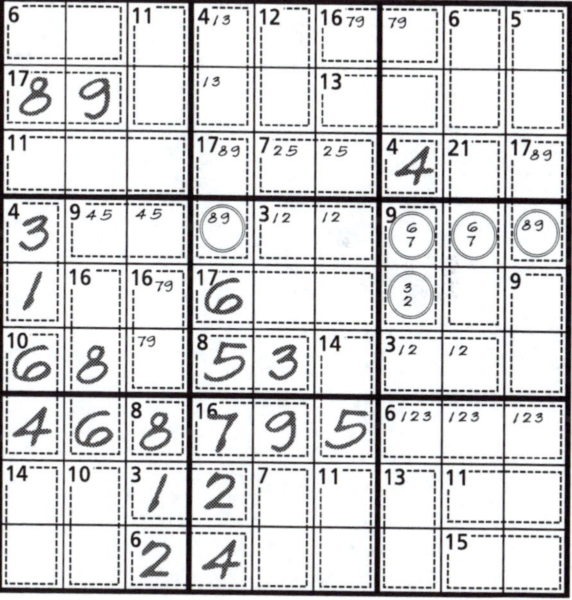

The key thing to remember is that whenever you place a number in Killer, you can then delete the options for that number in its row, column and mini-grid in the usual way. You can also delete that number option anywhere within the dotted lines.

Let's concentrate on row 4 and the stack of mini-grids on the right.

Only two boxes on row 4 remain completely empty. All the others have numbers placed in them or they hold definite options—no multi-options have been placed so far. So let's count along the row from 1 to 9 to find which options should be placed in the empty boxes.

We have twins (note there is only one set of options listed in this classic combination) for numbers 1 and 2, number 3 has already been placed, numbers 4 and 5 are powerful twins along the row.

Numbers 6 and 7 haven't been placed. However, we have a pair of twins with number options 8 and 9 in (column 4, row 4) and (column 9, row 4). These are twins as they are definite options (not multi-options) and they share the same row. So just as in the normal game of Sudoku, this defines them as a pair of twins. Note that their dotted line partners on row 3 also make a pair of twins for exactly the same reason.

So we know for sure that the missing numbers 6 and 7 must be placed in our empty boxes in row 4.

Let's write them in but **do not** write them as joint options on the same line, as you would in a normal game of Sudoku.

The number options must be written on separate lines as they form different options for the boxes.

OK so far? Now let's analyze these two boxes further. The box in (column 7, row 4) is contained within a dotted line with a sum total of 9, so now we can use this to write the partnered options in the other box (column 7, row 5).

If number 6 is to be placed in (column 7, row 4) then with a quick bit of mental arithmetic:

$$9 - 6 = 3$$

it would be partnered by number 3 in (column 7, row 5). Write it in, making sure that the number option 3 is at the top of the box to show that it is partnered with the number 6 option above.

Equally **if** number 7 is to be placed in (column 7, row 4) then with another bit of mental arithmetic:

$$9 - 7 = 2$$

it would be partnered by number 2 in (column 7, row 5). Write it in, making sure that the number option 2 is at the bottom of the box to show that it is partnered with the number 7 option in the box above.

Remember, if any set of options is completely crossed out in any of the boxes then that set of options is wrong for the whole of the dotted line and you can delete all details of that set of options throughout the dotted line.

Now let's look at the information within the mini-grid itself. We have a definite pair of twins with number options 1 and 2 on row 6. This means that we have to delete all other number options for 1 and 2 within that row and mini-grid. Doing this means that we can delete the option for number 2 in (column 7, row 5).

By deleting this option we have now deleted all numbers in that set of options in that box. This means that set of options cannot be correct throughout the whole of the dotted line, which has a sum total of 9. Now we must delete all reference to that set of options throughout that dotted line.

In this case, it means we now delete the number option 7 from (column 7, row 4) which leaves us with a definite lone number of 6. Write it in and delete all other number options for 6 in its row, column and mini-grid.

We are also left with a lone number option for 3 in (column 7, row 5). Write that in now and delete all the relevant options for 3 as usual.

Finally we are left with a lone number 7 in (column 8, row 4). Fill it in.

So you can see just how important it is to be absolutely clear about multi-options. Don't ever confuse them with options in a classic Sudoku, they can be much more devious.

ADDING UP TO 45

I know that so far in all our extreme puzzles you haven't had to do much mental arithmetic. Well, now you're going to have to start adding up some simple numbers between 1 and 9.

It's time to work with rows, columns, dotted lines and mini-grids.

In order to follow the basic rules of Sudoku (which Killer does) each row, column and mini-grid must contain the numbers 1 to 9. If you add up the numbers from 1 to 9 you get:

$$1 + 2 + 3 + 4 + 5 + 6 + 7 + 8 + 9 = 45$$

45 is the sum total of every row, column and mini-grid. We can use this simple fact to prise apart a Killer.

Look at the bottom right mini-grid in the grid overleaf. Notice that all the dotted lines are contained within that mini-grid (unusual in Killer but useful). Now add up the sum totals of all those dotted lines and you will get:

$$6 + 11 + 13 + 15 = 45$$

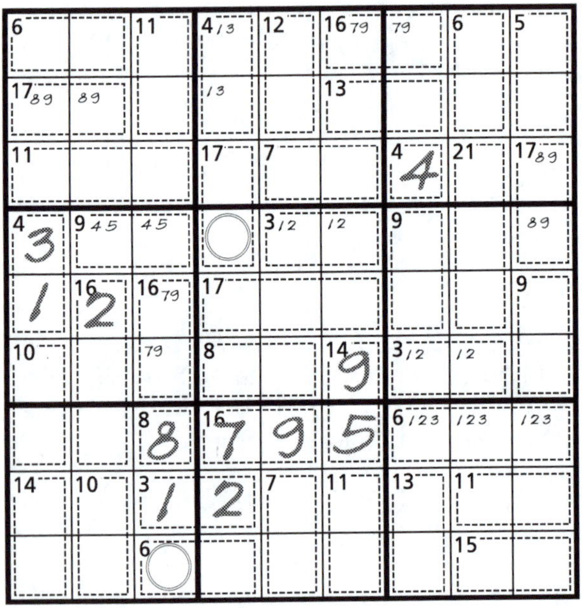

We can't do anything with this mini-grid but we can use the "45 rule" particularly well when we have been given the information for all the boxes in an individual row, column or mini-grid or in a group of them.

Watch closely.

We're going to try to find the answer for the box in (column 4, row 4).

Look at the central mini-grid where we have three sets of dotted lines for totals of 3, 17 and 8. Together they account for seven boxes in the mini-grid. We have a number 9 written into (column 6, row 6) so let's add up the totals for those eight boxes in the mini-grid.

3 + 17 + 8 + 9 = 37

Now deduct this total from the total for the mini-grid, which is 45, to get the answer.

45 - 37 = 8

You can now write number 8 into (column 4, row 4).

Let's look again and use a combination of mini-grids. Look at the left stack of mini-grids.

The numbers in each mini-grid will add up to 45 so if we are considering three mini-grids together, the sum total of the three will be 135 because:

3 x 45 = 135

This left stack of three mini-grids contains many dotted lines. It also has two extra boxes at the bottom of column 3 which do not belong in the same dotted lines. Let's start by adding up the dotted line totals which account for 25 out of the 27 boxes in the stack:

6 + 11 + 17 + 11 + 4 + 9 + 16 + 16 + 10 + 14 + 10 + 8 = 132

We also have one rogue box in (column 3, row 8) with a number 1, so add that to the total for 26 out of the 27 boxes:

132 + 1 = 133

The total for all 27 boxes in the mini-grids should be 135 and we have just one blank box in (column 3, row 9). So to find the number in our 27th box simply do a bit of subtraction:

135 - 133 = 2

We can now write number 2 into (column 3, row 9).

Sometimes you will be able to look at a Killer and find answers using this method at the beginning of your solution, but more often these "adding up to 45" situations arise once you've started to enter some numbers. Look out for this whenever you can and get to know your Killer grid.

Remember each row, column and mini-grid adds up to 45.

Use it or lose it.

SUMMARY

First of all fill in the single boxes, if any have been given.

Write all classic combinations in the dotted lines where there is only one possible combination of number options.

Use these as definite twins and triplets to delete options in other rows, columns and mini-grids.

Whenever you place a number, immediately delete those number options in its row, column, mini-grid and within the rest of its dotted line.

You should be able to complete quite a few numbers like this.

Look at missing numbers in rows, columns and mini-grids and use the usual Sudoku information with the "adding up" information from dotted lines to give further numbers or to delete further options.

Always look out for twins emerging when options are deleted, as they are extremely powerful in Killer.

Remember all individual rows, columns and mini-grids add up to 45. Use individuals, or groups of them together, to find the answer for a rogue box.

SUMMARY

Keep analyzing dotted lines, where one or more numbers have been placed, to see if you can narrow down your options in its remaining boxes.

Only start to write multi-options when you can go no further using the methods above. Multi-options are wonderful but it's cleaner and less confusing to keep them to a minimum within the grid.

KILLER START TO FINISH

Well I hope you enjoyed the tips and tricks in the "How To Do Killer" section. Now I'm going to put it all together so that you can tackle all the Killers which follow.

Be aware that when you're working with a Killer you might need to hop around the grid much more than you would with a classic Sudoku. Let's begin.

Have a look at the Killer over the page. The average time to complete a Killer of this grade would be about 40 minutes. I'm going to show you every single step. However, when you become more used to Killers you will learn to use natural shortcuts in your head, just as you now do with classic Sudoku.

The first thing to do is search for "single boxes" where the dotted line contains only a single box and a sum total. In other words, the sum total gives you the answer to the box straight away. Sadly in this Sudoku we haven't been given any of these easy clues. Let's move on.

The next thing you must do is search for dotted lines with classic combinations. Look at the classic combinations table on page 316 to check as you work your way around any grid.

39 456 789	456 789	456 789	**7** 124	**4** 13	**23** 689	**14**		**10**
456 789	456 789	124	124	13	689	689		
456 789	**6** 123	123	**16** 79	79	**12**	**21**		
22	123	**7**		**23**		**4** 13		**22**
		16 79				13		
	19	79	**4** 13		**17** 89	89	**10**	
7 124			13	**7**				**35**
124	**15**	**21**		**17** 89	**7** 124	124		
124				89	124			

In this grid we have 13 separate situations of dotted lines which must contain Classic Combinations. Let's fill them in now. I will put the sum totals for each dotted line in ' ' for ease of explanation and a rough guide to the position of each dotted line to which I'm referring.

Dotted line '6' in top left mini-grid gives number options 1 2 3.
Dotted line '7' in top center mini-grid gives number options 1 2 4.
Dotted line '4' in column 5 gives number options 1 3.
Dotted line '7' in bottom center mini-grid gives number options 1 2 4.
Dotted line '4' in column 7 gives number options 1 3.
Dotted line '4' in column 4 gives number options 1 3.

Dotted line '7' in column 1 gives number options 1 2 4.
Dotted line '16' on row 3 gives number options 7 9.
Dotted line '23' in top center mini-grid gives number options 6 8 9.
Dotted line '16' in column 3 gives number options 7 9.
Dotted line '17' on row 6 gives number options 8 9.
Dotted line '17' in column 5 gives number options 8 9.

All these can be written on the same line within each box as they are definite options and can all be treated as twins or triplets.

Our final classic combination is to be placed in the top left mini-grid. The dotted line has a sum total of 39 and holds 6 boxes. We know that the only numbers to be placed in there can be 4 5 6 7 8 9. It's difficult to fit all of those numbers on one line in each box so for one of the very few occasions, and as we know these are definite options, we can spread our number options onto a couple of lines in each box. Do make a note in your head of what you've done so that it doesn't cause any confusion with multi-options later on.

Now we've placed our twins and triplets we can start to use their strength to cross out options in other boxes.

It's good to work methodically with these, as we don't want to miss any clues. So, starting with:

Column 1 – triplets 1 2 4. Cross out those options in the column and mini-grid.
Column 3 – twins 7 9. Cross out those options in the column and mini-grid.
Column 4 – twins 1 3. Cross out those options in the column.

Column 5 – twins 1 3. Cross out those options in the column and mini-grid.
Column 5 – twins 8 9. Cross out those options in the column and mini-grid.

This gives us a lone number 7 in (column 5, row 3). Cross out options for 7 in its row, column, dotted line and mini-grid.

This gives us lone number 9 in (column 4, row 3). Write it in and cross out options for 9 in its row, column, dotted line and mini-grid.

This leaves us with twins 6 8 in column 6 in this top center mini-grid, so using these twins we can now cross out options for 6 8 in its column, dotted line and mini-grid.

This leaves us with lone number 9 in (column 6, row 6). Fill it in and delete options.

Now we have lone number 8 in (column 7, row 6). Fill it in and delete options.

We now have lone number 7 in (column 3, row 6) and number 9 in (column 3, row 5). Fill them in and delete options.

We have been left with a lone number 9 in (column 7, row 2) so fill it in and delete the options.

Let's go back up to the top left mini-grid where the only possible position for number option 1 in the dotted line '7' is in (column 3, row 2). Fill it in and delete the relevant options.

This immediately gives us lone number 3 in (column 5, row 2) and also lone number 1 in (column 5, row 1). Fill them in and delete options.

We are also able to see that the only place for number 1 in dotted line '6' in the left stack of mini-grids is in (column 2, row 4). Write it in and delete options.

This in turn gives lone number 3 in (column 7, row 4) and number 1 in (column 7, row 5). Fill in and delete options.

We're doing well.

39 56789	456789	4568	**7** 24	**4** 1	**23** 68	**14**		**10**
5678	45678	1	24	3	68	9		
568	**6** 23	23	**16** 9	7	**12**	**21**		
22	1	**7**		**23**		**4** 3		**22**
		16 9				1		
	19	7	**4** 13		**17** 9	8	**10**	
7 124			13	**7**				**35**
124	**15**	**21**		**17** 89	**7** 124	24		
124				89	124			

It's time now for a bit of traditional slicing and dicing. Slice and dice number 1 into (column 4, row 6) and then delete options. We're left with lone number 3 in (column 4, row 7). Delete options.

Now look at the options for dotted line '12' contained in column 6. The full list of multi-options is 3 9, 4 8, and 5 7.

Well we know that it can't be 3 9 as 9 has already been placed in that column. We also know that it can't be 4 8 as we have 8 contained with twins in the same column. Therefore, the definite number options for dotted line '12' are 5 7. Write them in. Now look along row 3 to see that number 7 has already been placed so that leaves us with the only option for (column 6, row 3) which is number 5. Fill it in and delete its options and then place the other option for that dotted line which is number 7 in (column 6, row 4).

Now slice and dice number 1 into the top right mini-grid. With traditional slicing and dicing, we are left with two boxes in (column 8, row 3) and (column 9, row 3), but where do we place the number 1?

Well, have a look now at the dotted line of '21'. We know by looking through options that we can't possibly place a number 1 into that dotted line. If we did, the numbers in the other two boxes couldn't be large enough to make the total. Therefore, we can eliminate (column 8, row 3) and place number 1 into (column 9, row 3) with confidence. Do it now and then delete its relevant options.

Time for a bit of mental arithmetic. We're going to add up the dotted lines and stray numbers across the top band of mini-grids, then deduct 135 from the number (the sum total of all three mini-grids is 3 x 45 = 135) to find the correct number for (column 8, row 4).

So we have:

39 + 6 + 7 + 4 + 23 + 14 + 10 + 16 + 12 + 21 = 152

Then subtract the numbers, which lie within those dotted lines but outside the top band of mini-grids, which are number 1 (column 2, row 4) and number 7 (column 6, row 4).

152 - 1 - 7 = 144

Now we can deduct 135 from this number:

144 - 135 = 9

Write number 9 into (column 8, row 4).

Now we can analyze dotted line '7' in row 4. The full list of options are 1 6, 2 5, and 3 4. It can't be 1 6 as number 1 has already been placed in that row. It can't be 3 4 as number 3 has also been placed in row 4. Therefore, it must be number options 2 5 but which number goes in which box? Well we can't place number 2 in (column 4, row 4) as we have twins in that same column, which include the number 2. So we can place number 5 into (column 4, row 4) and then number 2 into (column 3, row 4).

Crossing out the options for these numbers in their row, columns, dotted lines and mini-grids means that we can now place the following numbers.

Lone number 3 into (column 3, row 3).
Lone number 2 into (column 2, row 3).

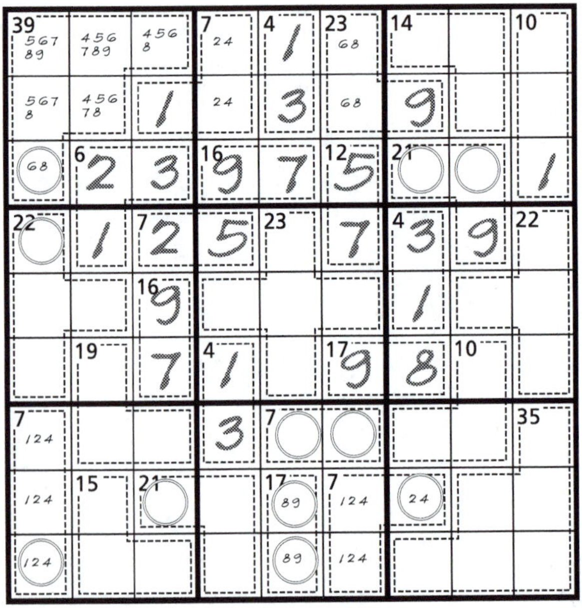

We're going to concentrate on row 3 and the dotted line '21' in the top right mini-grid. We know that one of the numbers already placed inside this dotted line is number 9. So now we also know that the two empty boxes must add up to a total of 21 – 9 = 12.

The full list of options for our new temporary dotted line '12' with two boxes is 3 9, 4 8 and 5 7. We know that it can't be 3 9 or 5 7 as these numbers have already been placed on that row so the dotted line must contain numbers 4 and 8. We also know that number 8 already exists in column 7 so the only option left for (column 7, row 3) is number 4. Write it in and then complete the dotted line with number 8 in (column 8, row 3). Delete the relevant options to give us our final missing number 6 on the row in (column 1, row 3).

Now look at dotted line '7' on row 7. The full list of options is 1 6, 2 5 and 3 4. It can't be 1 6 as we already have twins containing the number 1 in the same mini-grid. It can't be 3 4 as number 3 is already placed on that row, so it must be options 2 5. Now look at column 6 where we've already placed a number 5. So now we know the only number to be placed in (column 6, row 7) is number 2 and that number 5 then fits into (column 5, row 7). Fill them in now and delete the options.

Deleting the number 2 options from the bottom center mini-grid means that we now have twins of numbers 1 and 4 in column 7 contained within the same mini-grid and the same dotted line. We can now delete those options throughout its column, mini-grid and dotted line. This then gives us a lone number 2 in (column 7, row 8). Fill it in and delete the options.

Look at row 4 where we have missing numbers 4 6 and 8. (Column 1, row 4) can't contain numbers 4 or 6 (look at the column in detail to see why) so we can immediately place a number 8 into that box. We can't place any more numbers on row 4 with certainty so let's move on to another part of the Killer.

Let's add up the left stack of mini-grids to find the number to be placed in (column 3, row 8). We're going to add up the dotted lines and stray numbers across the left stack of mini-grids, then deduct that number from 135 (the sum total of all three mini-grids is 3 x 45 = 135) to find the correct number for (column 3, row 8).

So we have:

39 + 6 + 22 + 16 + 19 + 7 + 15 = 124

Then add the numbers which lie outside those dotted lines but within the left stack of mini-grids which are number 1 (column 3, row 2) and number 2 (column 3, row 4).

124 + 1 + 2 = 127

Now we can deduct this number from 135:

135 - 127 = 8

Write number 8 into (column 3, row 8).

Deleting options for number 8 gives us lone number 9 in (column 5, row 8) and then lone number 8 in (column 5, row 9). Delete options in the usual way.

Now returning to the dotted line of '21' we can see that the other two boxes must add up to a total of 21 - 8 = 13. The full list of options for '13' are 4 9, 5 8 and 6 7. We know it can't be options 4 9 or 5 8 as those numbers have already been placed in that mini-grid. Therefore, the dotted line must contain the options 6 7 which become a nice pair of twins in column 4. Write them in.

Now look at the grid opposite. Slice and dice number 3 into (column 6, row 5) and number 8 into (column 4, row 5). Delete options.

In column 3 we have missing numbers 4 5 and 6. We cannot place the 4 in (column 3, row 7) as we have twins in that mini-grid containing options for number 4. Nor can we place missing number 5 in that box as 5 has already been placed on row 7. The only number left is number 6. Write it in now and delete its options.

Now we can place number 5 in (column 3, row 9) and number 4 in (column 3, row 1). Excellent. Remember to delete the relevant options as you go. This gives lone number 2 in (column 4, row 1) and then lone number 4 in (column 4, row 2).

Looking at column 5 we have missing numbers 2 4 and 6. We can't place any of these just yet but we can happily place them as options in the boxes in the central mini-grid, only writing 4 6 into (column 5, row 4) as number 2 has already been placed on row 4.

The middle left mini-grid now has enough information for us to perform a special "adding to 45" trick. Add the numbers from the dotted lines together with the stray numbers to find the missing number in (column 2, row 6).

$$22 + 1 + 2 + 9 + 7 = 41$$

$$45 - 41 = 4$$

So write number 4 into (column 2, row 6) and delete options.

Now we can look at the dotted line '19' to find out its missing number.

$$19 - 4 - 6 = 9$$

Write number 9 into (column 2, row 7) now and then slice and dice number 9 into (column 1, row 1). Lovely. We're doing well.

39 9	578	4	7 2	4 1	23 68	14		10
57	578	1	4	3	68	9		
6	6 2	3	16 9	7	12 5	21 4	8	1
22 8	1	7 2	5	23 46	7	4 3	9	22
		16 9	8	246	3	1		
	19 4	7	4 1	26	17 9	8	10	
7 14	9	6	3	7 5	2			35
14	15	21 8	67	17 9	7 14	2		
2		5	67	8	14			

Let's find the missing numbers in the bottom left mini-grid, which are numbers 3 and 7. We can write these as twins and then delete options for these numbers around the mini-grid and up the column. This means that we are now left with a powerful pair of twins with number options 5 and 8 at the top of column 2. We can now delete those number options throughout that mini-grid and throughout the dotted line in which they are contained. This leaves us with a lone number 7 in (column 1, row 2).

So now we have a final missing number 6 to write into (column 2, row 5).

In column 7 we have three missing numbers which are 5 6 and 7.

Place number 7 into (column 7, row 7) as number 5 and 6 have already been placed in that row.

Then place number 6 in (column 7, row 9) and number 5 in (column 7, row 1).

This gives a list of lone numbers. Every time you fill one in please then delete the relevant options before you move on to the next number.

Number 8 in (column 2, row 1).
Number 5 in (column 2, row 2).
Number 6 in (column 6, row 1).
Number 8 in (column 6, row 2).
Number 7 in (column 4, row 9).
Number 6 in (column 4, row 8).

Deleting options gives us number 3 in (column 2, row 9) and number 7 in (column 2, row 8).

Now look at column 1 with missing numbers 3 and 5. We can place number 5 into (column 1, row 5) as number 3 has already been placed on that row and then number 3 in (column 1, row 6).

When you look at the Killer now you'll see that the right hand side is still fairly empty. That's because we didn't have many classic combinations over on that side when we began. Have no fear. Look at the top right mini-grid.

In row 1 we have missing numbers 3 and 7.
In row 2 we have missing numbers 2 and 6.

The dotted lines '10 and '14' are unable to reduce our options so we have to write the options in on separate lines.

Now look at dotted line '10' which begins in column 8. We have already placed a number 7 within it, so we know that the remaining two boxes must add up to 10 - 7 = 3. Two boxes with a sum total of 3 gives us a classic combination of numbers 1 and 2 so we can place number 2 in (column 8, row 6) as number 1 has already been placed in that row and can't be repeated. Then place number 1 in (column 8, row 7). Delete options.

Now we can complete column 1 with:
Number 4 in (column 1, row 7) and
Number 1 in (column 1, row 8).

9	8	4	2	1	6	5	3 7	3 7
7	5	1	4	3	8	9	6 2	6 2
6	2	3	9	7	5	4	8	1
8	1	2	5	4 6	7	3	9	
5	6	9	8	2 4	3	1		
3	4	7	1	6	9	8		
4	9	6	3	5	2	7	1	8
1	7	8	6	9	4	2		
2	3	5	7	8	1	6	4	9

Number 4 in (column 6, row 8).
Number 1 in (column 6, row 9).

Slice and dice number 8 into (column 9, row 7) and then slice and dice number 9 into (column 9, row 9).

Now complete the final number 4 in row 9.

We have now placed a number 2 in column 8 so crossing out options in (column 8, row 2) means that we can now place number 6 in that box and then number 3 in (column 8, row 1). Moving on we can now place the following, always deleting options as we go.

Number 7 in (column 9, row 1).
Number 2 in (column 9, row 2).
Number 6 in (column 5, row 6).
Number 4 in (column 5, row 4).
Number 2 in (column 5, row 5).
Number 6 in (column 9, row 4).
Number 5 in (column 9, row 6).
Number 4 in (column 9, row 5).
Number 3 in (column 9, row 8).
Number 5 in (column 8, row 8).
Number 7 in (column 8, row 5).

We're done. We've conquered the Killer. Time for a treat.

226

6		11	4	12	16		6	5
17					13			
11			17	7		4	21	17
4	9			3		9		
	16	16	17					9
10			8		14	3		
		8	16			6		
14	10	3		7	11	13	11	
		6					15	

Scoring:
Less than 12 mins = 15
12–20 mins = 10
over 20 mins = 5

Time:

Score:

227

16	4		7	17		15		
	7			30			3	10
11	17	20		8				
			4		10	10	11	
12			14	7			11	
3				10			14	17
7	9	21	16		8			
						14		3
16			13			10		

Scoring:
Less than 12 mins = 15
12–20 mins = 10
over 20 mins = 5

Time:

Score:

228

Scoring:
Less than 12 mins = 15
12–20 mins = 10
over 20 mins = 5

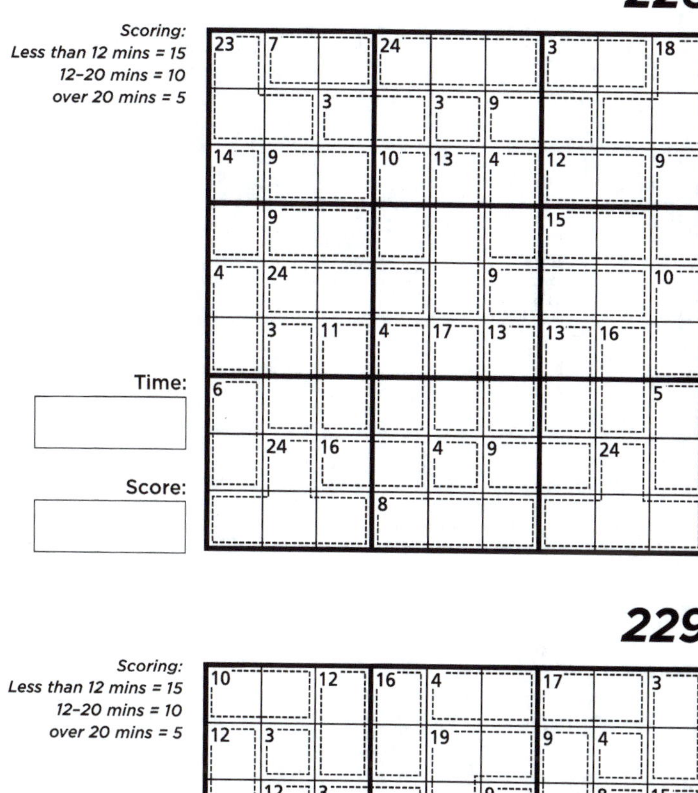

Time:

Score:

229

Scoring:
Less than 12 mins = 15
12–20 mins = 10
over 20 mins = 5

Time:

Score:

230

11	14			15	3	10		11
	16	4				17		
16		23		13		10	9	
				7	7			
5		14			13		11	
16		13	8		11		21	
20			4				10	
	8		8	15	17			4
	3				18			

Scoring:
Less than 12 mins = 15
12–20 mins = 10
over 20 mins = 5

Time:

Score:

231

17	10		12	11	14		3	
	9	8			15	11		9
6				3		5	13	
		10			15			16
13	17		11			4		
	11	4		16	14		7	
8		8	17		6	5	10	
	16			10				13
5		7				16		

Scoring:
Less than 12 mins = 15
12–20 mins = 10
over 20 mins = 5

Time:

Score:

232

Scoring:
Less than 12 mins = 15
12–20 mins = 10
over 20 mins = 5

Time:

Score:

233

Scoring:
Less than 12 mins = 15
12–20 mins = 10
over 20 mins = 5

Time:

Score:

234

16		3		4	10	20		15
20	15						4	
	17	10	16	7	11			8
					9		17	
	4	11		8	3			
		13		15	17	11		13
16	6	18				6		
			4	11	15			
	11				5		16	

Scoring:
Less than 12 mins = 15
12–20 mins = 10
over 20 mins = 5

Time:

Score:

235

10		6		13	12	10		4
3	17		13			11	16	
	12	7		11				7
9		10			14			
	9		18			7		15
23		4		5	11		11	
	3	14	12		14	4		12
10				15		4		
	9				10		10	

Scoring:
Less than 12 mins = 15
12–20 mins = 10
over 20 mins = 5

Time:

Score:

236

Scoring:
Less than 12 mins = 15
12–20 mins = 10
over 20 mins = 5

10	14			10	14	9		7
	17	3				16		
16		18		6		6	24	
				23	2			
10		11			4		11	
13		17	3		19		15	
16			3				7	
	4		16	9	17			13
	10				12			

Time:

Score:

237

Scoring:
Less than 12 mins = 15
12–20 mins = 10
over 20 mins = 5

23	9	8		8	3	17	11	
		16					9	7
	4		10	13	9			
22					11			
4		13		4	10		14	
7	16			3	16	17		
	8	12				8		23
		8	4	17	13		3	
16					9			

Time:

Score:

238

12		9	14		15		15	6
5	15			4		15		
		29						
8		12		23	13		8	
	17		6			4		16
8					11		14	
23	7		27					9
	10		4		14	3		
		12					17	

Scoring:
Less than 12 mins = 15
12–20 mins = 10
over 20 mins = 5

Time:

Score:

239

31		16			8		17	
		7	24	6		21		
4					6		15	
	14		5	16				8
16		4			17		3	
	3	18	9		7	7		17
22				23			30	
			9					
		16		6				

Scoring:
Less than 12 mins = 15
12–20 mins = 10
over 20 mins = 5

Time:

Score:

240

Scoring:
Less than 12 mins = 15
12–20 mins = 10
over 20 mins = 5

6		9		9	6		16	
16	22				13			6
	4		19			13		
14		14	15		4	9	12	
3				11			9	
4	13	6			17		6	13
		7		19	13			
12						23		
17		12			10		3	

Time:

Score:

241

Scoring:
Less than 12 mins = 15
12–20 mins = 10
over 20 mins = 5

10	17		7	16	11		4	
	13	7			19			16
				9	9	15		
34	3	4				14		
		11		2	10		10	14
	9	10	12	7	16			
					4		9	
	23			11	3	14		12
4		16						

Time:

Score:

242

Scoring:
Less than 12 mins = 15
12–20 mins = 10
over 20 mins = 5

Time:

Score:

243

Scoring:
Less than 12 mins = 15
12–20 mins = 10
over 20 mins = 5

Time:

Score:

244

Scoring:
Less than 12 mins = 15
12–20 mins = 10
over 20 mins = 5

15	11		17		5	4	6	
	1	12	15				7	19
3	11		4		16		11	
		12		21	16			
11			11			11	4	
13	12				9		12	16
		6		9		11		
	8	9	16				3	3
11				7		17		

Time:

Score:

245

Scoring:
Less than 12 mins = 15
12–20 mins = 10
over 20 mins = 5

16			10		4		20	
4	17		16	7	17		1	
		12			13			3
23			13		13	9	8	
	6	5	4	4				23
9				11		5		
	19			4	9		19	11
21	3	13						
		3		16		14		

Time:

Score:

246

13		16		12	4		6	
12			19		19	15		
7	3						12	17
		6		17	10			
16		12	5		11	9	3	
7				26			12	
15	5					5		12
	24			4	7			
8		6			16		14	

Scoring:
Less than 12 mins = 15
12–20 mins = 10
over 20 mins = 5

Time:

Score:

247

7	17	16		8	3	13	4	
		11					6	19
	9		9	16	17			
6					19			
13		6		8	4		14	
23	14			10	9	12		
	6	16				9		7
		4	11	3	14		16	
12					14			

Scoring:
Less than 12 mins = 15
12–20 mins = 10
over 20 mins = 5

Time:

Score:

248

Scoring:
Less than 12 mins = 15
12–20 mins = 10
over 20 mins = 5

Time:

Score:

249

Scoring:
Less than 12 mins = 15
12–20 mins = 10
over 20 mins = 5

Time:

Score:

250

10	3		27			9		9
	11	17	3			17	9	
17			4	12				4
	8			23	13	16		
		20					11	
7	13				7	7		14
	17	4	16				11	
10			22	3				16
	9					6		

Scoring:
Less than 12 mins = 15
12–20 mins = 10
over 20 mins = 5

Time:

Score:

251

15		14	5		9	15		7
4	10		23	5		8	15	
		9			4			
15			10			5	10	
7	5	11	22				8	
			4	9		17	13	
14		10		15			4	16
17			11	3		9		
	4			15			8	

Scoring:
Less than 12 mins = 15
12–20 mins = 10
over 20 mins = 5

Time:

Score:

252

Scoring:
Less than 12 mins = 15
12–20 mins = 10
over 20 mins = 5

11		12		14	6		10	
14	10				12			13
	14		10			13		
15		12	10		4	17	6	
5				12			10	
4	17	10			16		11	3
		15		12	17			
17						17		
9		4			10		13	

Time:

Score:

253

Scoring:
Less than 12 mins = 15
12–20 mins = 10
over 20 mins = 5

13	12	4		18		8		17
		7	9		4		8	
16	1			14		13		20
		7		24				
7		16			7		13	
14		17			9		6	
	12		6		13	17	4	
12		14		16			9	7
	4				7			

Time:

Score:

254

27		7		23			16	
		23	11		6	15		
	7		17					16
5				12	4		3	
	16	11			14			13
10		15	3		7	7	16	
	25		11					26
				17				
		6			16			

Scoring:
Less than 12 mins = 15
12–20 mins = 10
over 20 mins = 5

Time:

Score:

255

17	13		12		3		9	16
	4	8			17	9		
15		13	8				8	9
			28		3			
16		12			8		7	
6		8				16	20	
	4	16	4	14			3	
7	14			20	9			9
		3				17		

Scoring:
Less than 12 mins = 15
12–20 mins = 10
over 20 mins = 5

Time:

Score:

256

Scoring:
Less than 12 mins = 15
12–20 mins = 10
over 20 mins = 5

15		9	11	10		8		4
17	6			13		13	9	
	4	6			10		6	16
		24		18		9		
12		12			10		6	
9	7		4				11	14
		8		23	16			
4	7				8	5	5	
	17		6				13	

Time:

Score:

257

Scoring:
Less than 12 mins = 15
12–20 mins = 10
over 20 mins = 5

9		4		12	15		13	
23			17		10	14		
6	8						3	16
		9		16	12			
8		16	6		8	17	4	
12				15			11	
15	3					11		11
	24			13	7			
7		6			13		11	

Time:

Score:

258

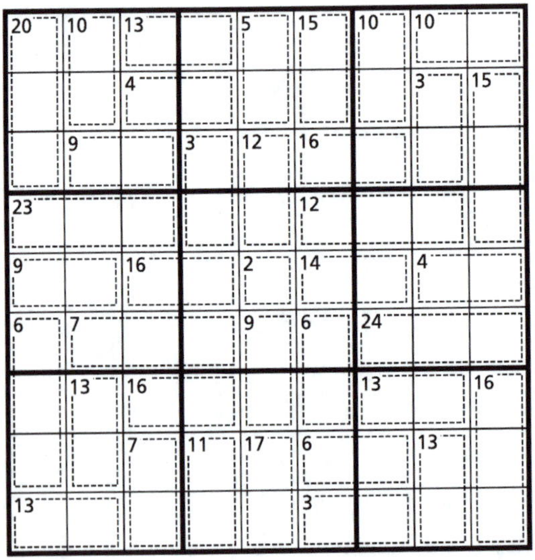

Scoring:
Less than 12 mins = 15
12–20 mins = 10
over 20 mins = 5

Time:

Score:

259

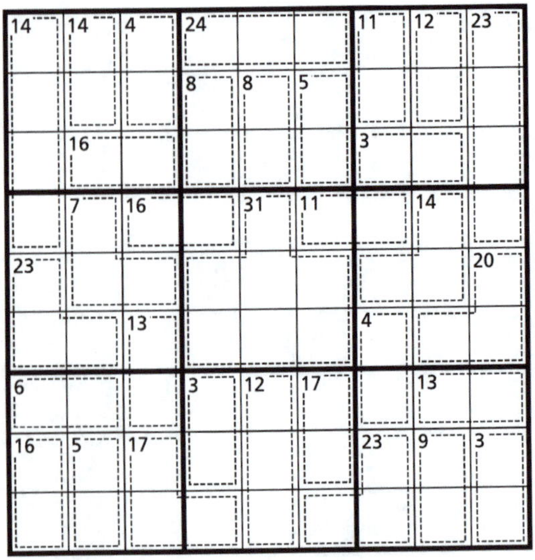

Scoring:
Less than 12 mins = 15
12–20 mins = 10
over 20 mins = 5

Time:

Score:

260

Scoring:
Less than 12 mins = 15
12–20 mins = 10
over 20 mins = 5

15			10		22	7		13
12	3	24				5		
			4			20	9	12
17		14	13	9				
8				3	3		17	
8	16		17				7	
			7	9		29	8	3
11	12							
	4			17		17		

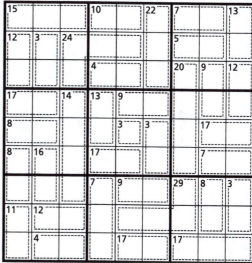

Time:

Score:

261

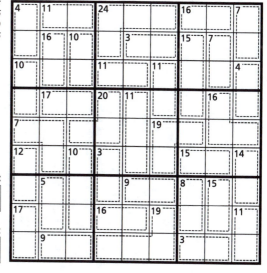

Scoring:
Less than 18 mins = 15
18–40 mins = 10
over 40 mins = 5

4	11		24			16		7
	16	10		3		15	7	
10			11		11			4
	17		20	11			16	
7					19			
12		10	3			15		14
	5			9		8	15	
17			16		19			11
	9					3		

Time:

Score:

262

Scoring:
Less than 18 mins = 15
18–40 mins = 10
over 40 mins = 5

Time:

Score:

263

Scoring:
Less than 18 mins = 15
18–40 mins = 10
over 40 mins = 5

Time:

Score:

264

Scoring:
Less than 18 mins = 15
18–40 mins = 10
over 40 mins = 5

Time:

Score:

265

Scoring:
Less than 18 mins = 15
18–40 mins = 10
over 40 mins = 5

Time:

Score:

266

12		12	13	10	3	15	5	
12							8	
7	3		19			9		15
	19			18	10			
13	15	9			8		13	15
		8	11		10	15		
	16			12			10	
		5			10			
17			6			22		

Scoring:
Less than 18 mins = 15
18–40 mins = 10
over 40 mins = 5

Time:

Score:

267

15			21	3	17		16	8
6	14				9			
	17	3			17	3		16
6			29					
	16		11			8		9
17		9				16	14	
	7			17				17
16		4		15		9		
		14				6		

Scoring:
Less than 18 mins = 15
18–40 mins = 10
over 40 mins = 5

Time:

Score:

268

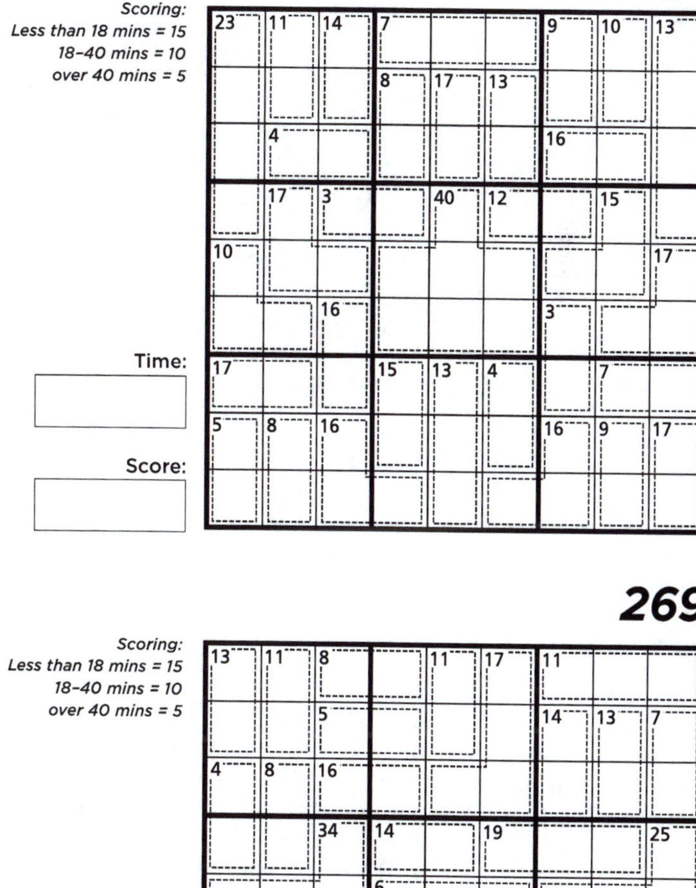

Scoring:
Less than 18 mins = 15
18–40 mins = 10
over 40 mins = 5

Time:

Score:

269

Scoring:
Less than 18 mins = 15
18–40 mins = 10
over 40 mins = 5

Time:

Score:

270

19	12	7	7			14	12	12
			15	12	11			
	10					9		
	23	13		28	13		13	
12								17
		10				14		
11			10	23	3		11	
6	7	17				10	9	15

Scoring:
Less than 18 mins = 15
18–40 mins = 10
over 40 mins = 5

Time:

Score:

271

7	17		9		3		8	9
	7		14	16		10		
5	12			4			17	
	9			18	17	18		15
11		24	4					
					7			15
13		3	10		8	11		
16	10		6			17		4
		10		14		7		

Scoring:
Less than 18 mins = 15
18–40 mins = 10
over 40 mins = 5

Time:

Score:

272

Scoring:
Less than 18 mins = 15
18–40 mins = 10
over 40 mins = 5

17	12		14	10	6	12		18
	13					3		
	10	7		10	15		9	
22		8			7			23
			15					
	8	6		10	15		16	
9		7			8			15
	10		16	9	14	8		
	17					6		

Time:

Score:

273

Scoring:
Less than 18 mins = 15
18–40 mins = 10
over 40 mins = 5

17		3	17	7		13		10
22				13		17		
	4	9			10		3	9
		19		24		4		
9		9			7		17	
3	17		10				11	22
		9		6	11			
11					17	7	12	
	16		10					

Time:

Score:

274

Scoring:
Less than 18 mins = 15
18–40 mins = 10
over 40 mins = 5

Time:

Score:

275

Scoring:
Less than 18 mins = 15
18–40 mins = 10
over 40 mins = 5

Time:

Score:

276

Scoring:
Less than 18 mins = 15
18–40 mins = 10
over 40 mins = 5

11		11	18		12		12	11
4	16			3		13		
		29						
16		4		16	12		10	
	14		15			6		16
3					15		13	
18	8		23					8
	12		8		19	3		
		9					17	

Time:

Score:

277

Scoring:
Less than 18 mins = 15
18–40 mins = 10
over 40 mins = 5

4		17		9		16	15	
13		30		6				
	7			24		3	20	
16		9						
	7		10			11		17
22		9	15		9		8	
			13		30			7
26		3						
			9		4		16	

Time:

Score:

278

11		16		17	8		18	
5	12	10			6			
			10		12	17		
24		14				15	9	
		11	11				9	
4			17	16			18	
25	12			7		4		17
	12			11	14			
		4					9	

Scoring:
Less than 18 mins = 15
18–40 mins = 10
over 40 mins = 5

Time:

Score:

279

19			17		6		17	
16				10		16		
17	10		17		14			15
		17		3			6	
	8		19			8		
3		6	11		10		24	17
	12			9				
23			10		24	14		
						7		

Scoring:
Less than 18 mins = 15
18–40 mins = 10
over 40 mins = 5

Time:

Score:

280

Scoring:
Less than 18 mins = 15
18–40 mins = 10
over 40 mins = 5

23		3		18		29		
	24				3			13
9				15	19			
	9	14						16
7		24					4	
	18	18		4	17			23
					22			
	29	4		27				10
					3			

Time:

Score:

281

Scoring:
Less than 18 mins = 15
18–40 mins = 10
over 40 mins = 5

10		8		9		20		
	24			12	7	6		14
10	6	15				13		
		9	15	15			16	
24					15	3	17	
		8						7
6	16		5	12	17			
					18			12
16			11		9			

Time:

Score:

282

14	16	6		10	14			10
		10				10		
4	3		7	12	17		11	
	17				10		9	
15			9			21		
6		15		12	10	4		13
11		8				11		
9	10		23		3		7	10
	19				9			

Scoring:
Less than 18 mins = 15
18–40 mins = 10
over 40 mins = 5

Time:

Score:

283

5		18		14	17		11	
11		13				3	11	
16			12		19		24	
	9			4			7	
10		14			10			3
	16	3	24			10	14	
			13	18	11			
13						13		
13		6			8		12	

Scoring:
Less than 18 mins = 15
18–40 mins = 10
over 40 mins = 5

Time:

Score:

284

Scoring:
Less than 18 mins = 15
18–40 mins = 10
over 40 mins = 5

25		24			3		21	
		18	21	11		15		
3					6		17	
	17			13				11
9		3			7		11	
	4	14	12		25	21		9
32							21	
			9					
		5		18				

Time:

Score:

285

Scoring:
Less than 18 mins = 15
18–40 mins = 10
over 40 mins = 5

24	4		3	12	10	13		9
	8					16		
	6	12		17	4		10	
24		16			7			26
			16					
	10	15		4	3		15	
7		7			17			14
	12		8	8	16	6		
	17					9		

Time:

Score:

286

18	12	12	9			10	9	22
			15	10	11			
	8					11		
	17	7		34	17		7	
17								14
		3				15		
10			6	21	11		5	
5	17	16				9	15	12

Scoring:
Less than 25 mins = 15
25–60 mins = 10
over 60 mins = 5

Time:

Score:

287

6		10		8		24		
	15			8	13	10		9
12	21	14				9		
		4	5	25			17	
15					15	14	14	
		16						3
17	14		12	10	4			
					12			17
7			17		8			

Scoring:
Less than 25 mins = 15
25–60 mins = 10
over 60 mins = 5

Time:

Score:

288

Scoring:
Less than 25 mins = 15
25–60 mins = 10
over 60 mins = 5

9		17		11	8		9	
6			9		15	22		
16		11				8	14	
12			12					12
	11	3		17	14		5	
13		16			8			21
		9		16		8		
10			15		16		13	
16							3	

Time:

Score:

289

Scoring:
Less than 25 mins = 15
25–60 mins = 10
over 60 mins = 5

16		16	23	9			14	
					10	15		
22		11	13				15	15
					10			
6	10		21			8		
	16	3		13		17	25	
		12	10					
23				23		11	11	
		7						

Time:

Score:

290

15	16		10			17		16
		12		9	12			
	19				9			
22	16		4	12	11	3		29
		3				7		
11			18					14
		15		3	13			
16	5	11			15		12	3
		27						

Scoring:
Less than 25 mins = 15
25–60 mins = 10
over 60 mins = 5

Time:

Score:

291

13		10	15	10	8	14	5	
10							5	
9	11		12			15		13
	9			15	16			
14	9	5			11		11	11
		14	15		14	7		
	14			16			16	
		5			8			
19			6			20		

Scoring:
Less than 25 mins = 15
25–60 mins = 10
over 60 mins = 5

Time:

Score:

292

Scoring:
Less than 25 mins = 15
25–60 mins = 10
over 60 mins = 5

15			15		16		12	
13				9		22		
22	17		4		18			13
		13		5			10	
	3		16			10		
6		14	16		8		15	17
	21			6				
10			18		19	6		
						16		

Time:

Score:

293

Scoring:
Less than 25 mins = 15
25–60 mins = 10
over 60 mins = 5

13		11	10		4	3		10
11			14			23		
11	24			12	13			6
		13				10		
10			12			15	9	
5	10		19		18		15	
	18	5						
11			12	10		5	11	
	9			9			14	

Time:

Score:

294

9		15		8	11		4	
15	12				16			16
	5		17			10		
12		11	10		9	17	8	
8				12			8	
7	11	15			6		9	10
		12		21	11			
14						16		
9		10			11		10	

Scoring:
Less than 25 mins = 15
25–60 mins = 10
over 60 mins = 5

Time:

Score:

295

13		13		12	4		28	
6	11	13			11			
			17		13	7		
15		18				17	3	
		3	11				15	
16			6	13			13	
24	11			11		12		8
	12			10	9			
		13					17	

Scoring:
Less than 25 mins = 15
25–60 mins = 10
over 60 mins = 5

Time:

Score:

296

Scoring:
Less than 25 mins = 15
25–60 mins = 10
over 60 mins = 5

Time:

Score:

297

Scoring:
Less than 25 mins = 15
25–60 mins = 10
over 60 mins = 5

Time:

Score:

298

21		26				6		
	7		5	7		20		
12	15			15	18		12	
		9				17		
	18		18			12		20
17			7	21			6	
					8			
19			6			14		15
11			23					

Scoring:
Less than 25 mins = 15
25–60 mins = 10
over 60 mins = 5

Time:

Score:

299

32		13			17	3		16
			24			23		
				7				11
7			35		23			
	25	16						15
						30		
	11		3				35	
14			14					
	16			15				

Scoring:
Less than 25 mins = 15
25–60 mins = 10
over 60 mins = 5

Time:

Score:

300

Scoring:
Less than 25 mins = 15
25–60 mins = 10
over 60 mins = 5

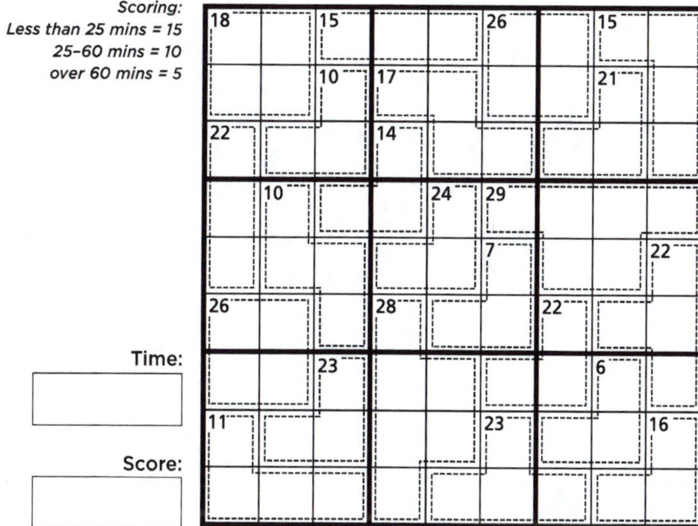

Time:

Score:

ANSWERS

ANSWERS: CLASSIC

1 CLASSIC

1	7	6	2	5	4	9	3	8
8	2	9	3	6	1	4	7	5
4	5	3	8	7	9	2	6	1
2	3	5	6	9	8	7	1	4
6	9	4	1	3	7	5	8	2
7	1	8	4	2	5	6	9	3
3	6	7	5	1	2	8	4	9
5	8	1	9	4	6	3	2	7
9	4	2	7	8	3	1	5	6

Score: __________

2 CLASSIC

6	1	9	7	5	2	4	8	3
4	3	7	1	6	8	5	9	2
8	2	5	4	9	3	6	7	1
7	5	2	8	3	9	1	6	4
3	4	1	6	2	7	8	5	9
9	6	8	5	1	4	3	2	7
5	7	3	9	4	6	2	1	8
1	9	4	2	8	5	7	3	6
2	8	6	3	7	1	9	4	5

Score: __________

3 CLASSIC

7	3	4	2	5	8	6	9	1
9	6	5	1	4	3	8	2	7
1	8	2	6	9	7	4	3	5
4	9	3	7	8	1	5	6	2
5	1	8	4	2	6	3	7	9
2	7	6	5	3	9	1	8	4
3	4	9	8	1	2	7	5	6
8	5	7	9	6	4	2	1	3
6	2	1	3	7	5	9	4	8

Score: __________

4 CLASSIC

6	7	8	5	3	4	1	9	2
4	2	3	7	1	9	6	5	8
9	5	1	6	2	8	4	3	7
2	1	7	3	4	6	9	8	5
3	8	9	1	5	7	2	6	4
5	6	4	8	9	2	7	1	3
8	4	6	9	7	3	5	2	1
1	9	2	4	8	5	3	7	6
7	3	5	2	6	1	8	4	9

Score: __________

5 CLASSIC

8	5	4	9	2	7	1	6	3
1	7	9	6	3	4	2	5	8
2	6	3	5	8	1	4	7	9
3	8	7	2	1	9	5	4	6
6	2	5	4	7	3	8	9	1
9	4	1	8	6	5	3	2	7
4	9	8	1	5	6	7	3	2
7	1	6	3	4	2	9	8	5
5	3	2	7	9	8	6	1	4

Score: __________

6 CLASSIC

6	7	8	5	1	2	4	9	3
9	4	5	3	8	7	1	2	6
2	1	3	6	4	9	8	5	7
4	5	6	8	9	3	7	1	2
1	3	7	4	2	5	9	6	8
8	2	9	7	6	1	5	3	4
5	6	4	1	3	8	2	7	9
3	9	1	2	7	4	6	8	5
7	8	2	9	5	6	3	4	1

Score: __________

7 CLASSIC

4	2	3	5	6	8	7	9	1
6	9	7	4	1	2	8	3	5
1	5	8	7	3	9	2	4	6
9	7	2	3	8	6	5	1	4
8	4	6	9	5	1	3	7	2
5	3	1	2	4	7	6	8	9
2	1	9	8	7	5	4	6	3
3	8	5	6	9	4	1	2	7
7	6	4	1	2	3	9	5	8

Score: __________

8 CLASSIC

8	6	7	2	4	9	3	1	5
9	2	1	6	5	3	7	4	8
5	4	3	8	7	1	6	2	9
1	5	8	4	3	7	9	6	2
7	9	4	5	6	2	8	3	1
6	3	2	1	9	8	5	7	4
4	8	5	7	2	6	1	9	3
3	1	6	9	8	4	2	5	7
2	7	9	3	1	5	4	8	6

Score: __________

9 CLASSIC

6	2	7	3	9	4	8	5	1
8	4	1	7	5	6	9	3	2
5	3	9	8	2	1	4	6	7
1	9	6	5	4	2	3	7	8
4	5	3	1	8	7	6	2	9
7	8	2	6	3	9	5	1	4
3	1	4	9	7	5	2	8	6
9	6	5	2	1	8	7	4	3
2	7	8	4	6	3	1	9	5

Score: __________

10 CLASSIC

3	9	8	6	2	5	1	7	4
5	1	4	8	7	3	2	9	6
2	7	6	9	1	4	5	8	3
7	4	1	3	6	2	9	5	8
6	2	5	7	9	8	4	3	1
9	8	3	4	5	1	6	2	7
1	6	9	2	8	7	3	4	5
4	5	7	1	3	9	8	6	2
8	3	2	5	4	6	7	1	9

Score: __________

11 CLASSIC

8	5	2	6	4	9	1	7	3
1	7	3	2	8	5	9	6	4
4	9	6	1	7	3	5	2	8
7	4	8	5	3	6	2	9	1
6	1	9	8	2	7	4	3	5
3	2	5	4	9	1	7	8	6
2	6	1	7	5	8	3	4	9
5	3	4	9	6	2	8	1	7
9	8	7	3	1	4	6	5	2

Score: __________

12 CLASSIC

9	2	5	8	1	7	6	4	3
6	1	3	4	5	9	2	8	7
7	4	8	3	2	6	5	9	1
1	5	2	9	3	4	8	7	6
8	7	4	2	6	1	3	5	9
3	9	6	5	7	8	1	2	4
4	3	9	6	8	2	7	1	5
2	6	7	1	4	5	9	3	8
5	8	1	7	9	3	4	6	2

Score: __________

13 CLASSIC

8	6	5	4	9	3	1	7	2
4	1	7	2	5	6	3	8	9
9	2	3	7	1	8	6	4	5
3	7	6	9	4	5	2	1	8
1	5	8	6	3	2	7	9	4
2	4	9	1	8	7	5	6	3
5	3	4	8	7	1	9	2	6
6	9	1	5	2	4	8	3	7
7	8	2	3	6	9	4	5	1

Score: __________

14 CLASSIC

2	5	6	3	4	1	7	8	9
7	4	9	2	5	8	1	6	3
1	3	8	9	7	6	4	5	2
9	7	3	4	8	5	6	2	1
5	6	1	7	3	2	8	9	4
8	2	4	1	6	9	5	3	7
3	9	5	8	1	4	2	7	6
6	1	2	5	9	7	3	4	8
4	8	7	6	2	3	9	1	5

Score: __________

15 CLASSIC

3	4	1	9	6	7	5	2	8
9	5	2	8	1	3	6	4	7
8	6	7	5	4	2	9	3	1
4	3	8	6	7	9	1	5	2
5	1	6	2	8	4	7	9	3
7	2	9	1	3	5	8	6	4
1	8	3	4	9	6	2	7	5
2	9	4	7	5	1	3	8	6
6	7	5	3	2	8	4	1	9

Score: __________

16 CLASSIC

8	4	9	5	3	6	1	2	7
1	7	5	9	4	2	8	6	3
3	2	6	1	7	8	4	9	5
9	6	7	3	8	5	2	4	1
4	3	2	7	9	1	5	8	6
5	1	8	6	2	4	3	7	9
2	9	1	8	6	3	7	5	4
6	8	3	4	5	7	9	1	2
7	5	4	2	1	9	6	3	8

Score: __________

ANSWERS: CLASSIC

17 CLASSIC

3	1	5	7	2	6	8	4	9
9	8	2	4	5	1	6	7	3
4	7	6	8	9	3	1	2	5
2	3	1	5	6	7	4	9	8
6	9	7	3	4	8	5	1	2
5	4	8	9	1	2	7	3	6
7	6	4	2	3	5	9	8	1
8	5	3	1	7	9	2	6	4
1	2	9	6	8	4	3	5	7

Score: ________

18 CLASSIC

3	7	5	2	8	9	4	6	1
1	2	4	5	6	3	8	9	7
9	6	8	1	4	7	5	2	3
7	5	6	3	1	8	9	4	2
8	1	2	7	9	4	3	5	6
4	9	3	6	5	2	1	7	8
2	4	7	8	3	5	6	1	9
6	3	9	4	7	1	2	8	5
5	8	1	9	2	6	7	3	4

Score: ________

19 CLASSIC

5	2	8	3	9	6	7	4	1
3	1	9	2	7	4	6	8	5
4	7	6	5	1	8	9	3	2
9	8	5	4	2	1	3	7	6
2	3	4	6	8	7	1	5	9
7	6	1	9	5	3	8	2	4
6	4	2	7	3	9	5	1	8
8	9	3	1	4	5	2	6	7
1	5	7	8	6	2	4	9	3

Score: ________

20 CLASSIC

1	8	6	2	5	7	4	9	3
2	9	5	1	4	3	7	6	8
3	4	7	8	9	6	1	2	5
9	3	8	4	2	1	6	5	7
5	6	2	3	7	9	8	1	4
7	1	4	6	8	5	9	3	2
6	5	1	7	3	4	2	8	9
8	7	9	5	6	2	3	4	1
4	2	3	9	1	8	5	7	6

Score: ________

21 CLASSIC

6	7	1	3	8	2	4	5	9
2	5	4	9	7	1	6	3	8
9	8	3	6	4	5	7	1	2
5	6	8	7	9	4	3	2	1
7	4	9	1	2	3	5	8	6
1	3	2	8	5	6	9	4	7
8	2	6	4	3	9	1	7	5
3	9	7	5	1	8	2	6	4
4	1	5	2	6	7	8	9	3

Score: ________

22 CLASSIC

1	5	2	6	8	3	7	9	4
6	8	9	7	4	5	2	3	1
7	4	3	1	2	9	8	5	6
9	7	5	3	1	4	6	8	2
2	3	6	5	7	8	4	1	9
8	1	4	9	6	2	3	7	5
3	9	8	2	5	6	1	4	7
4	6	1	8	9	7	5	2	3
5	2	7	4	3	1	9	6	8

Score: ________

23 CLASSIC

2	1	5	9	3	8	6	4	7
8	4	7	1	2	6	9	5	3
6	3	9	5	4	7	1	2	8
4	9	6	8	1	2	3	7	5
1	5	3	7	6	4	8	9	2
7	2	8	3	9	5	4	1	6
5	7	1	6	8	9	2	3	4
3	8	4	2	5	1	7	6	9
9	6	2	4	7	3	5	8	1

Score: ________

24 CLASSIC

7	6	9	4	5	8	2	1	3
4	1	3	6	7	2	5	9	8
8	2	5	1	9	3	4	7	6
3	5	8	9	1	7	6	4	2
6	7	1	2	8	4	3	5	9
2	9	4	5	3	6	1	8	7
9	3	6	8	4	1	7	2	5
5	4	7	3	2	9	8	6	1
1	8	2	7	6	5	9	3	4

Score: ________

25 CLASSIC

1	6	4	5	3	7	8	2	9
2	5	8	6	9	4	3	1	7
7	9	3	2	8	1	6	5	4
6	8	2	7	1	9	5	4	3
9	3	1	8	4	5	2	7	6
5	4	7	3	2	6	9	8	1
8	2	6	1	7	3	4	9	5
4	1	5	9	6	8	7	3	2
3	7	9	4	5	2	1	6	8

Score: __________

26 CLASSIC

5	6	1	8	7	9	3	4	2
7	2	9	4	6	3	5	8	1
8	3	4	5	2	1	7	6	9
3	7	6	2	9	4	8	1	5
1	9	2	6	5	8	4	7	3
4	5	8	3	1	7	9	2	6
2	4	3	1	8	5	6	9	7
9	1	5	7	4	6	2	3	8
6	8	7	9	3	2	1	5	4

Score: __________

27 CLASSIC

7	2	4	1	6	8	9	5	3
1	6	9	7	3	5	8	2	4
8	5	3	9	2	4	6	7	1
4	7	8	3	5	1	2	9	6
9	3	6	4	7	2	5	1	8
5	1	2	8	9	6	3	4	7
2	4	5	6	8	7	1	3	9
6	9	1	2	4	3	7	8	5
3	8	7	5	1	9	4	6	2

Score: __________

28 CLASSIC

9	4	5	1	2	3	7	6	8
7	2	8	9	6	4	5	1	3
3	1	6	5	7	8	4	9	2
2	9	4	6	1	5	3	8	7
5	8	7	3	9	2	1	4	6
1	6	3	8	4	7	9	2	5
8	7	2	4	3	9	6	5	1
4	3	1	2	5	6	8	7	9
6	5	9	7	8	1	2	3	4

Score: __________

29 CLASSIC

6	1	3	7	5	9	2	8	4
7	2	5	4	6	8	9	3	1
9	4	8	3	1	2	6	7	5
5	6	7	1	2	4	8	9	3
2	9	4	5	8	3	1	6	7
8	3	1	9	7	6	5	4	2
1	7	9	8	3	5	4	2	6
4	5	6	2	9	7	3	1	8
3	8	2	6	4	1	7	5	9

Score: __________

30 CLASSIC

3	7	4	9	5	2	1	8	6
5	6	1	4	8	3	2	9	7
8	2	9	7	6	1	3	4	5
4	1	8	3	9	6	7	5	2
2	9	3	5	1	7	4	6	8
7	5	6	8	2	4	9	3	1
9	4	2	6	7	5	8	1	3
6	8	7	1	3	9	5	2	4
1	3	5	2	4	8	6	7	9

Score: __________

31 CLASSIC

2	7	4	6	5	9	3	8	1
1	3	9	8	2	7	4	5	6
5	6	8	1	4	3	2	7	9
8	2	1	4	7	6	5	9	3
3	5	6	9	1	8	7	4	2
9	4	7	2	3	5	1	6	8
7	9	5	3	6	1	8	2	4
4	8	3	7	9	2	6	1	5
6	1	2	5	8	4	9	3	7

Score: __________

32 CLASSIC

6	1	3	9	7	5	2	8	4
7	9	2	8	4	6	1	3	5
5	8	4	3	1	2	9	7	6
2	3	9	5	6	4	8	1	7
1	4	5	7	3	8	6	9	2
8	7	6	1	2	9	4	5	3
3	2	8	6	9	7	5	4	1
9	6	7	4	5	1	3	2	8
4	5	1	2	8	3	7	6	9

Score: __________

ANSWERS: CLASSIC

33 CLASSIC

9	1	6	5	3	2	7	8	4
4	8	2	6	7	1	3	9	5
3	5	7	4	8	9	1	2	6
8	9	5	7	6	4	2	1	3
7	6	1	3	2	8	4	5	9
2	4	3	9	1	5	6	7	8
6	2	4	8	9	7	5	3	1
5	7	9	1	4	3	8	6	2
1	3	8	2	5	6	9	4	7

Score: __________

34 CLASSIC

9	4	5	7	8	2	1	3	6
2	6	3	9	4	1	7	8	5
7	8	1	3	5	6	4	9	2
3	5	2	4	1	7	8	6	9
1	9	4	8	6	5	2	7	3
8	7	6	2	3	9	5	4	1
6	3	7	5	2	8	9	1	4
5	1	8	6	9	4	3	2	7
4	2	9	1	7	3	6	5	8

Score: __________

35 CLASSIC

3	7	8	2	4	9	6	1	5
9	1	2	6	5	3	8	7	4
4	5	6	7	1	8	3	9	2
5	2	9	3	7	1	4	8	6
8	4	1	9	6	2	5	3	7
6	3	7	4	8	5	9	2	1
7	8	4	1	3	6	2	5	9
2	6	5	8	9	7	1	4	3
1	9	3	5	2	4	7	6	8

Score: __________

36 CLASSIC

5	1	3	8	6	2	7	9	4
2	4	8	9	7	3	5	6	1
9	7	6	4	1	5	3	8	2
1	6	9	5	2	4	8	7	3
4	5	7	3	8	6	2	1	9
3	8	2	1	9	7	6	4	5
6	9	4	2	3	8	1	5	7
7	3	5	6	4	1	9	2	8
8	2	1	7	5	9	4	3	6

Score: __________

37 CLASSIC

3	2	1	7	5	8	6	4	9
9	4	7	1	6	3	8	5	2
8	5	6	4	2	9	3	1	7
1	9	5	3	4	7	2	8	6
4	6	8	9	1	2	7	3	5
2	7	3	5	8	6	4	9	1
6	1	2	8	3	5	9	7	4
5	8	9	6	7	4	1	2	3
7	3	4	2	9	1	5	6	8

Score: __________

38 CLASSIC

8	9	6	3	1	2	7	5	4
5	3	2	7	4	9	6	8	1
7	1	4	6	5	8	3	2	9
3	4	5	8	7	6	9	1	2
9	2	7	5	3	1	8	4	6
1	6	8	2	9	4	5	7	3
4	7	1	9	8	3	2	6	5
6	8	3	1	2	5	4	9	7
2	5	9	4	6	7	1	3	8

Score: __________

39 CLASSIC

7	3	9	5	6	8	1	2	4
2	6	8	9	4	1	3	5	7
4	1	5	2	7	3	6	8	9
5	2	6	1	9	4	7	3	8
9	8	4	3	2	7	5	6	1
1	7	3	6	8	5	4	9	2
6	9	1	4	5	2	8	7	3
3	5	7	8	1	9	2	4	6
8	4	2	7	3	6	9	1	5

Score: __________

40 CLASSIC

1	3	8	4	7	6	5	9	2
9	2	6	8	5	1	7	4	3
5	7	4	3	9	2	8	1	6
7	6	1	5	2	9	3	8	4
4	9	3	6	1	8	2	7	5
8	5	2	7	3	4	1	6	9
3	8	5	9	6	7	4	2	1
2	4	9	1	8	3	6	5	7
6	1	7	2	4	5	9	3	8

Score: __________

41 CLASSIC

1	9	6	7	3	2	5	4	8
5	3	8	4	6	9	1	2	7
2	4	7	5	8	1	9	6	3
7	5	2	1	4	8	3	9	6
8	1	3	2	9	6	7	5	4
9	6	4	3	7	5	2	8	1
4	7	9	8	2	3	6	1	5
3	2	1	6	5	4	8	7	9
6	8	5	9	1	7	4	3	2

Score: ____________

42 CLASSIC

5	9	1	6	2	7	4	3	8
4	8	7	5	3	9	6	2	1
3	2	6	4	8	1	5	9	7
9	1	5	2	4	3	7	8	6
2	4	8	7	9	6	3	1	5
6	7	3	8	1	5	9	4	2
8	5	9	3	6	2	1	7	4
7	3	2	1	5	4	8	6	9
1	6	4	9	7	8	2	5	3

Score: ____________

43 CLASSIC

9	4	5	8	6	1	2	3	7
7	8	3	2	4	5	6	9	1
6	2	1	9	7	3	5	4	8
5	1	8	3	9	7	4	2	6
3	9	2	6	1	4	7	8	5
4	7	6	5	2	8	3	1	9
1	6	9	7	3	2	8	5	4
8	3	4	1	5	6	9	7	2
2	5	7	4	8	9	1	6	3

Score: ____________

44 CLASSIC

7	8	4	3	6	2	5	1	9
2	3	5	1	9	4	6	7	8
6	1	9	7	8	5	4	3	2
1	9	6	4	2	8	3	5	7
8	2	7	5	1	3	9	6	4
5	4	3	6	7	9	8	2	1
9	6	2	8	5	7	1	4	3
4	5	8	2	3	1	7	9	6
3	7	1	9	4	6	2	8	5

Score: ____________

45 CLASSIC

2	1	3	8	6	9	4	7	5
5	4	8	3	2	7	1	9	6
9	7	6	5	4	1	3	2	8
4	9	1	7	5	8	6	3	2
8	3	5	6	9	2	7	1	4
7	6	2	4	1	3	8	5	9
3	8	9	2	7	4	5	6	1
6	2	7	1	8	5	9	4	3
1	5	4	9	3	6	2	8	7

Score: ____________

46 CLASSIC

5	2	8	4	6	7	3	1	9
9	4	3	1	5	8	7	6	2
6	7	1	9	3	2	5	8	4
1	6	7	5	2	4	9	3	8
4	8	2	3	9	6	1	5	7
3	5	9	8	7	1	4	2	6
2	9	4	6	1	5	8	7	3
7	3	5	2	8	9	6	4	1
8	1	6	7	4	3	2	9	5

Score: ____________

47 CLASSIC

3	7	1	5	9	2	6	8	4
8	6	4	1	3	7	2	5	9
9	2	5	6	4	8	3	7	1
7	5	3	4	2	9	1	6	8
1	4	9	8	6	3	5	2	7
6	8	2	7	5	1	9	4	3
5	9	6	3	8	4	7	1	2
2	1	8	9	7	5	4	3	6
4	3	7	2	1	6	8	9	5

Score: ____________

48 CLASSIC

5	2	1	8	4	6	7	3	9
3	7	4	1	2	9	8	6	5
9	8	6	3	7	5	2	4	1
1	9	3	4	8	2	5	7	6
7	4	5	6	3	1	9	8	2
8	6	2	5	9	7	4	1	3
6	1	7	9	5	8	3	2	4
2	3	9	7	1	4	6	5	8
4	5	8	2	6	3	1	9	7

Score: ____________

ANSWERS: CLASSIC

49 CLASSIC

8	6	1	2	5	7	4	3	9
9	4	2	6	3	8	1	5	7
5	3	7	1	4	9	8	6	2
1	8	6	3	7	2	9	4	5
4	9	5	8	1	6	7	2	3
2	7	3	4	9	5	6	8	1
6	1	9	5	2	4	3	7	8
3	5	8	7	6	1	2	9	4
7	2	4	9	8	3	5	1	6

Score: ________

50 CLASSIC

3	5	4	1	9	2	7	6	8
8	9	7	3	4	6	2	5	1
6	2	1	8	5	7	4	9	3
9	1	6	7	3	5	8	4	2
4	3	8	6	2	1	9	7	5
2	7	5	4	8	9	1	3	6
5	6	2	9	7	8	3	1	4
1	4	9	2	6	3	5	8	7
7	8	3	5	1	4	6	2	9

Score: ________

51 CLASSIC

3	7	9	5	2	1	8	4	6
6	8	4	9	7	3	1	5	2
2	1	5	6	4	8	7	3	9
8	4	2	1	3	5	9	6	7
9	5	6	7	8	4	2	1	3
7	3	1	2	6	9	5	8	4
1	6	7	4	5	2	3	9	8
5	2	3	8	9	6	4	7	1
4	9	8	3	1	7	6	2	5

Score: ________

52 CLASSIC

9	4	2	3	6	7	5	1	8
1	6	7	5	9	8	4	3	2
5	3	8	4	1	2	7	9	6
2	9	3	8	7	1	6	5	4
4	1	5	2	3	6	8	7	9
8	7	6	9	4	5	1	2	3
3	5	9	1	8	4	2	6	7
7	8	1	6	2	3	9	4	5
6	2	4	7	5	9	3	8	1

Score: ________

53 CLASSIC

7	2	8	9	3	6	5	4	1
3	4	9	5	8	1	6	2	7
6	5	1	7	4	2	9	3	8
4	3	7	8	1	9	2	6	5
2	1	5	3	6	7	4	8	9
9	8	6	2	5	4	1	7	3
5	7	4	1	2	8	3	9	6
1	9	2	6	7	3	8	5	4
8	6	3	4	9	5	7	1	2

Score: ________

54 CLASSIC

9	8	3	7	4	5	6	2	1
7	2	1	8	3	6	9	4	5
5	6	4	1	2	9	3	7	8
6	9	7	5	8	1	4	3	2
8	1	2	4	6	3	7	5	9
3	4	5	9	7	2	1	8	6
2	3	8	6	9	4	5	1	7
4	5	9	2	1	7	8	6	3
1	7	6	3	5	8	2	9	4

Score: ________

55 CLASSIC

2	8	4	5	7	9	6	1	3
5	6	9	2	1	3	7	4	8
3	7	1	8	4	6	9	5	2
4	5	8	3	2	7	1	6	9
6	3	7	9	5	1	8	2	4
1	9	2	4	6	8	5	3	7
8	4	6	7	3	5	2	9	1
7	1	3	6	9	2	4	8	5
9	2	5	1	8	4	3	7	6

Score: ________

56 CLASSIC

7	4	9	5	2	3	8	1	6
3	6	8	9	7	1	5	4	2
2	5	1	4	8	6	3	7	9
5	8	3	1	9	4	6	2	7
9	2	4	6	3	7	1	8	5
1	7	6	2	5	8	4	9	3
4	1	2	3	6	9	7	5	8
8	3	5	7	4	2	9	6	1
6	9	7	8	1	5	2	3	4

Score: ________

57 CLASSIC

3	2	9	5	1	7	8	6	4
4	1	7	8	6	3	5	9	2
6	5	8	9	2	4	3	7	1
8	6	1	7	9	2	4	5	3
2	9	5	4	3	6	1	8	7
7	3	4	1	5	8	9	2	6
1	8	3	6	7	9	2	4	5
5	4	6	2	8	1	7	3	9
9	7	2	3	4	5	6	1	8

Score: ________

58 CLASSIC

7	8	5	3	2	9	6	4	1
3	9	1	7	4	6	5	2	8
6	2	4	8	5	1	9	7	3
1	7	8	5	6	2	3	9	4
2	5	3	9	8	4	7	1	6
4	6	9	1	7	3	8	5	2
9	4	6	2	3	5	1	8	7
5	3	7	4	1	8	2	6	9
8	1	2	6	9	7	4	3	5

Score: ________

59 CLASSIC

1	6	9	4	5	2	3	7	8
3	8	2	9	7	1	4	6	5
4	7	5	6	3	8	2	9	1
7	4	6	8	2	9	1	5	3
2	1	3	5	4	7	6	8	9
5	9	8	1	6	3	7	2	4
6	2	1	3	8	5	9	4	7
9	5	7	2	1	4	8	3	6
8	3	4	7	9	6	5	1	2

Score: ________

60 CLASSIC

7	1	9	4	5	8	6	3	2
6	3	5	9	1	2	7	4	8
8	2	4	6	7	3	9	5	1
5	8	2	1	4	7	3	9	6
4	9	7	3	8	6	1	2	5
3	6	1	2	9	5	8	7	4
1	5	3	8	2	9	4	6	7
2	4	6	7	3	1	5	8	9
9	7	8	5	6	4	2	1	3

Score: ________

61 CLASSIC

7	6	1	4	9	8	5	3	2
3	8	5	2	1	6	4	9	7
4	2	9	7	3	5	6	1	8
5	3	4	6	7	1	2	8	9
1	9	8	3	2	4	7	5	6
6	7	2	8	5	9	3	4	1
8	1	7	5	6	3	9	2	4
2	4	3	9	8	7	1	6	5
9	5	6	1	4	2	8	7	3

Score: ________

62 CLASSIC

5	9	3	7	1	4	6	8	2
6	7	1	3	8	2	4	9	5
4	8	2	9	6	5	3	1	7
7	5	8	6	2	1	9	4	3
2	1	9	5	4	3	7	6	8
3	6	4	8	9	7	2	5	1
8	4	7	1	3	6	5	2	9
9	2	5	4	7	8	1	3	6
1	3	6	2	5	9	8	7	4

Score: ________

63 CLASSIC

9	6	2	3	1	4	7	5	8
4	5	1	7	6	8	2	9	3
8	3	7	2	5	9	4	6	1
2	8	3	9	7	5	6	1	4
6	4	9	8	2	1	3	7	5
1	7	5	4	3	6	9	8	2
7	1	6	5	4	2	8	3	9
3	9	4	1	8	7	5	2	6
5	2	8	6	9	3	1	4	7

Score: ________

64 CLASSIC

8	2	9	5	7	3	1	4	6
3	6	4	1	8	9	2	5	7
7	1	5	6	2	4	9	3	8
1	5	6	3	9	2	7	8	4
9	7	8	4	1	5	6	2	3
2	4	3	8	6	7	5	9	1
5	8	7	9	4	1	3	6	2
4	3	1	2	5	6	8	7	9
6	9	2	7	3	8	4	1	5

Score: ________

ANSWERS: CLASSIC

65 *CLASSIC*

1	8	2	6	4	5	7	9	3
7	3	4	2	8	9	1	6	5
9	6	5	3	1	7	2	4	8
3	9	6	5	7	2	4	8	1
5	1	8	4	6	3	9	7	2
2	4	7	8	9	1	5	3	6
6	7	3	1	2	4	8	5	9
8	2	9	7	5	6	3	1	4
4	5	1	9	3	8	6	2	7

Score: ____________

66 *CLASSIC*

8	9	4	7	5	3	1	2	6
6	7	1	8	2	9	3	5	4
5	2	3	1	6	4	8	9	7
3	6	8	5	9	2	7	4	1
9	4	2	3	1	7	5	6	8
1	5	7	4	8	6	2	3	9
7	3	5	6	4	8	9	1	2
4	1	9	2	7	5	6	8	3
2	8	6	9	3	1	4	7	5

Score: ____________

67 *CLASSIC*

6	9	1	3	4	7	2	8	5
4	3	2	1	5	8	9	6	7
8	7	5	6	2	9	4	3	1
7	1	8	4	9	3	5	2	6
5	6	3	8	1	2	7	9	4
2	4	9	7	6	5	8	1	3
9	8	4	5	3	6	1	7	2
3	5	7	2	8	1	6	4	9
1	2	6	9	7	4	3	5	8

Score: ____________

68 *CLASSIC*

5	1	2	4	9	3	7	8	6
7	3	4	8	6	5	9	2	1
8	9	6	1	7	2	3	4	5
6	7	5	2	1	9	8	3	4
4	8	3	7	5	6	2	1	9
1	2	9	3	8	4	5	6	7
9	4	1	5	2	8	6	7	3
3	6	8	9	4	7	1	5	2
2	5	7	6	3	1	4	9	8

Score: ____________

69 *CLASSIC*

3	2	8	1	4	5	9	7	6
7	6	4	3	9	8	2	5	1
9	1	5	6	7	2	3	4	8
1	3	2	5	8	7	6	9	4
4	5	6	9	2	3	8	1	7
8	7	9	4	1	6	5	3	2
2	8	1	7	3	9	4	6	5
5	9	7	2	6	4	1	8	3
6	4	3	8	5	1	7	2	9

Score: ____________

70 *CLASSIC*

1	8	2	4	5	7	6	3	9
9	5	6	2	3	1	7	4	8
3	7	4	8	9	6	1	5	2
8	4	9	7	1	2	3	6	5
5	2	7	6	8	3	9	1	4
6	3	1	5	4	9	8	2	7
2	9	5	1	6	8	4	7	3
7	1	8	3	2	4	5	9	6
4	6	3	9	7	5	2	8	1

Score: ____________

71 *CLASSIC*

4	6	2	3	8	5	1	7	9
8	9	5	7	1	6	4	3	2
3	1	7	4	2	9	8	6	5
1	7	4	5	9	3	2	8	6
5	8	9	2	6	1	3	4	7
6	2	3	8	4	7	5	9	1
7	5	8	9	3	2	6	1	4
2	3	6	1	7	4	9	5	8
9	4	1	6	5	8	7	2	3

Score: ____________

72 *CLASSIC*

3	6	7	1	4	5	2	9	8
4	1	9	8	7	2	5	3	6
2	8	5	3	6	9	4	7	1
5	2	8	6	3	7	9	1	4
9	7	3	5	1	4	8	6	2
1	4	6	2	9	8	3	5	7
6	9	2	7	8	3	1	4	5
7	5	4	9	2	1	6	8	3
8	3	1	4	5	6	7	2	9

Score: ____________

73 *CLASSIC*

7	5	9	6	4	1	3	8	2
4	3	2	7	8	5	1	9	6
8	6	1	9	3	2	5	4	7
3	1	8	4	5	7	6	2	9
5	7	6	2	9	8	4	1	3
9	2	4	3	1	6	7	5	8
1	9	5	8	7	3	2	6	4
2	4	3	1	6	9	8	7	5
6	8	7	5	2	4	9	3	1

Score: ________

74 *CLASSIC*

1	3	2	6	9	5	4	8	7
4	7	6	8	1	2	5	3	9
5	9	8	4	7	3	2	1	6
9	8	3	7	2	4	1	6	5
6	1	7	5	3	9	8	2	4
2	5	4	1	6	8	7	9	3
7	2	1	3	5	6	9	4	8
8	6	5	9	4	1	3	7	2
3	4	9	2	8	7	6	5	1

Score: ________

75 *CLASSIC*

6	9	4	8	3	7	5	2	1
1	5	7	9	6	2	4	8	3
3	2	8	1	4	5	6	7	9
8	1	9	4	5	6	7	3	2
5	6	3	2	7	1	8	9	4
7	4	2	3	9	8	1	6	5
9	3	1	7	8	4	2	5	6
2	7	6	5	1	3	9	4	8
4	8	5	6	2	9	3	1	7

Score: ________

76 *CLASSIC*

9	8	1	4	3	7	6	2	5
5	2	6	8	9	1	7	4	3
3	7	4	2	5	6	9	8	1
7	1	9	5	2	8	3	6	4
2	3	8	6	7	4	5	1	9
4	6	5	3	1	9	2	7	8
6	4	2	9	8	5	1	3	7
1	9	3	7	4	2	8	5	6
8	5	7	1	6	3	4	9	2

Score: ________

77 *CLASSIC*

5	1	6	2	8	3	9	7	4
2	8	9	6	4	7	5	3	1
3	4	7	9	1	5	6	8	2
4	2	8	5	3	9	1	6	7
9	6	5	4	7	1	3	2	8
1	7	3	8	6	2	4	9	5
6	9	4	7	5	8	2	1	3
8	3	2	1	9	4	7	5	6
7	5	1	3	2	6	8	4	9

Score: ________

78 *CLASSIC*

8	9	5	3	4	2	7	1	6
2	7	1	5	6	9	3	4	8
3	6	4	7	8	1	2	9	5
7	5	3	9	2	6	4	8	1
6	1	2	4	5	8	9	7	3
9	4	8	1	3	7	5	6	2
5	3	6	8	9	4	1	2	7
4	8	7	2	1	3	6	5	9
1	2	9	6	7	5	8	3	4

Score: ________

79 *CLASSIC*

8	3	7	4	2	9	6	5	1
1	9	4	8	5	6	2	7	3
5	2	6	1	3	7	8	4	9
4	8	5	2	1	3	9	6	7
7	6	2	5	9	4	1	3	8
3	1	9	7	6	8	4	2	5
2	5	8	3	4	1	7	9	6
6	4	1	9	7	5	3	8	2
9	7	3	6	8	2	5	1	4

Score: ________

80 *CLASSIC*

4	8	1	9	5	7	2	3	6
5	2	3	4	1	6	9	7	8
9	6	7	2	3	8	1	5	4
1	4	8	5	2	3	7	6	9
6	9	2	1	7	4	5	8	3
7	3	5	8	6	9	4	1	2
3	1	4	6	9	5	8	2	7
2	7	9	3	8	1	6	4	5
8	5	6	7	4	2	3	9	1

Score: ________

ANSWERS: CLASSIC

81 CLASSIC

8	2	4	1	9	6	3	5	7
7	5	1	4	3	2	6	9	8
9	6	3	5	8	7	2	4	1
5	4	8	6	7	9	1	3	2
3	1	9	8	2	4	7	6	5
2	7	6	3	5	1	9	8	4
4	3	7	9	1	5	8	2	6
6	8	2	7	4	3	5	1	9
1	9	5	2	6	8	4	7	3

Score: ____________

82 CLASSIC

8	1	9	2	7	5	3	6	4
7	4	2	8	3	6	5	9	1
6	3	5	9	1	4	7	2	8
9	8	1	3	5	7	6	4	2
4	2	7	1	6	8	9	5	3
3	5	6	4	9	2	8	1	7
2	9	4	5	8	3	1	7	6
5	6	8	7	4	1	2	3	9
1	7	3	6	2	9	4	8	5

Score: ____________

83 CLASSIC

7	4	6	8	5	1	3	2	9
3	5	9	2	7	4	8	6	1
1	8	2	6	9	3	5	7	4
4	2	8	5	3	9	6	1	7
5	6	3	1	2	7	4	9	8
9	1	7	4	8	6	2	5	3
6	7	1	3	4	5	9	8	2
8	3	5	9	1	2	7	4	6
2	9	4	7	6	8	1	3	5

Score: ____________

84 CLASSIC

5	4	2	1	6	8	7	9	3
6	7	1	9	5	3	2	8	4
8	3	9	4	7	2	5	1	6
2	1	8	7	4	9	6	3	5
7	6	3	5	2	1	9	4	8
4	9	5	3	8	6	1	7	2
3	5	7	6	1	4	8	2	9
9	2	6	8	3	7	4	5	1
1	8	4	2	9	5	3	6	7

Score: ____________

85 CLASSIC

7	5	8	4	1	3	9	6	2
1	9	6	7	2	8	4	3	5
2	4	3	6	9	5	1	7	8
8	3	5	1	6	9	7	2	4
4	2	9	5	8	7	6	1	3
6	7	1	3	4	2	8	5	9
9	6	7	2	3	4	5	8	1
3	1	4	8	5	6	2	9	7
5	8	2	9	7	1	3	4	6

Score: ____________

86 CLASSIC

2	9	7	5	6	3	4	1	8
8	3	6	4	1	2	5	9	7
1	5	4	8	9	7	6	3	2
5	1	8	2	3	6	7	4	9
3	4	2	7	8	9	1	6	5
6	7	9	1	5	4	2	8	3
9	6	5	3	7	1	8	2	4
4	8	1	9	2	5	3	7	6
7	2	3	6	4	8	9	5	1

Score: ____________

87 CLASSIC

6	7	4	3	1	9	5	8	2
5	9	2	4	8	6	1	7	3
1	8	3	5	2	7	4	6	9
4	6	9	2	3	5	8	1	7
8	3	1	9	7	4	2	5	6
2	5	7	1	6	8	3	9	4
3	1	5	7	9	2	6	4	8
9	2	8	6	4	1	7	3	5
7	4	6	8	5	3	9	2	1

Score: ____________

88 CLASSIC

3	5	9	8	6	1	7	4	2
7	1	2	3	5	4	9	8	6
4	8	6	9	7	2	3	5	1
9	6	5	4	2	8	1	3	7
1	4	7	6	3	9	5	2	8
8	2	3	7	1	5	6	9	4
2	7	8	1	9	3	4	6	5
6	9	4	5	8	7	2	1	3
5	3	1	2	4	6	8	7	9

Score: ____________

89 CLASSIC

1	8	7	3	6	5	4	2	9
4	9	2	8	7	1	6	5	3
3	5	6	9	4	2	8	7	1
6	1	3	5	2	9	7	8	4
9	7	4	6	1	8	2	3	5
8	2	5	7	3	4	9	1	6
7	4	9	2	5	3	1	6	8
2	3	1	4	8	6	5	9	7
5	6	8	1	9	7	3	4	2

Score: __________

90 CLASSIC

2	1	3	5	9	7	4	8	6
5	7	6	4	1	8	3	2	9
9	8	4	2	6	3	5	1	7
1	3	7	9	2	4	6	5	8
4	5	2	1	8	6	9	7	3
8	6	9	3	7	5	1	4	2
6	9	1	7	4	2	8	3	5
7	4	5	8	3	9	2	6	1
3	2	8	6	5	1	7	9	4

Score: __________

91 CLASSIC

7	6	9	5	1	3	2	4	8
4	3	2	6	8	9	5	1	7
1	8	5	4	2	7	9	3	6
9	4	3	2	6	8	7	5	1
6	5	7	9	3	1	8	2	4
2	1	8	7	4	5	6	9	3
3	2	6	8	9	4	1	7	5
8	7	1	3	5	2	4	6	9
5	9	4	1	7	6	3	8	2

Score: __________

92 CLASSIC

6	4	8	1	5	3	7	9	2
9	1	3	6	2	7	4	8	5
5	2	7	4	8	9	3	1	6
4	3	6	9	7	1	2	5	8
8	5	9	3	6	2	1	4	7
2	7	1	5	4	8	9	6	3
7	9	4	8	3	6	5	2	1
3	6	5	2	1	4	8	7	9
1	8	2	7	9	5	6	3	4

Score: __________

93 CLASSIC

5	1	9	6	7	8	2	4	3
8	2	6	4	3	5	9	1	7
3	7	4	2	9	1	5	8	6
7	3	1	8	6	9	4	5	2
4	9	8	5	2	7	3	6	1
2	6	5	3	1	4	8	7	9
9	8	3	1	4	6	7	2	5
1	4	7	9	5	2	6	3	8
6	5	2	7	8	3	1	9	4

Score: __________

94 CLASSIC

5	9	3	8	2	7	1	6	4
4	2	1	6	9	3	8	5	7
7	8	6	5	4	1	9	3	2
2	4	9	3	7	5	6	1	8
1	7	5	4	6	8	3	2	9
3	6	8	9	1	2	4	7	5
9	1	7	2	3	4	5	8	6
8	3	4	7	5	6	2	9	1
6	5	2	1	8	9	7	4	3

Score: __________

95 CLASSIC

9	1	6	4	8	2	5	7	3
4	7	3	9	6	5	8	2	1
5	8	2	7	1	3	6	4	9
3	4	1	5	9	7	2	6	8
2	6	5	1	4	8	9	3	7
8	9	7	3	2	6	1	5	4
1	5	4	6	3	9	7	8	2
6	3	8	2	7	1	4	9	5
7	2	9	8	5	4	3	1	6

Score: __________

96 CLASSIC

6	4	5	7	2	1	3	9	8
2	8	7	3	5	9	4	6	1
1	3	9	4	6	8	5	7	2
4	7	8	6	1	5	2	3	9
9	6	3	8	4	2	1	5	7
5	2	1	9	3	7	6	8	4
8	5	2	1	7	3	9	4	6
3	9	4	2	8	6	7	1	5
7	1	6	5	9	4	8	2	3

Score: __________

ANSWERS: CLASSIC

97 CLASSIC

4	6	9	1	8	5	7	3	2
8	3	5	7	2	9	6	4	1
2	1	7	3	4	6	5	8	9
5	4	8	2	9	7	1	6	3
7	9	1	6	3	8	2	5	4
3	2	6	4	5	1	9	7	8
6	8	3	9	7	2	4	1	5
1	5	2	8	6	4	3	9	7
9	7	4	5	1	3	8	2	6

Score: ___________

98 CLASSIC

2	8	7	3	6	1	5	9	4
9	5	3	8	4	7	2	1	6
6	4	1	9	2	5	3	8	7
4	1	2	7	5	9	8	6	3
7	9	8	6	3	2	1	4	5
5	3	6	4	1	8	9	7	2
8	6	4	5	9	3	7	2	1
3	2	9	1	7	4	6	5	8
1	7	5	2	8	6	4	3	9

Score: ___________

99 CLASSIC

9	1	6	3	5	7	4	8	2
5	7	2	1	8	4	6	9	3
8	4	3	2	6	9	7	5	1
1	8	9	4	2	5	3	7	6
6	3	5	7	1	8	9	2	4
7	2	4	9	3	6	8	1	5
2	6	1	8	9	3	5	4	7
4	5	8	6	7	2	1	3	9
3	9	7	5	4	1	2	6	8

Score: ___________

100 CLASSIC

8	2	1	9	4	5	3	6	7
3	7	5	6	8	1	9	4	2
9	6	4	3	7	2	1	5	8
2	1	9	8	6	7	4	3	5
4	5	8	1	2	3	7	9	6
6	3	7	5	9	4	2	8	1
7	9	2	4	5	6	8	1	3
5	8	3	7	1	9	6	2	4
1	4	6	2	3	8	5	7	9

Score: ___________

101 CLASSIC

6	2	4	3	8	1	5	7	9
5	8	3	9	7	6	4	1	2
1	9	7	4	5	2	8	3	6
8	3	6	1	4	9	2	5	7
2	1	5	6	3	7	9	4	8
4	7	9	8	2	5	1	6	3
7	5	1	2	6	8	3	9	4
3	6	2	5	9	4	7	8	1
9	4	8	7	1	3	6	2	5

Score: ___________

102 CLASSIC

1	6	3	7	5	2	9	4	8
7	8	5	4	9	3	2	6	1
9	4	2	1	8	6	5	3	7
5	2	8	3	6	9	1	7	4
4	1	6	8	7	5	3	9	2
3	7	9	2	4	1	8	5	6
2	9	1	6	3	4	7	8	5
6	3	7	5	1	8	4	2	9
8	5	4	9	2	7	6	1	3

Score: ___________

103 CLASSIC

3	6	4	8	1	2	9	5	7
2	1	5	9	3	7	4	6	8
7	8	9	5	6	4	3	2	1
9	4	3	2	8	5	1	7	6
5	2	6	3	7	1	8	4	9
1	7	8	4	9	6	2	3	5
6	9	7	1	2	3	5	8	4
8	5	2	7	4	9	6	1	3
4	3	1	6	5	8	7	9	2

Score: ___________

104 CLASSIC

6	2	5	8	3	9	1	7	4
7	9	1	4	2	6	5	3	8
3	8	4	1	7	5	9	2	6
8	7	6	9	5	1	3	4	2
1	4	2	3	6	8	7	5	9
5	3	9	2	4	7	8	6	1
4	5	8	7	9	2	6	1	3
9	6	3	5	1	4	2	8	7
2	1	7	6	8	3	4	9	5

Score: ___________

105 *CLASSIC*

6	4	7	2	1	8	9	3	5
5	1	3	9	7	4	6	2	8
2	9	8	6	3	5	4	7	1
1	3	6	7	8	9	5	4	2
9	8	4	3	5	2	7	1	6
7	2	5	4	6	1	3	8	9
4	5	1	8	9	3	2	6	7
8	7	2	5	4	6	1	9	3
3	6	9	1	2	7	8	5	4

Score: ________

106 *CLASSIC*

1	9	7	6	3	5	8	4	2
8	6	5	4	1	2	3	7	9
3	4	2	8	7	9	5	6	1
7	1	9	2	5	3	6	8	4
6	5	3	1	4	8	2	9	7
2	8	4	9	6	7	1	5	3
9	7	8	5	2	1	4	3	6
5	2	6	3	9	4	7	1	8
4	3	1	7	8	6	9	2	5

Score: ________

107 *CLASSIC*

7	2	1	4	3	9	5	6	8
8	3	9	5	2	6	4	7	1
4	6	5	1	8	7	2	3	9
5	9	2	6	7	4	1	8	3
1	8	4	3	9	2	7	5	6
3	7	6	8	5	1	9	2	4
9	5	8	7	4	3	6	1	2
6	4	7	2	1	8	3	9	5
2	1	3	9	6	5	8	4	7

Score: ________

108 *CLASSIC*

2	5	4	3	8	6	9	7	1
6	9	1	7	4	5	8	2	3
8	3	7	1	9	2	5	6	4
5	4	9	6	2	3	1	8	7
1	6	8	4	5	7	2	3	9
3	7	2	8	1	9	6	4	5
9	8	3	2	7	1	4	5	6
4	1	6	5	3	8	7	9	2
7	2	5	9	6	4	3	1	8

Score: ________

109 *CLASSIC*

6	3	5	4	8	7	9	2	1
9	7	1	6	3	2	4	8	5
8	2	4	5	9	1	3	7	6
4	8	6	7	1	9	5	3	2
7	9	3	2	4	5	1	6	8
1	5	2	8	6	3	7	9	4
2	6	7	3	5	4	8	1	9
5	1	8	9	7	6	2	4	3
3	4	9	1	2	8	6	5	7

Score: ________

110 *CLASSIC*

8	9	6	2	1	4	5	3	7
4	1	5	3	9	7	2	6	8
7	3	2	5	6	8	4	9	1
9	5	1	4	8	2	6	7	3
2	7	3	6	5	1	9	8	4
6	4	8	7	3	9	1	2	5
1	8	7	9	2	5	3	4	6
3	2	4	1	7	6	8	5	9
5	6	9	8	4	3	7	1	2

Score: ________

111 *CLASSIC*

7	1	4	5	8	6	3	9	2
2	9	8	1	3	4	6	5	7
6	3	5	9	7	2	4	8	1
8	2	1	3	4	5	7	6	9
5	4	6	8	9	7	1	2	3
9	7	3	6	2	1	5	4	8
1	6	2	7	5	8	9	3	4
4	5	9	2	1	3	8	7	6
3	8	7	4	6	9	2	1	5

Score: ________

112 *CLASSIC*

6	7	8	4	2	1	5	3	9
4	2	9	8	3	5	7	1	6
5	1	3	7	6	9	8	2	4
2	5	7	6	4	3	1	9	8
9	6	4	1	8	2	3	5	7
3	8	1	9	5	7	4	6	2
7	9	6	3	1	4	2	8	5
8	3	2	5	7	6	9	4	1
1	4	5	2	9	8	6	7	3

Score: ________

ANSWERS: CLASSIC

113 CLASSIC

7	9	1	8	2	4	3	6	5
8	3	5	6	1	7	9	4	2
4	6	2	9	3	5	8	1	7
9	5	7	4	6	8	2	3	1
2	8	6	1	7	3	4	5	9
1	4	3	2	5	9	6	7	8
6	7	4	5	8	2	1	9	3
3	1	8	7	9	6	5	2	4
5	2	9	3	4	1	7	8	6

Score: __________

114 CLASSIC

7	1	9	3	8	6	4	5	2
5	4	3	7	2	9	6	8	1
6	8	2	4	5	1	3	9	7
2	5	7	9	1	3	8	6	4
9	3	1	8	6	4	7	2	5
8	6	4	5	7	2	9	1	3
3	9	6	1	4	5	2	7	8
4	7	5	2	9	8	1	3	6
1	2	8	6	3	7	5	4	9

Score: __________

115 CLASSIC

3	5	4	7	9	2	6	8	1
9	6	7	1	3	8	2	4	5
2	1	8	4	5	6	3	9	7
1	7	9	8	2	4	5	3	6
5	4	2	3	6	1	9	7	8
6	8	3	9	7	5	1	2	4
8	3	5	2	1	7	4	6	9
4	9	6	5	8	3	7	1	2
7	2	1	6	4	9	8	5	3

Score: __________

116 CLASSIC

3	6	8	2	9	4	5	7	1
4	9	1	5	7	8	6	3	2
2	7	5	1	6	3	8	9	4
7	8	9	3	2	6	1	4	5
6	5	2	4	1	7	3	8	9
1	4	3	8	5	9	2	6	7
9	1	6	7	3	2	4	5	8
5	3	4	9	8	1	7	2	6
8	2	7	6	4	5	9	1	3

Score: __________

117 CLASSIC

3	9	7	2	4	8	1	5	6
5	2	6	1	7	9	3	8	4
8	4	1	3	5	6	2	9	7
1	5	8	6	9	3	4	7	2
6	7	9	4	8	2	5	3	1
4	3	2	7	1	5	9	6	8
7	8	3	5	2	4	6	1	9
2	1	5	9	6	7	8	4	3
9	6	4	8	3	1	7	2	5

Score: __________

118 CLASSIC

2	8	4	5	3	7	1	6	9
7	5	1	4	6	9	3	8	2
9	3	6	2	8	1	4	7	5
1	6	5	3	7	8	2	9	4
8	4	9	1	2	6	7	5	3
3	2	7	9	4	5	8	1	6
6	7	3	8	5	2	9	4	1
5	1	2	7	9	4	6	3	8
4	9	8	6	1	3	5	2	7

Score: __________

119 CLASSIC

2	4	9	3	6	1	8	5	7
3	1	8	2	7	5	9	4	6
5	7	6	4	8	9	3	1	2
6	5	7	1	3	4	2	8	9
4	8	2	5	9	7	6	3	1
1	9	3	6	2	8	5	7	4
8	6	5	7	1	2	4	9	3
7	2	4	9	5	3	1	6	8
9	3	1	8	4	6	7	2	5

Score: __________

120 CLASSIC

9	4	7	3	1	6	8	5	2
3	6	1	2	8	5	4	7	9
8	5	2	7	9	4	1	6	3
7	2	6	5	4	1	3	9	8
1	3	9	6	2	8	5	4	7
4	8	5	9	7	3	6	2	1
6	9	4	8	3	2	7	1	5
2	1	8	4	5	7	9	3	6
5	7	3	1	6	9	2	8	4

Score: __________

121 CLASSIC

4	3	5	8	6	9	2	7	1
7	8	1	3	2	5	4	9	6
6	2	9	4	1	7	3	5	8
3	1	8	7	9	2	5	6	4
9	7	4	6	5	8	1	2	3
2	5	6	1	4	3	9	8	7
8	9	7	5	3	1	6	4	2
1	4	2	9	8	6	7	3	5
5	6	3	2	7	4	8	1	9

Score: ________

122 CLASSIC

9	2	5	3	4	8	7	1	6
3	1	4	7	6	2	5	9	8
7	6	8	5	1	9	2	3	4
8	3	6	1	2	5	4	7	9
2	4	9	8	3	7	6	5	1
5	7	1	4	9	6	8	2	3
4	9	7	2	8	1	3	6	5
1	5	3	6	7	4	9	8	2
6	8	2	9	5	3	1	4	7

Score: ________

123 CLASSIC

6	4	7	2	3	1	5	9	8
1	9	8	7	5	4	3	6	2
2	5	3	6	8	9	1	7	4
7	8	1	9	2	3	4	5	6
5	3	4	1	7	6	8	2	9
9	2	6	8	4	5	7	3	1
8	6	2	3	1	7	9	4	5
4	7	9	5	6	8	2	1	3
3	1	5	4	9	2	6	8	7

Score: ________

124 CLASSIC

3	8	4	1	9	6	7	2	5
9	6	5	7	2	4	1	8	3
2	1	7	3	5	8	6	9	4
4	5	1	8	6	7	2	3	9
7	2	3	5	4	9	8	1	6
8	9	6	2	3	1	4	5	7
5	4	9	6	8	2	3	7	1
1	3	2	4	7	5	9	6	8
6	7	8	9	1	3	5	4	2

Score: ________

125 CLASSIC

8	9	7	5	4	2	1	3	6
3	2	4	6	1	9	8	5	7
5	6	1	7	3	8	4	2	9
7	1	9	4	2	5	3	6	8
4	5	6	8	7	3	9	1	2
2	8	3	1	9	6	5	7	4
9	3	5	2	6	4	7	8	1
6	7	8	9	5	1	2	4	3
1	4	2	3	8	7	6	9	5

Score: ________

126 CLASSIC

6	4	2	8	7	3	9	1	5
1	7	3	6	9	5	8	4	2
5	8	9	1	4	2	6	7	3
2	1	6	4	3	9	7	5	8
9	5	4	2	8	7	3	6	1
7	3	8	5	1	6	4	2	9
4	6	1	3	5	8	2	9	7
3	9	5	7	2	4	1	8	6
8	2	7	9	6	1	5	3	4

Score: ________

127 CLASSIC

3	6	9	4	1	2	7	5	8
5	7	1	9	8	3	4	6	2
8	4	2	7	6	5	1	3	9
2	9	6	3	5	7	8	1	4
1	3	8	2	4	6	5	9	7
7	5	4	1	9	8	3	2	6
6	1	5	8	2	4	9	7	3
9	8	3	6	7	1	2	4	5
4	2	7	5	3	9	6	8	1

Score: ________

128 CLASSIC

8	3	5	9	7	6	2	1	4
6	9	2	1	3	4	7	5	8
4	7	1	2	5	8	6	9	3
7	8	4	6	9	1	5	3	2
3	1	9	8	2	5	4	7	6
5	2	6	3	4	7	9	8	1
1	4	7	5	6	3	8	2	9
2	6	8	7	1	9	3	4	5
9	5	3	4	8	2	1	6	7

Score: ________

ANSWERS: CLASSIC

129 CLASSIC

7	2	9	5	4	3	8	6	1
8	4	1	6	9	7	3	5	2
3	5	6	8	2	1	4	7	9
4	3	7	1	6	2	9	8	5
1	9	5	4	3	8	6	2	7
6	8	2	7	5	9	1	3	4
5	1	8	3	7	4	2	9	6
2	7	4	9	8	6	5	1	3
9	6	3	2	1	5	7	4	8

Score: ________

130 CLASSIC

5	2	8	3	4	6	7	9	1
7	4	9	8	1	5	2	3	6
6	3	1	9	7	2	4	8	5
9	5	3	7	8	1	6	2	4
1	7	4	2	6	3	8	5	9
2	8	6	5	9	4	1	7	3
8	6	2	1	3	9	5	4	7
4	9	5	6	2	7	3	1	8
3	1	7	4	5	8	9	6	2

Score: ________

131 CLASSIC

8	5	7	1	3	6	4	9	2
6	3	1	2	9	4	7	5	8
2	9	4	7	5	8	3	1	6
9	6	5	4	8	7	2	3	1
1	8	3	5	2	9	6	4	7
4	7	2	3	6	1	9	8	5
3	1	9	8	7	2	5	6	4
5	2	8	6	4	3	1	7	9
7	4	6	9	1	5	8	2	3

Score: ________

132 CLASSIC

5	6	7	3	9	8	4	1	2
9	4	3	5	2	1	6	7	8
1	8	2	4	7	6	5	3	9
3	2	8	6	4	5	1	9	7
6	7	9	1	8	2	3	5	4
4	1	5	9	3	7	8	2	6
2	5	1	8	6	9	7	4	3
8	9	4	7	1	3	2	6	5
7	3	6	2	5	4	9	8	1

Score: ________

133 CLASSIC

3	2	6	9	5	8	7	1	4
5	4	9	2	1	7	3	8	6
8	7	1	6	4	3	2	5	9
9	6	4	7	8	5	1	3	2
2	3	8	1	6	4	9	7	5
7	1	5	3	9	2	4	6	8
6	9	3	8	2	1	5	4	7
1	5	2	4	7	6	8	9	3
4	8	7	5	3	9	6	2	1

Score: ________

134 CLASSIC

7	8	3	4	2	9	5	1	6
5	9	6	8	7	1	4	2	3
1	2	4	3	6	5	9	8	7
4	6	2	9	3	7	8	5	1
8	7	1	5	4	2	6	3	9
3	5	9	1	8	6	7	4	2
9	4	5	7	1	3	2	6	8
6	3	7	2	5	8	1	9	4
2	1	8	6	9	4	3	7	5

Score: ________

135 CLASSIC

6	2	5	7	8	4	9	1	3
3	9	4	1	2	6	8	7	5
8	7	1	9	3	5	6	2	4
9	4	6	5	7	1	2	3	8
7	1	8	2	4	3	5	6	9
2	5	3	8	6	9	1	4	7
5	8	7	3	1	2	4	9	6
1	6	9	4	5	7	3	8	2
4	3	2	6	9	8	7	5	1

Score: ________

136 CLASSIC

3	6	4	1	2	9	7	5	8
2	8	1	5	3	7	9	6	4
7	5	9	4	6	8	3	2	1
9	7	2	3	5	4	8	1	6
4	1	8	7	9	6	2	3	5
6	3	5	8	1	2	4	7	9
1	2	3	9	4	5	6	8	7
8	9	6	2	7	1	5	4	3
5	4	7	6	8	3	1	9	2

Score: ________

137 *CLASSIC*

7	4	3	8	5	6	9	2	1
1	8	9	3	4	2	5	6	7
6	2	5	9	7	1	3	8	4
9	3	4	1	8	7	2	5	6
5	1	7	6	2	9	4	3	8
2	6	8	4	3	5	1	7	9
8	9	1	2	6	3	7	4	5
3	7	6	5	1	4	8	9	2
4	5	2	7	9	8	6	1	3

Score: ________

138 *CLASSIC*

3	1	2	5	7	6	9	8	4
4	9	6	1	2	8	7	3	5
5	7	8	4	3	9	6	1	2
9	8	4	7	5	3	2	6	1
6	3	5	2	8	1	4	9	7
7	2	1	6	9	4	3	5	8
8	6	7	3	4	5	1	2	9
2	5	3	9	1	7	8	4	6
1	4	9	8	6	2	5	7	3

Score: ________

139 *CLASSIC*

7	4	2	3	9	8	5	6	1
8	6	3	7	5	1	2	4	9
9	5	1	2	4	6	8	7	3
5	9	8	6	3	4	1	2	7
3	1	4	8	2	7	6	9	5
2	7	6	9	1	5	4	3	8
4	2	9	1	8	3	7	5	6
6	8	5	4	7	9	3	1	2
1	3	7	5	6	2	9	8	4

Score: ________

140 *CLASSIC*

1	4	9	6	5	8	3	2	7
8	2	6	4	3	7	1	5	9
5	3	7	9	1	2	8	6	4
2	1	3	8	4	5	7	9	6
7	8	4	2	6	9	5	1	3
9	6	5	3	7	1	4	8	2
6	5	1	7	2	4	9	3	8
4	9	2	1	8	3	6	7	5
3	7	8	5	9	6	2	4	1

Score: ________

141 *CLASSIC*

3	4	6	2	5	7	9	1	8
8	5	1	3	6	9	2	4	7
2	7	9	8	4	1	6	5	3
1	3	4	9	8	5	7	6	2
7	9	5	6	2	4	8	3	1
6	2	8	1	7	3	5	9	4
5	1	3	7	9	2	4	8	6
4	8	7	5	1	6	3	2	9
9	6	2	4	3	8	1	7	5

Score: ________

142 *CLASSIC*

5	3	6	2	8	1	4	7	9
1	4	9	5	7	6	3	2	8
2	8	7	4	3	9	5	1	6
6	5	4	1	2	8	9	3	7
9	7	8	3	6	4	2	5	1
3	2	1	9	5	7	8	6	4
4	6	5	7	9	2	1	8	3
8	1	3	6	4	5	7	9	2
7	9	2	8	1	3	6	4	5

Score: ________

143 *CLASSIC*

2	7	6	9	3	4	5	8	1
1	9	4	2	5	8	3	6	7
5	3	8	7	6	1	2	4	9
4	1	2	5	8	3	7	9	6
8	6	9	4	7	2	1	3	5
7	5	3	6	1	9	4	2	8
9	2	1	8	4	7	6	5	3
3	4	5	1	9	6	8	7	2
6	8	7	3	2	5	9	1	4

Score: ________

144 *CLASSIC*

8	2	1	9	7	3	6	5	4
6	3	7	4	5	1	9	8	2
4	9	5	2	8	6	1	3	7
2	8	4	5	1	7	3	6	9
7	5	9	6	3	4	8	2	1
3	1	6	8	2	9	7	4	5
1	4	8	3	9	5	2	7	6
5	7	3	1	6	2	4	9	8
9	6	2	7	4	8	5	1	3

Score: ________

ANSWERS: CLASSIC

145 *CLASSIC*

3	8	6	5	1	4	7	9	2
4	2	1	6	7	9	3	8	5
9	7	5	8	3	2	1	4	6
1	6	4	2	8	7	5	3	9
5	9	2	3	4	6	8	1	7
7	3	8	1	9	5	6	2	4
6	4	3	9	5	1	2	7	8
8	5	7	4	2	3	9	6	1
2	1	9	7	6	8	4	5	3

Score: ________

146 *CLASSIC*

8	2	7	3	9	4	1	5	6
6	3	4	1	5	7	8	9	2
9	1	5	2	6	8	7	3	4
4	9	3	7	8	6	5	2	1
2	6	8	5	3	1	9	4	7
5	7	1	9	4	2	3	6	8
7	5	6	4	1	3	2	8	9
1	4	9	8	2	5	6	7	3
3	8	2	6	7	9	4	1	5

Score: ________

147 *CLASSIC*

6	8	9	5	7	4	3	2	1
5	7	2	3	8	1	4	9	6
1	4	3	6	2	9	5	8	7
7	5	1	4	6	8	9	3	2
4	2	6	9	5	3	7	1	8
3	9	8	2	1	7	6	5	4
9	1	4	7	3	2	8	6	5
8	3	5	1	4	6	2	7	9
2	6	7	8	9	5	1	4	3

Score: ________

148 *CLASSIC*

1	9	2	5	8	6	7	4	3
8	3	4	9	1	7	5	2	6
7	6	5	2	3	4	1	8	9
6	2	3	4	5	9	8	1	7
9	4	7	8	2	1	6	3	5
5	1	8	7	6	3	2	9	4
2	5	6	3	9	8	4	7	1
4	8	9	1	7	5	3	6	2
3	7	1	6	4	2	9	5	8

Score: ________

149 *CLASSIC*

8	1	2	3	7	6	4	5	9
5	3	4	2	8	9	6	1	7
7	9	6	5	1	4	2	8	3
6	2	3	4	9	1	8	7	5
9	4	7	8	5	3	1	2	6
1	8	5	6	2	7	9	3	4
3	5	1	9	4	2	7	6	8
2	6	9	7	3	8	5	4	1
4	7	8	1	6	5	3	9	2

Score: ________

150 *CLASSIC*

9	1	3	7	4	2	5	8	6
4	7	5	8	9	6	2	3	1
8	2	6	3	1	5	7	4	9
2	4	8	6	7	1	9	5	3
7	5	1	9	3	8	4	6	2
3	6	9	2	5	4	1	7	8
5	8	4	1	2	3	6	9	7
1	3	7	5	6	9	8	2	4
6	9	2	4	8	7	3	1	5

Score: ________

151 *CLASSIC*

9	8	5	2	3	4	1	6	7
7	1	3	8	6	9	5	2	4
4	2	6	1	7	5	8	3	9
6	4	8	3	9	1	7	5	2
1	7	9	5	2	6	4	8	3
3	5	2	4	8	7	9	1	6
2	6	1	7	4	8	3	9	5
8	9	7	6	5	3	2	4	1
5	3	4	9	1	2	6	7	8

Score: ________

152 *CLASSIC*

4	7	9	5	8	1	3	2	6
6	8	3	2	7	4	1	5	9
1	5	2	6	9	3	8	7	4
8	4	1	3	6	7	5	9	2
5	2	6	9	1	8	4	3	7
9	3	7	4	5	2	6	1	8
2	1	4	8	3	9	7	6	5
3	6	8	7	2	5	9	4	1
7	9	5	1	4	6	2	8	3

Score: ________

153 CLASSIC

3	9	8	7	4	1	2	6	5
2	7	6	5	9	3	1	8	4
4	1	5	6	2	8	3	9	7
8	2	7	4	5	6	9	1	3
1	4	9	2	3	7	8	5	6
6	5	3	8	1	9	4	7	2
7	8	2	1	6	4	5	3	9
5	3	1	9	7	2	6	4	8
9	6	4	3	8	5	7	2	1

Score: ____________

154 CLASSIC

7	3	4	8	1	5	2	9	6
1	8	2	9	7	6	5	3	4
6	9	5	4	3	2	1	8	7
5	1	7	3	8	4	6	2	9
8	2	9	1	6	7	3	4	5
3	4	6	5	2	9	8	7	1
9	5	8	2	4	1	7	6	3
4	7	3	6	5	8	9	1	2
2	6	1	7	9	3	4	5	8

Score: ____________

155 CLASSIC

2	3	4	6	9	7	5	8	1
8	5	7	1	3	4	9	6	2
1	9	6	8	5	2	3	7	4
5	7	9	4	2	6	1	3	8
6	2	8	9	1	3	4	5	7
3	4	1	7	8	5	6	2	9
9	1	2	3	6	8	7	4	5
4	6	5	2	7	9	8	1	3
7	8	3	5	4	1	2	9	6

Score: ____________

156 CLASSIC

3	4	2	6	9	8	7	5	1
8	5	6	3	7	1	2	4	9
9	7	1	4	2	5	6	3	8
2	8	3	7	6	4	9	1	5
1	6	4	5	3	9	8	7	2
5	9	7	8	1	2	4	6	3
4	2	5	1	8	6	3	9	7
7	1	8	9	4	3	5	2	6
6	3	9	2	5	7	1	8	4

Score: ____________

157 CLASSIC

6	3	4	7	2	1	5	8	9
7	5	9	6	4	8	2	1	3
1	2	8	5	3	9	4	6	7
8	7	3	2	1	5	6	9	4
9	6	2	3	8	4	7	5	1
4	1	5	9	6	7	8	3	2
2	8	6	1	7	3	9	4	5
5	4	1	8	9	2	3	7	6
3	9	7	4	5	6	1	2	8

Score: ____________

158 CLASSIC

5	3	1	8	6	9	4	2	7
4	9	8	2	7	3	1	6	5
2	6	7	5	4	1	9	3	8
8	4	9	1	3	2	5	7	6
3	7	2	9	5	6	8	4	1
1	5	6	7	8	4	2	9	3
9	2	5	6	1	7	3	8	4
7	8	4	3	2	5	6	1	9
6	1	3	4	9	8	7	5	2

Score: ____________

159 CLASSIC

9	3	8	6	2	7	4	1	5
5	6	1	9	4	3	2	8	7
2	4	7	8	5	1	9	6	3
7	1	3	2	9	5	8	4	6
4	2	5	1	6	8	7	3	9
6	8	9	7	3	4	1	5	2
8	5	2	4	7	6	3	9	1
3	9	4	5	1	2	6	7	8
1	7	6	3	8	9	5	2	4

Score: ____________

160 CLASSIC

4	2	7	5	6	1	9	3	8
3	1	5	8	7	9	4	6	2
6	9	8	3	4	2	1	7	5
5	8	2	4	9	7	6	1	3
9	4	3	6	1	5	2	8	7
7	6	1	2	3	8	5	9	4
8	7	6	9	5	4	3	2	1
2	5	9	1	8	3	7	4	6
1	3	4	7	2	6	8	5	9

Score: ____________

161 CLASSIC

9	7	1	4	2	8	3	5	6
5	8	6	9	3	1	4	7	2
4	3	2	6	5	7	1	9	8
3	4	9	5	8	2	7	6	1
8	1	5	7	6	4	9	2	3
2	6	7	1	9	3	5	8	4
6	9	4	2	1	5	8	3	7
7	5	8	3	4	6	2	1	9
1	2	3	8	7	9	6	4	5

Score: ________

162 CLASSIC

3	6	5	9	8	2	1	7	4
2	1	9	7	4	3	5	8	6
7	8	4	5	6	1	9	3	2
1	3	2	4	5	8	7	6	9
5	4	6	3	9	7	2	1	8
9	7	8	1	2	6	3	4	5
8	5	7	2	1	4	6	9	3
4	2	3	6	7	9	8	5	1
6	9	1	8	3	5	4	2	7

Score: ________

163 CLASSIC

3	4	9	5	8	2	7	6	1
8	7	5	1	6	4	3	9	2
6	2	1	3	9	7	8	4	5
2	5	7	6	1	9	4	3	8
1	6	8	4	5	3	2	7	9
9	3	4	7	2	8	5	1	6
7	1	2	8	4	6	9	5	3
5	8	3	9	7	1	6	2	4
4	9	6	2	3	5	1	8	7

Score: ________

164 CLASSIC

7	5	3	6	9	2	1	4	8
9	4	2	8	1	7	6	3	5
8	1	6	5	4	3	7	9	2
4	9	7	2	3	6	8	5	1
5	2	1	7	8	4	9	6	3
6	3	8	9	5	1	2	7	4
3	7	9	1	2	5	4	8	6
2	8	4	3	6	9	5	1	7
1	6	5	4	7	8	3	2	9

Score: ________

165 CLASSIC

1	4	8	6	2	9	7	5	3
5	3	7	1	8	4	9	6	2
6	2	9	5	3	7	1	8	4
2	6	1	9	4	3	5	7	8
8	9	5	7	6	2	3	4	1
3	7	4	8	1	5	6	2	9
7	1	6	4	9	8	2	3	5
4	5	2	3	7	1	8	9	6
9	8	3	2	5	6	4	1	7

Score: ________

166 CLASSIC

2	1	5	3	9	6	7	4	8
4	3	9	8	7	1	5	2	6
8	7	6	4	2	5	1	9	3
1	9	2	6	8	7	3	5	4
5	6	8	9	4	3	2	7	1
3	4	7	1	5	2	6	8	9
9	5	1	7	6	8	4	3	2
7	8	3	2	1	4	9	6	5
6	2	4	5	3	9	8	1	7

Score: ________

167 CLASSIC

2	1	7	5	6	8	9	3	4
4	6	9	1	7	3	5	8	2
3	8	5	2	9	4	1	7	6
7	2	4	9	8	5	3	6	1
1	3	8	7	4	6	2	9	5
5	9	6	3	2	1	8	4	7
8	5	3	4	1	7	6	2	9
6	4	2	8	5	9	7	1	3
9	7	1	6	3	2	4	5	8

Score: ________

168 CLASSIC

8	7	9	1	2	4	6	5	3
4	3	2	6	5	7	9	1	8
6	1	5	8	9	3	4	2	7
2	8	3	4	1	5	7	9	6
7	5	6	2	3	9	8	4	1
1	9	4	7	8	6	5	3	2
9	2	7	3	4	8	1	6	5
3	4	8	5	6	1	2	7	9
5	6	1	9	7	2	3	8	4

Score: ________

169 *CLASSIC*

9	8	2	1	6	3	4	7	5
6	7	5	2	8	4	3	9	1
4	3	1	7	9	5	2	8	6
7	4	6	5	1	8	9	3	2
2	5	9	4	3	7	1	6	8
3	1	8	6	2	9	5	4	7
8	9	7	3	5	1	6	2	4
5	6	4	9	7	2	8	1	3
1	2	3	8	4	6	7	5	9

Score: ________

170 *CLASSIC*

6	9	3	2	1	7	8	4	5
8	7	4	6	9	5	3	1	2
1	2	5	8	3	4	7	6	9
3	5	7	4	6	2	1	9	8
4	1	6	7	8	9	2	5	3
2	8	9	3	5	1	6	7	4
5	6	1	9	2	8	4	3	7
7	3	2	5	4	6	9	8	1
9	4	8	1	7	3	5	2	6

Score: ________

171 *CLASSIC*

3	5	8	1	4	9	6	2	7
7	1	9	3	2	6	8	5	4
6	2	4	5	8	7	1	3	9
8	9	6	7	5	1	2	4	3
4	7	2	8	6	3	5	9	1
5	3	1	2	9	4	7	6	8
9	8	3	6	7	2	4	1	5
1	6	7	4	3	5	9	8	2
2	4	5	9	1	8	3	7	6

Score: ________

172 *CLASSIC*

9	8	5	7	6	2	3	1	4
3	1	4	5	8	9	2	7	6
6	2	7	3	4	1	8	9	5
8	4	9	2	5	3	1	6	7
5	3	1	4	7	6	9	2	8
7	6	2	9	1	8	4	5	3
2	7	3	6	9	4	5	8	1
4	5	8	1	2	7	6	3	9
1	9	6	8	3	5	7	4	2

Score: ________

173 *CLASSIC*

2	9	4	1	7	5	3	8	6
1	7	6	3	8	4	5	2	9
8	3	5	6	2	9	4	7	1
9	6	7	4	5	2	1	3	8
3	1	2	9	6	8	7	5	4
4	5	8	7	3	1	6	9	2
7	2	3	8	1	6	9	4	5
5	4	1	2	9	7	8	6	3
6	8	9	5	4	3	2	1	7

Score: ________

174 *CLASSIC*

8	4	5	1	9	3	7	6	2
2	3	6	7	5	4	9	1	8
1	7	9	8	2	6	5	3	4
9	2	8	5	6	1	4	7	3
3	5	4	2	7	8	1	9	6
7	6	1	3	4	9	2	8	5
6	1	2	4	3	7	8	5	9
4	9	7	6	8	5	3	2	1
5	8	3	9	1	2	6	4	7

Score: ________

175 *CLASSIC*

4	9	7	8	6	3	1	2	5
6	2	1	5	7	4	8	3	9
5	8	3	9	1	2	4	6	7
8	4	5	6	3	1	9	7	2
2	7	6	4	9	5	3	8	1
1	3	9	7	2	8	5	4	6
3	1	8	2	5	6	7	9	4
9	6	4	1	8	7	2	5	3
7	5	2	3	4	9	6	1	8

Score: ________

176 *SQUIFFY*

5	6	1	4	3	9	2	8	7
9	7	6	8	4	2	5	1	3
8	1	2	3	5	7	6	4	9
3	4	7	6	9	1	8	2	5
6	9	5	2	1	3	4	7	8
4	2	3	7	8	5	1	9	6
1	3	8	9	6	4	7	5	2
7	8	4	5	2	6	9	3	1
2	5	9	1	7	8	3	6	4

Score: ________

ANSWERS: SQUIFFY

177 SQUIFFY

2	5	9	7	1	3	6	4	8
8	1	4	6	5	2	9	7	3
9	7	3	2	4	8	1	5	6
6	4	1	9	8	5	7	3	2
3	9	8	5	7	4	2	6	1
1	2	7	4	3	6	5	8	9
7	6	5	8	2	9	3	1	4
5	8	2	3	6	1	4	9	7
4	3	6	1	9	7	8	2	5

Score: ________

178 SQUIFFY

6	9	3	7	1	5	4	2	8
4	5	2	8	9	1	6	7	3
7	1	6	4	3	2	8	9	5
1	4	8	9	5	3	7	6	2
8	7	5	3	6	9	2	1	4
9	3	4	1	2	6	5	8	7
5	2	9	6	7	8	3	4	1
3	6	7	2	8	4	1	5	9
2	8	1	5	4	7	9	3	6

Score: ________

179 SQUIFFY

7	4	1	9	5	8	3	6	2
2	3	6	7	1	4	9	5	8
6	5	8	4	3	7	1	2	9
8	1	2	5	4	9	6	3	7
9	6	3	8	7	1	2	4	5
5	2	4	1	9	6	7	8	3
3	7	5	6	8	2	4	9	1
1	8	9	2	6	3	5	7	4
4	9	7	3	2	5	8	1	6

Score: ________

180 SQUIFFY

4	5	1	6	3	8	9	2	7
7	1	2	8	6	9	5	4	3
2	7	4	1	9	5	8	3	6
6	8	3	2	4	7	1	9	5
3	9	5	7	8	2	4	6	1
5	4	6	9	7	1	3	8	2
1	3	8	5	2	4	6	7	9
9	6	7	4	1	3	2	5	8
8	2	9	3	5	6	7	1	4

Score: ________

181 SQUIFFY

7	8	5	3	6	2	4	9	1
2	4	6	1	9	8	3	5	7
9	5	3	8	2	4	7	1	6
5	9	7	6	8	3	1	4	2
8	3	1	4	5	7	6	2	9
6	2	4	9	7	1	5	3	8
3	1	8	7	4	9	2	6	5
1	6	9	2	3	5	8	7	4
4	7	2	5	1	6	9	8	3

Score: ________

182 SQUIFFY

1	5	2	8	9	7	3	6	4
3	4	6	7	1	2	8	5	9
9	7	1	3	4	6	5	2	8
2	8	5	9	6	3	4	1	7
6	9	4	2	3	1	7	8	5
7	1	3	6	5	8	9	4	2
5	2	7	4	8	9	6	3	1
8	6	9	5	2	4	1	7	3
4	3	8	1	7	5	2	9	6

Score: ________

183 SQUIFFY

5	3	8	9	1	2	6	4	7
7	1	4	5	8	9	3	2	6
9	2	6	7	3	4	1	5	8
8	4	9	2	5	6	7	1	3
3	7	1	6	2	5	8	9	4
4	5	7	3	9	8	2	6	1
6	8	2	4	7	1	5	3	9
1	9	5	8	6	3	4	7	2
2	6	3	1	4	7	9	8	5

Score: ________

184 SQUIFFY

9	5	7	8	3	1	2	6	4
6	7	2	1	5	9	3	4	8
8	4	9	3	6	7	1	5	2
1	3	5	6	2	4	8	9	7
2	9	4	7	1	3	6	8	5
4	6	8	2	9	5	7	1	3
7	1	3	5	4	8	9	2	6
5	8	6	9	7	2	4	3	1
3	2	1	4	8	6	5	7	9

Score: ________

185 SQUIFFY

1	9	6	4	2	5	8	3	7
3	5	7	8	1	9	6	2	4
4	2	3	5	7	8	1	9	6
7	1	9	2	4	6	3	5	8
8	6	5	7	9	2	4	1	3
2	8	4	1	3	7	5	6	9
6	3	8	9	5	4	2	7	1
5	7	1	6	8	3	9	4	2
9	4	2	3	6	1	7	8	5

Score: ________

186 SQUIFFY

8	1	3	6	7	5	4	9	2
6	5	9	4	3	1	2	7	8
9	7	8	2	6	4	3	1	5
4	2	6	5	1	7	9	8	3
7	9	5	3	2	8	1	6	4
3	8	1	9	4	6	5	2	7
2	6	4	7	9	3	8	5	1
1	4	2	8	5	9	7	3	6
5	3	7	1	8	2	6	4	9

Score: ________

187 SQUIFFY

3	8	9	1	5	6	7	4	2
6	2	7	5	9	3	1	8	4
9	3	4	7	2	1	5	6	8
1	4	5	6	7	8	2	9	3
2	5	3	8	6	4	9	7	1
5	7	1	4	8	2	6	3	9
8	1	2	9	4	7	3	5	6
4	9	6	3	1	5	8	2	7
7	6	8	2	3	9	4	1	5

Score: ________

188 SQUIFFY

7	3	5	9	1	4	6	8	2
4	9	7	2	8	3	5	1	6
1	5	8	6	4	2	7	3	9
3	7	2	8	9	6	1	4	5
5	4	9	1	2	7	3	6	8
2	1	3	5	6	8	4	9	7
9	6	4	7	3	5	8	2	1
8	2	6	3	7	1	9	5	4
6	8	1	4	5	9	2	7	3

Score: ________

189 SQUIFFY

8	1	7	2	9	6	4	3	5
3	6	9	4	5	7	8	2	1
7	5	2	8	1	3	6	9	4
1	9	6	5	7	4	2	8	3
9	3	4	6	2	8	1	5	7
2	7	8	1	4	5	3	6	9
6	4	5	3	8	9	7	1	2
5	8	1	7	3	2	9	4	6
4	2	3	9	6	1	5	7	8

Score: ________

190 SQUIFFY

7	4	9	1	5	8	2	6	3
6	1	3	8	2	4	7	5	9
2	5	6	4	7	9	3	1	8
4	9	7	5	1	3	8	2	6
1	3	8	2	6	7	5	9	4
8	7	1	9	4	2	6	3	5
9	6	4	3	8	5	1	7	2
5	8	2	7	3	6	9	4	1
3	2	5	6	9	1	4	8	7

Score: ________

191 SQUIFFY

8	6	2	5	4	9	1	7	3
2	4	8	7	3	5	6	9	1
7	5	1	9	6	8	2	3	4
6	3	7	2	1	4	9	8	5
1	2	4	8	7	3	5	6	9
9	8	5	3	2	6	4	1	7
3	1	9	4	5	7	8	2	6
5	7	6	1	9	2	3	4	8
4	9	3	6	8	1	7	5	2

Score: ________

192 SQUIFFY

4	8	3	5	1	7	9	2	6
2	7	1	6	9	4	3	5	8
6	5	9	4	3	8	2	7	1
8	1	7	2	5	9	4	6	3
3	4	6	1	7	2	5	8	9
7	2	5	9	8	3	6	1	4
9	3	2	8	6	1	7	4	5
1	6	4	3	2	5	8	9	7
5	9	8	7	4	6	1	3	2

Score: ________

ANSWERS: SQUIFFY

193 SQUIFFY

8	7	1	9	6	3	5	2	4
5	4	3	8	2	7	6	1	9
7	1	4	2	5	6	8	9	3
6	3	8	5	4	9	2	7	1
2	9	6	3	7	1	4	8	5
9	5	2	7	3	4	1	6	8
4	6	5	1	9	8	7	3	2
3	8	7	4	1	2	9	5	6
1	2	9	6	8	5	3	4	7

Score: __________

194 SQUIFFY

9	1	3	8	4	6	5	2	7
5	4	7	6	2	8	3	1	9
2	8	1	4	7	9	6	3	5
4	2	8	9	6	1	7	5	3
7	9	6	2	3	5	1	4	8
1	3	9	5	8	4	2	7	6
8	7	4	1	5	3	9	6	2
6	5	2	3	9	7	4	8	1
3	6	5	7	1	2	8	9	4

Score: __________

195 SQUIFFY

3	5	2	4	8	6	9	1	7
5	6	9	7	2	1	3	8	4
1	9	4	8	7	2	5	3	6
4	7	1	9	5	8	2	6	3
2	1	8	3	6	4	7	5	9
7	8	3	6	1	9	4	2	5
6	2	7	5	9	3	8	4	1
9	3	6	2	4	5	1	7	8
8	4	5	1	3	7	6	9	2

Score: __________

196 SQUIFFY

8	6	3	7	9	4	5	2	1
4	7	5	2	1	8	3	6	9
1	3	6	9	4	7	2	5	8
3	9	7	1	6	2	4	8	5
7	2	8	4	5	1	6	9	3
9	5	1	6	8	3	7	4	2
6	1	9	3	2	5	8	7	4
5	4	2	8	7	9	1	3	6
2	8	4	5	3	6	9	1	7

Score: __________

197 SQUIFFY

2	5	3	8	4	7	6	1	9
4	1	9	2	7	8	5	3	6
9	6	5	1	3	2	4	7	8
8	4	7	5	6	9	1	2	3
7	3	8	9	1	6	2	5	4
1	2	6	3	5	4	9	8	7
5	9	1	4	8	3	7	6	2
3	7	4	6	2	5	8	9	1
6	8	2	7	9	1	3	4	5

Score: __________

198 SQUIFFY

4	7	9	1	3	2	5	8	6
6	8	3	2	5	7	1	4	9
8	1	2	5	9	4	3	6	7
5	9	4	6	8	1	7	3	2
7	6	5	4	2	9	8	1	3
1	3	7	9	6	5	4	2	8
9	5	8	3	1	6	2	7	4
3	2	1	7	4	8	6	9	5
2	4	6	8	7	3	9	5	1

Score: __________

199 SQUIFFY

9	5	4	2	7	6	3	8	1
4	3	2	8	5	9	7	1	6
6	9	7	1	8	3	2	4	5
7	4	3	5	1	8	6	9	2
5	2	8	6	4	1	9	3	7
8	7	9	3	2	5	1	6	4
3	6	1	7	9	4	5	2	8
2	1	6	4	3	7	8	5	9
1	8	5	9	6	2	4	7	3

Score: __________

200 SQUIFFY

7	6	5	4	2	3	9	8	1
1	3	7	9	6	8	5	4	2
9	5	8	3	1	4	6	2	7
2	4	6	8	7	1	3	9	5
6	8	3	2	5	9	7	1	4
4	7	9	1	3	6	2	5	8
8	1	2	5	9	7	4	3	6
5	9	4	6	8	2	1	7	3
3	2	1	7	4	5	8	6	9

Score: __________

201 SUDOKU 16

5	11	15	6	16	2	14	8	10	3	7	9	1	4	12	13
4	7	9	12	11	15	13	1	5	8	16	6	14	3	10	2
10	13	14	3	4	5	6	9	2	12	15	1	16	7	11	8
16	1	2	8	3	12	10	7	4	14	11	13	15	6	9	5
3	6	16	14	5	8	7	15	9	4	12	2	11	10	13	1
9	8	13	4	1	16	11	2	3	6	10	7	12	5	14	15
12	10	11	1	14	6	9	3	16	15	13	5	4	2	8	7
2	15	5	7	13	10	4	12	14	1	8	11	3	9	6	16
8	4	12	16	6	11	1	5	15	2	3	10	9	13	7	14
1	14	7	2	8	9	3	13	12	11	6	4	5	15	16	10
11	3	6	5	10	7	15	16	13	9	14	8	2	12	1	4
13	9	10	15	12	14	2	4	1	7	5	16	8	11	3	6
14	2	8	9	15	13	16	6	11	10	4	12	7	1	5	3
15	12	3	10	7	4	5	11	8	13	1	14	6	16	2	9
6	16	1	13	2	3	12	14	7	5	9	15	10	8	4	11
7	5	4	11	9	1	8	10	6	16	2	3	13	14	15	12

Score: ____________

202 SUDOKU 16

6	15	3	10	2	16	4	13	8	12	7	1	14	5	9	11
5	7	4	2	9	12	15	6	16	10	14	11	13	8	1	3
13	1	9	11	8	10	5	14	4	3	6	15	12	7	16	2
14	12	8	16	3	11	7	1	13	2	5	9	10	6	15	4
3	2	11	13	5	4	16	12	6	1	10	7	15	14	8	9
1	16	7	12	13	15	11	9	14	8	4	3	5	2	6	10
8	10	15	5	6	14	3	7	9	16	2	13	4	1	11	12
9	6	14	4	1	8	10	2	12	11	15	5	7	13	3	16
7	14	2	15	11	3	13	8	1	5	12	4	16	9	10	6
16	9	10	3	12	5	1	4	15	13	8	6	2	11	7	14
11	13	12	8	14	7	6	15	10	9	16	2	1	3	4	5
4	5	6	1	10	9	2	16	11	7	3	14	8	12	13	15
2	4	16	6	7	13	9	10	3	14	1	12	11	15	5	8
12	11	5	14	15	1	8	3	7	4	9	16	6	10	2	13
15	8	1	9	4	2	14	11	5	6	13	10	3	16	12	7
10	3	13	7	16	6	12	5	2	15	11	8	9	4	14	1

Score: ____________

203 SUDOKU 16

8	1	16	10	12	11	9	4	14	13	5	7	2	15	6	3
2	15	14	11	5	7	13	3	4	6	9	12	1	10	16	8
3	4	6	9	8	1	2	14	11	10	16	15	7	5	12	13
5	13	12	7	6	10	16	15	8	3	2	1	9	4	11	14
10	7	11	2	14	12	4	13	3	1	15	8	6	9	5	16
16	5	4	3	15	6	7	2	12	9	13	10	14	8	1	11
14	12	15	8	1	9	10	16	5	4	6	11	3	13	7	2
6	9	1	13	3	8	11	5	2	16	7	14	10	12	4	15
7	2	9	15	13	16	8	11	1	12	14	5	4	6	3	10
11	6	10	16	7	3	14	9	13	15	4	2	5	1	8	12
12	14	3	5	10	4	1	6	16	8	11	9	15	2	13	7
1	8	13	4	2	15	5	12	6	7	10	3	11	16	14	9
15	10	8	6	4	5	3	7	9	11	12	13	16	14	2	1
13	3	5	12	16	14	15	10	7	2	1	6	8	11	9	4
9	16	7	14	11	2	12	1	15	5	8	4	13	3	10	6
4	11	2	1	9	13	6	8	10	14	3	16	12	7	15	5

Score: ____________

204 SUDOKU 16

13	12	14	16	15	9	5	1	7	6	10	8	4	3	11	2
2	11	10	1	4	3	13	7	16	5	9	15	12	14	6	8
8	7	3	15	6	16	11	12	14	4	2	13	5	1	9	10
5	6	9	4	14	2	8	10	1	11	3	12	7	15	13	16
6	10	4	7	11	5	15	9	8	14	12	16	13	2	3	1
16	13	11	8	1	4	12	2	5	3	7	6	9	10	15	14
14	5	1	3	10	13	7	16	11	9	15	2	8	6	4	12
15	2	12	9	8	6	14	3	4	13	1	10	16	7	5	11
7	8	5	14	12	15	16	6	13	10	11	3	1	9	2	4
1	9	6	12	3	11	2	4	15	8	16	5	10	13	14	7
3	4	16	13	7	1	10	8	6	2	14	9	11	5	12	15
11	15	2	10	13	14	9	5	12	1	4	7	6	8	16	3
10	16	13	11	5	8	4	14	3	15	6	1	2	12	7	9
9	3	8	5	16	12	1	15	2	7	13	4	14	11	10	6
12	1	7	6	2	10	3	11	9	16	5	14	15	4	8	13
4	14	15	2	9	7	6	13	10	12	8	11	3	16	1	5

Score: ____________

205 SUDOKU 16

1	16	2	10	14	5	8	15	7	13	6	11	9	4	3	12
15	7	6	4	9	1	3	11	12	16	5	10	2	8	14	13
5	11	12	9	13	10	4	6	2	3	8	14	7	15	1	16
8	14	3	13	12	16	7	2	15	1	4	9	5	10	11	6
12	15	7	3	2	13	6	8	5	9	1	16	10	11	4	14
13	2	9	11	16	7	15	4	14	12	10	8	6	3	5	1
14	10	16	6	3	9	1	5	11	4	7	15	8	13	12	2
4	8	1	5	11	14	10	12	3	6	2	13	16	7	9	15
10	13	14	7	4	6	2	3	9	5	16	1	15	12	8	11
2	1	11	12	5	8	9	10	13	14	15	3	4	16	6	7
3	5	8	16	7	15	12	13	6	2	11	4	14	1	10	9
6	9	4	15	1	11	14	16	10	8	12	7	3	2	13	5
16	4	15	14	6	12	13	1	8	7	3	5	11	9	2	10
7	3	5	2	10	4	11	9	1	15	13	6	12	14	16	8
9	6	10	1	8	2	16	7	4	11	14	12	13	5	15	3
11	12	13	8	15	3	5	14	16	10	9	2	1	6	7	4

Score: ____________

206 SUDOKU 16

15	9	13	5	3	7	8	2	11	10	12	14	16	4	1	6
10	6	14	8	16	4	13	11	1	2	3	7	9	15	12	5
7	4	1	2	5	9	12	14	16	6	8	15	11	10	3	13
11	16	3	12	1	15	10	6	9	5	4	13	2	8	14	7
3	15	7	9	6	1	2	5	14	12	16	10	4	13	11	8
6	10	5	16	13	12	14	8	4	1	11	9	7	2	15	3
8	1	4	14	11	10	15	3	13	7	5	2	6	12	16	9
13	12	2	11	4	16	9	7	8	3	15	6	10	1	5	14
1	11	8	7	2	13	5	9	15	16	6	3	12	14	4	10
9	13	12	10	15	6	3	16	7	8	14	4	5	11	2	1
14	5	15	6	12	8	1	4	2	13	10	11	3	9	7	16
4	2	16	3	14	11	7	10	12	9	1	5	13	6	8	15
2	8	9	15	10	3	6	12	5	11	7	1	14	16	13	4
5	3	10	4	8	2	11	1	6	14	13	16	15	7	9	12
16	14	11	1	7	5	4	13	10	15	9	12	8	3	6	2
12	7	6	13	9	14	16	15	3	4	2	8	1	5	10	11

Score: ____________

207 SUDOKU 16

5	2	15	3	6	14	9	7	8	11	13	12	1	4	10	16
14	1	10	8	11	4	13	12	7	6	2	16	15	5	9	3
12	11	7	16	8	15	10	5	1	4	9	3	13	6	14	2
13	9	6	4	1	16	2	3	15	5	14	10	8	7	12	11
4	6	1	15	2	11	12	9	3	14	16	5	10	13	7	8
11	10	9	13	14	5	16	8	6	15	1	7	3	12	2	4
3	12	2	14	10	7	1	6	4	13	8	11	9	16	5	15
16	5	8	7	3	13	4	15	10	2	12	9	14	11	1	6
7	15	14	5	13	6	3	1	2	16	10	8	4	9	11	12
1	4	16	12	15	2	11	10	5	9	6	13	7	3	8	14
2	13	11	9	7	8	14	16	12	1	3	4	6	10	15	5
6	8	3	10	9	12	5	4	11	7	15	14	2	1	16	13
10	3	13	1	4	9	8	14	16	12	11	2	5	15	6	7
15	14	12	2	5	3	7	11	9	10	4	6	16	8	13	1
9	7	4	11	16	1	6	2	13	8	5	15	12	14	3	10
8	16	5	6	12	10	15	13	14	3	7	1	11	2	4	9

Score: ____________

208 SUDOKU 16

13	12	1	16	10	14	7	8	11	2	15	6	9	4	3	5
3	14	6	11	15	5	2	1	4	7	9	13	12	8	10	16
4	8	10	5	11	13	16	9	3	12	14	1	15	6	2	7
15	7	9	2	3	6	12	4	10	5	8	16	13	14	11	1
6	15	2	7	1	10	11	16	14	9	3	8	5	12	4	13
16	13	4	1	8	2	3	15	5	6	12	11	7	10	9	14
14	11	12	9	5	7	13	6	15	16	10	4	3	1	8	2
8	10	5	3	14	4	9	12	13	1	7	2	16	11	6	15
11	5	3	8	16	9	1	14	2	13	4	7	10	15	12	6
10	6	16	15	13	11	8	5	12	14	1	9	4	2	7	3
9	1	7	14	2	12	4	10	6	15	5	3	8	16	13	11
12	2	13	4	6	3	15	7	8	11	16	10	14	5	1	9
5	16	8	10	12	1	6	2	9	3	13	14	11	7	15	4
7	3	14	13	4	15	5	11	1	10	2	12	6	9	16	8
1	9	11	12	7	8	14	3	16	4	6	15	2	13	5	10
2	4	15	6	9	16	10	13	7	8	11	5	1	3	14	12

Score: ____________

209 SUDOKU 16

10	13	9	16	8	5	12	3	14	6	15	4	7	2	11	1
4	14	7	5	1	15	10	2	3	16	13	11	6	9	12	8
2	15	1	6	11	7	4	14	8	12	10	9	3	5	13	16
11	3	8	12	6	9	16	13	5	7	2	1	10	15	4	14
12	4	3	15	7	14	9	1	13	10	11	5	2	8	16	6
9	8	16	7	2	6	5	10	15	1	4	12	13	3	14	11
6	1	5	14	4	8	13	11	16	3	9	2	12	7	10	15
13	2	11	10	15	12	3	16	7	14	6	8	4	1	9	5
7	11	14	9	10	3	8	5	12	13	1	15	16	6	2	4
1	10	15	8	13	16	6	4	2	11	5	3	14	12	7	9
3	12	13	4	9	2	1	7	6	8	16	14	5	11	15	10
5	16	6	2	12	11	14	15	9	4	7	10	1	13	8	3
16	7	4	1	5	10	2	8	11	9	3	13	15	14	6	12
14	9	2	13	3	1	11	6	4	15	12	16	8	10	5	7
15	5	10	11	14	4	7	12	1	2	8	6	9	16	3	13
8	6	12	3	16	13	15	9	10	5	14	7	11	4	1	2

Score: ____________

210 SUDOKU 16

2	4	12	15	16	3	6	7	1	14	8	9	11	5	10	13
6	14	13	8	5	11	15	2	10	3	7	4	16	9	1	12
11	9	5	7	12	1	8	10	6	2	16	13	14	15	3	4
3	10	1	16	13	14	9	4	11	5	15	12	6	2	7	8
13	16	7	2	9	10	4	11	5	12	6	8	1	3	15	14
12	11	3	1	8	7	16	6	13	15	2	14	5	4	9	10
14	6	4	10	1	13	5	15	16	11	9	3	7	8	12	2
15	8	9	5	14	2	3	12	7	1	4	10	13	6	16	11
1	7	6	14	10	5	13	3	4	8	12	16	15	11	2	9
9	3	16	13	2	12	11	1	15	6	10	5	8	14	4	7
8	15	11	12	4	6	14	9	2	13	1	7	10	16	5	3
10	5	2	4	15	8	7	16	3	9	14	11	12	13	6	1
4	12	10	3	6	16	2	14	8	7	13	15	9	1	11	5
16	2	8	11	7	15	10	13	9	4	5	1	3	12	14	6
7	13	14	9	3	4	1	5	12	16	11	6	2	10	8	15
5	1	15	6	11	9	12	8	14	10	3	2	4	7	13	16

Score: ____________

211 SUDOKU 16

1	3	2	9	5	8	12	10	13	7	11	14	15	16	6	4
6	16	14	10	4	13	7	11	15	9	8	12	5	3	1	2
8	5	15	12	1	14	2	3	4	10	16	6	9	13	11	7
4	13	11	7	9	16	6	15	5	1	3	2	12	14	8	10
12	11	10	5	2	4	14	16	7	3	15	13	6	1	9	8
9	14	8	4	3	10	13	7	6	12	1	16	2	11	15	5
15	1	3	16	6	12	5	9	8	11	2	10	4	7	13	14
13	6	7	2	11	15	1	8	14	4	9	5	3	12	10	16
16	7	1	13	10	2	9	14	12	5	6	11	8	15	4	3
10	4	5	8	15	3	11	12	1	13	14	7	16	9	2	6
11	2	9	14	13	5	16	6	3	8	4	15	1	10	7	12
3	12	6	15	8	7	4	1	16	2	10	9	11	5	14	13
7	10	4	6	12	9	15	5	2	16	13	1	14	8	3	11
14	8	13	3	16	11	10	2	9	15	12	4	7	6	5	1
2	15	16	1	7	6	3	13	11	14	5	8	10	4	12	9
5	9	12	11	14	1	8	4	10	6	7	3	13	2	16	15

Score: ____________

212 SUDOKU 16

15	11	7	2	5	6	1	16	12	10	13	4	3	14	9	8
12	3	10	4	15	2	11	14	9	16	8	6	1	13	5	7
9	8	5	14	10	3	13	7	1	2	11	15	16	4	6	12
1	13	16	6	8	12	4	9	3	5	7	14	15	10	2	11
10	7	8	12	2	5	16	4	6	3	9	11	13	15	14	1
14	15	2	5	11	9	8	10	13	12	4	1	6	7	16	3
6	16	9	1	7	13	15	3	14	8	2	10	12	5	11	4
3	4	11	13	1	14	6	12	16	15	5	7	10	2	8	9
11	9	1	10	3	16	2	6	4	14	12	5	7	8	13	15
2	14	4	15	13	8	12	11	10	7	6	16	9	3	1	5
13	6	3	16	9	10	7	5	8	1	15	2	11	12	4	14
8	5	12	7	4	15	14	1	11	13	3	9	2	16	10	6
5	12	13	11	16	7	9	8	2	4	1	3	14	6	15	10
7	2	14	9	12	11	5	13	15	6	10	8	4	1	3	16
16	1	15	3	6	4	10	2	5	9	14	12	8	11	7	13
4	10	6	8	14	1	3	15	7	11	16	13	5	9	12	2

Score: ____________

213 *SUDOKU 16*

11	1	14	12	6	3	7	15	2	9	13	16	8	5	4	10
10	3	8	16	13	2	12	1	15	4	6	5	11	14	7	9
13	7	4	15	5	14	16	9	10	3	8	11	2	6	12	1
6	5	2	9	11	10	4	8	1	7	14	12	16	3	13	15
2	13	16	10	8	15	5	7	9	12	3	6	4	1	11	14
12	14	6	5	9	16	11	2	4	1	15	10	13	7	3	8
8	15	11	7	1	4	6	3	5	14	16	13	10	12	9	2
9	4	3	1	10	12	13	14	8	11	2	7	5	15	16	6
3	8	7	11	15	6	2	10	14	16	1	4	12	9	5	13
15	12	1	14	16	5	3	4	13	2	11	9	6	8	10	7
16	2	9	6	14	7	8	13	12	5	10	3	15	11	1	4
5	10	13	4	12	9	1	11	6	8	7	15	14	16	2	3
4	6	10	3	7	8	9	5	16	13	12	14	1	2	15	11
14	11	5	2	4	13	15	16	3	6	9	1	7	10	8	12
1	16	15	8	3	11	14	12	7	10	4	2	9	13	6	5
7	9	12	13	2	1	10	6	11	15	5	8	3	4	14	16

Score: ____________

214 *SUDOKU 16*

10	15	8	13	2	6	9	14	12	3	5	11	16	7	1	4
4	2	1	9	10	12	5	16	13	6	7	8	15	3	11	14
7	3	5	16	1	15	8	11	14	4	9	2	13	12	6	10
14	6	12	11	4	3	7	13	10	1	16	15	2	9	5	8
8	14	6	3	7	11	2	10	1	9	4	5	12	16	13	15
12	9	15	1	13	4	14	6	8	7	10	16	3	5	2	11
13	11	4	10	5	16	1	3	2	15	6	12	9	14	8	7
16	5	7	2	12	9	15	8	3	14	11	13	6	4	10	1
2	12	3	8	11	14	13	4	5	16	1	6	10	15	7	9
15	1	13	4	9	5	16	12	7	11	14	10	8	2	3	6
5	10	14	7	15	2	6	1	9	12	8	3	11	13	4	16
11	16	9	6	8	10	3	7	15	13	2	4	14	1	12	5
3	7	16	14	6	13	4	2	11	10	15	1	5	8	9	12
6	4	2	12	14	8	10	9	16	5	3	7	1	11	15	13
1	8	11	5	16	7	12	15	6	2	13	9	4	10	14	3
9	13	10	15	3	1	11	5	4	8	12	14	7	6	16	2

Score: ____________

215 *SUDOKU 16*

13	2	11	9	12	1	8	5	15	6	10	14	4	7	3	16
6	5	4	7	11	13	16	10	3	8	12	2	1	15	14	9
14	12	15	16	6	7	4	3	13	9	1	11	8	5	10	2
1	3	10	8	9	14	2	15	4	7	16	5	11	12	6	13
2	4	6	11	1	9	13	8	7	16	14	15	5	3	12	10
5	7	16	1	2	10	6	14	8	12	4	3	15	13	9	11
15	10	14	13	5	3	12	16	11	1	6	9	2	8	7	4
8	9	3	12	7	11	15	4	2	10	5	13	14	16	1	6
16	15	1	4	3	12	14	9	10	13	2	7	6	11	8	5
3	8	9	2	4	16	10	11	14	5	15	6	7	1	13	12
12	14	13	5	15	8	7	6	16	4	11	1	10	9	2	3
10	11	7	6	13	2	5	1	9	3	8	12	16	14	4	15
7	16	5	15	8	4	3	13	6	14	9	10	12	2	11	1
4	1	12	14	16	6	9	2	5	11	13	8	3	10	15	7
9	6	8	3	10	15	11	12	1	2	7	16	13	4	5	14
11	13	2	10	14	5	1	7	12	15	3	4	9	6	16	8

Score: ____________

216 *SUDOKU 16*

2	4	14	11	10	7	15	3	5	16	12	1	6	8	9	13
6	12	8	9	11	16	14	2	13	4	10	15	3	1	5	7
5	15	7	10	13	9	12	1	2	8	3	6	16	11	14	4
3	16	1	13	5	8	6	4	7	9	11	14	15	10	2	12
14	13	10	4	7	15	3	11	16	5	9	8	1	6	12	2
1	8	5	12	4	14	13	16	6	2	15	11	9	7	3	10
9	11	15	2	12	6	5	10	3	1	7	4	13	14	8	16
16	7	6	3	9	2	1	8	12	14	13	10	5	15	4	11
8	5	3	7	6	13	16	15	14	11	4	2	10	12	1	9
10	14	9	1	8	11	4	12	15	7	5	3	2	16	13	6
12	6	11	15	3	5	2	9	10	13	1	16	8	4	7	14
4	2	13	16	1	10	7	14	8	12	6	9	11	5	15	3
13	10	2	6	15	1	11	7	4	3	8	12	14	9	16	5
7	9	12	8	16	3	10	5	11	15	14	13	4	2	6	1
15	3	16	5	14	4	9	6	1	10	2	7	12	13	11	8
11	1	4	14	2	12	8	13	9	6	16	5	7	3	10	15

Score: ____________

217 *SUDOKU 16*

13	3	16	1	9	2	8	14	11	7	10	15	4	6	12	5
12	15	4	11	3	13	5	16	6	8	14	2	9	1	7	10
2	9	6	7	12	10	1	15	3	13	5	4	16	14	11	8
10	5	8	14	4	11	6	7	9	1	16	12	15	2	3	13
7	16	11	13	10	15	9	3	5	4	2	8	6	12	14	1
9	4	14	5	13	8	7	6	1	12	3	10	2	15	16	11
1	8	15	6	11	12	2	5	16	9	13	14	7	3	10	4
3	12	2	10	16	14	4	1	15	11	7	6	5	13	8	9
8	11	9	2	1	5	14	10	13	16	15	7	3	4	6	12
16	13	1	4	6	7	12	9	10	14	11	3	8	5	2	15
14	7	12	3	2	4	15	13	8	6	1	5	10	11	9	16
6	10	5	15	8	3	16	11	12	2	4	9	1	7	13	14
11	14	10	9	15	6	3	12	7	5	8	1	13	16	4	2
4	6	3	16	5	9	10	2	14	15	12	13	11	8	1	7
15	1	7	8	14	16	13	4	2	3	9	11	12	10	5	6
5	2	13	12	7	1	11	8	4	10	6	16	14	9	15	3

Score: ____________

218 *SUDOKU 16*

16	2	7	6	12	11	13	3	9	15	8	4	1	10	5	14
8	10	9	13	15	7	5	14	1	3	12	11	16	2	6	4
5	3	14	12	8	4	2	1	6	16	13	10	7	9	11	15
15	1	11	4	6	9	16	10	2	5	7	14	3	8	12	13
3	11	10	9	4	16	7	12	14	2	15	6	13	5	8	1
2	13	16	14	9	1	8	15	11	4	10	5	12	7	3	6
7	5	12	1	10	2	14	6	16	13	3	8	9	15	4	11
4	6	8	15	11	5	3	13	7	12	1	9	10	14	16	2
10	8	15	3	16	12	4	7	5	6	14	13	11	1	2	9
12	16	13	2	14	6	9	8	15	10	11	1	4	3	7	5
1	9	6	11	2	3	15	5	12	7	4	16	8	13	14	10
14	4	5	7	1	13	10	11	8	9	2	3	6	16	15	12
13	12	3	10	5	15	6	2	4	1	16	7	14	11	9	8
6	7	1	5	3	8	11	4	10	14	9	2	15	12	13	16
11	15	2	16	13	14	1	9	3	8	6	12	5	4	10	7
9	14	4	8	7	10	12	16	13	11	5	15	2	6	1	3

Score: ____________

ANSWERS: SUDOKU 16

219 SUDOKU 16

6	3	13	16	1	4	2	8	7	10	14	9	11	12	5	15
9	1	15	14	11	16	3	6	4	5	12	13	7	8	10	2
8	11	12	7	10	14	13	5	16	1	2	15	6	9	3	4
10	2	5	4	9	12	15	7	11	8	3	6	13	1	16	14
4	10	1	6	14	9	7	13	8	16	15	11	2	3	12	5
16	13	2	5	8	10	12	3	1	14	6	4	15	11	7	9
14	9	3	11	4	15	5	16	2	12	13	7	1	10	8	6
7	12	8	15	2	6	11	1	5	3	9	10	16	14	4	13
12	4	14	2	16	11	9	15	10	7	1	3	5	6	13	8
1	6	16	10	7	13	8	14	12	9	11	5	4	15	2	3
11	15	9	8	3	5	6	10	13	4	16	2	12	7	14	1
13	5	7	3	12	2	1	4	15	6	8	14	10	16	9	11
15	7	4	9	6	3	16	11	14	13	5	12	8	2	1	10
5	14	11	13	15	8	10	12	3	2	7	1	9	4	6	16
3	16	6	12	13	1	4	2	9	15	10	8	14	5	11	7
2	8	10	1	5	7	14	9	6	11	4	16	3	13	15	12

Score: ____________

220 SUDOKU 16

3	2	16	11	15	5	10	13	12	4	6	14	8	9	7	1
10	8	6	4	12	14	9	2	13	7	11	1	5	3	16	15
1	15	7	5	3	8	4	6	16	10	9	2	14	11	12	13
14	12	13	9	7	11	1	16	15	5	3	8	4	10	6	2
5	3	12	6	14	13	11	1	10	15	16	9	2	7	4	8
2	10	1	14	16	12	7	15	4	3	8	5	11	6	13	9
4	11	9	16	8	10	6	3	2	13	14	7	15	5	1	12
7	13	8	15	4	9	2	5	1	11	12	6	3	16	10	14
6	14	11	12	13	15	5	4	9	16	2	10	7	1	8	3
16	7	4	8	11	3	12	9	5	1	13	15	10	2	14	6
9	5	15	10	2	1	14	7	6	8	4	3	13	12	11	16
13	1	3	2	10	6	16	8	14	12	7	11	9	4	15	5
8	6	2	7	5	16	15	10	3	14	1	4	12	13	9	11
15	16	10	3	1	7	13	14	11	9	5	12	6	8	2	4
11	9	5	1	6	4	8	12	7	2	15	13	16	14	3	10
12	4	14	13	9	2	3	11	8	6	10	16	1	15	5	7

Score: ____________

221 SUDOKU 16

12	15	10	1	11	13	3	6	4	2	14	9	8	7	5	16
7	3	13	16	5	14	2	10	8	11	12	1	4	15	6	9
4	11	8	6	12	7	9	1	10	15	5	16	2	3	14	13
5	2	14	9	8	4	15	16	6	13	7	3	10	11	1	12
6	1	4	7	15	8	11	9	14	12	3	13	16	5	2	10
2	16	5	10	13	12	6	3	11	1	15	4	7	14	9	8
11	14	15	12	16	5	4	2	9	7	10	8	6	13	3	1
3	8	9	13	1	10	7	14	16	5	6	2	11	12	15	4
14	13	1	15	2	6	10	7	3	4	8	5	12	9	16	11
9	7	6	11	4	16	14	5	1	10	2	12	3	8	13	15
8	12	16	2	3	11	1	13	15	14	9	7	5	10	4	6
10	5	3	4	9	15	8	12	13	16	11	6	1	2	7	14
16	9	12	5	14	3	13	8	2	6	1	11	15	4	10	7
1	4	11	8	6	9	5	15	7	3	13	10	14	16	12	2
13	6	7	14	10	2	12	4	5	8	16	15	9	1	11	3
15	10	2	3	7	1	16	11	12	9	4	14	13	6	8	5

Score: ____________

222 SUDOKU 16

10	15	16	2	11	14	7	13	3	5	6	9	1	12	4	8
1	14	4	11	12	6	16	5	2	7	13	8	15	9	10	3
13	5	7	8	9	3	2	1	15	10	12	4	14	16	6	11
9	6	12	3	8	4	10	15	11	1	16	14	5	2	13	7
8	9	13	12	2	11	15	10	1	14	7	6	4	5	3	16
3	11	10	5	13	16	8	7	4	12	15	2	9	6	1	14
14	2	1	16	4	12	6	3	13	8	9	5	11	15	7	10
15	4	6	7	5	1	14	9	16	3	10	11	13	8	12	2
2	16	3	6	7	5	4	12	9	11	1	15	10	14	8	13
4	7	11	10	1	15	13	6	8	2	14	16	12	3	5	9
5	13	15	9	14	10	11	8	6	4	3	12	2	7	16	1
12	1	8	14	3	2	9	16	10	13	5	7	6	11	15	4
7	3	9	4	16	13	12	14	5	6	2	10	8	1	11	15
6	10	5	1	15	8	3	2	14	16	11	13	7	4	9	12
11	12	14	13	6	9	1	4	7	15	8	3	16	10	2	5
16	8	2	15	10	7	5	11	12	9	4	1	3	13	14	6

Score: ____________

223 SUDOKU 16

5	3	6	16	11	9	12	10	1	15	7	14	4	13	2	8
9	8	11	15	13	16	7	1	2	4	6	3	10	12	14	5
7	4	2	1	5	14	3	8	13	12	16	10	9	6	11	15
13	10	14	12	2	15	6	4	9	5	11	8	7	1	3	16
15	9	8	6	7	2	16	12	5	10	1	4	3	11	13	14
14	5	16	2	10	1	8	13	11	3	9	12	15	7	4	6
4	1	12	13	3	11	14	9	16	7	15	6	5	8	10	2
10	11	3	7	15	4	5	6	14	8	2	13	1	16	12	9
3	16	1	8	12	13	4	2	7	9	14	11	6	5	15	10
11	14	15	10	8	3	9	7	12	6	5	1	2	4	16	13
6	12	4	9	16	5	1	15	10	13	8	2	14	3	7	11
2	7	13	5	6	10	11	14	4	16	3	15	8	9	1	12
16	13	7	4	9	6	2	3	15	11	10	5	12	14	8	1
12	15	10	3	14	8	13	16	6	1	4	9	11	2	5	7
8	6	5	14	1	7	10	11	3	2	12	16	13	15	9	4
1	2	9	11	4	12	15	5	8	14	13	7	16	10	6	3

Score: ____________

224 SUDOKU 16

13	15	9	3	11	4	6	2	5	14	12	8	7	1	10	16
12	7	16	8	9	1	14	10	15	6	4	2	3	5	13	11
1	5	10	2	15	12	7	13	9	16	3	11	8	6	4	14
4	14	6	11	5	16	3	8	10	7	13	1	2	15	9	12
16	12	7	10	4	3	1	14	11	9	2	15	6	8	5	13
9	8	15	4	2	7	13	11	6	12	5	10	16	14	1	3
5	6	13	14	8	10	9	15	1	4	16	3	11	12	2	7
2	11	3	1	12	5	16	6	8	13	14	7	4	9	15	10
6	2	11	13	3	14	12	1	4	10	8	5	9	7	16	15
8	1	5	16	7	2	4	9	13	3	15	14	10	11	12	6
3	9	14	12	10	15	11	16	2	1	7	6	13	4	8	5
7	10	4	15	6	13	8	5	16	11	9	12	14	2	3	1
14	3	2	7	13	6	5	4	12	15	10	9	1	16	11	8
15	4	8	5	1	11	10	3	14	2	6	16	12	13	7	9
11	16	12	9	14	8	2	7	3	5	1	13	15	10	6	4
10	13	1	6	16	9	15	12	7	8	11	4	5	3	14	2

Score: ____________

225 *SUDOKU 16*

1	8	16	13	11	14	10	6	4	7	3	15	5	12	2	9
6	5	2	7	4	9	8	15	12	13	11	14	10	1	3	16
4	9	12	15	1	7	3	2	5	16	6	10	11	13	8	14
10	14	3	11	16	5	12	13	1	2	8	9	15	7	4	6
9	11	10	14	15	12	13	4	3	1	5	8	2	16	6	7
3	4	1	5	14	6	2	8	7	11	10	16	12	15	9	13
13	15	8	16	3	1	7	5	2	6	9	12	4	11	14	10
12	6	7	2	9	16	11	10	13	15	14	4	3	5	1	8
11	7	9	10	5	15	14	1	6	4	13	3	8	2	16	12
2	12	14	3	13	10	6	11	16	8	15	5	1	9	7	4
5	16	13	4	12	8	9	7	14	10	2	1	6	3	15	11
8	1	15	6	2	3	4	16	9	12	7	11	13	14	10	5
15	3	6	12	10	4	5	14	11	9	1	7	16	8	13	2
14	13	11	1	8	2	16	9	15	5	4	6	7	10	12	3
16	2	4	8	7	11	15	3	10	14	12	13	9	6	5	1
7	10	5	9	6	13	1	12	8	3	16	2	14	4	11	15

Score: ____________

226 *KILLER*

2	4	6	1	8	7	9	5	3
8	9	5	3	4	6	7	1	2
7	1	3	9	5	2	4	6	8
3	5	4	8	2	1	6	7	9
1	2	9	6	7	4	3	8	5
6	8	7	5	3	9	1	2	4
4	6	8	7	9	5	2	3	1
9	3	1	2	6	8	5	4	7
5	7	2	4	1	3	8	9	6

Score: ____________

227 *KILLER*

7	3	1	2	8	9	6	4	5
9	5	2	4	6	7	8	1	3
6	8	4	1	3	5	9	2	7
5	9	6	3	1	8	2	7	4
8	4	3	9	7	2	1	5	6
2	1	7	5	4	6	3	8	9
3	2	5	7	9	1	4	6	8
4	7	8	6	2	3	5	9	1
1	6	9	8	5	4	7	3	2

Score: ____________

228 *KILLER*

6	4	3	8	7	9	2	1	5
8	9	1	2	3	5	4	6	7
5	7	2	4	6	1	9	3	8
9	5	4	6	2	3	7	8	1
1	8	7	9	5	4	3	2	6
3	2	6	1	8	7	5	9	4
4	1	5	3	9	6	8	7	2
2	6	9	7	4	8	1	5	3
7	3	8	5	1	2	6	4	9

Score: ____________

229 *KILLER*

4	6	5	7	1	3	8	9	2
2	3	7	9	5	8	6	4	1
9	8	1	2	6	4	3	5	7
1	4	9	6	7	5	2	3	8
3	5	6	8	4	2	1	7	9
7	2	8	3	9	1	4	6	5
8	9	2	4	3	7	5	1	6
5	7	4	1	2	6	9	8	3
6	1	3	5	8	9	7	2	4

Score: ____________

230 *KILLER*

6	2	8	4	9	1	3	7	5
5	7	1	3	6	2	9	8	4
3	9	4	7	5	8	6	1	2
8	5	3	9	1	7	4	2	6
1	4	9	5	2	6	7	3	8
2	6	7	8	4	3	1	5	9
9	8	6	1	3	5	2	4	7
4	3	5	2	7	9	8	6	1
7	1	2	6	8	4	5	9	3

Score: ____________

ANSWERS: KILLER

231 KILLER

8	4	6	7	3	5	9	1	2
9	2	5	1	8	6	4	7	3
1	7	3	4	2	9	5	8	6
2	3	4	6	1	7	8	5	9
6	8	9	2	5	4	1	3	7
7	5	1	3	9	8	6	2	4
5	6	8	9	7	2	3	4	1
3	9	7	8	4	1	2	6	5
4	1	2	5	6	3	7	9	8

Score: ____________

232 KILLER

7	1	5	4	2	8	9	6	3
9	8	3	5	1	6	7	2	4
2	6	4	9	7	3	8	5	1
5	7	6	8	9	1	3	4	2
3	4	8	6	5	2	1	9	7
1	9	2	7	3	4	5	8	6
8	2	7	1	4	5	6	3	9
6	3	9	2	8	7	4	1	5
4	5	1	3	6	9	2	7	8

Score: ____________

233 KILLER

3	2	4	5	1	8	9	6	7
9	7	1	2	6	4	5	8	3
6	8	5	9	3	7	2	4	1
7	3	9	8	4	6	1	2	5
8	1	2	3	9	5	4	7	6
4	5	6	1	7	2	8	3	9
2	6	3	4	5	1	7	9	8
1	9	8	7	2	3	6	5	4
5	4	7	6	8	9	3	1	2

Score: ____________

234 KILLER

9	7	1	2	3	4	5	6	8
4	5	2	8	1	6	9	3	7
3	8	6	9	5	7	4	1	2
5	9	4	7	2	3	6	8	1
6	3	7	4	8	1	2	9	5
2	1	8	5	6	9	7	4	3
7	2	3	6	9	8	1	5	4
1	4	9	3	7	5	8	2	6
8	6	5	1	4	2	3	7	9

Score: ____________

235 KILLER

6	4	5	1	9	7	2	8	3
2	8	9	5	4	3	6	7	1
1	3	7	8	6	2	5	9	4
4	9	3	7	5	6	8	1	2
5	7	2	9	1	8	3	4	6
8	6	1	3	2	4	7	5	9
9	1	8	2	3	5	4	6	7
7	2	6	4	8	9	1	3	5
3	5	4	6	7	1	9	2	8

Score: ____________

236 KILLER

4	1	5	8	7	9	6	3	2
6	8	2	1	3	5	7	9	4
7	9	3	6	2	4	5	8	1
3	6	4	5	8	2	1	7	9
8	2	7	4	9	1	3	6	5
1	5	9	3	6	7	2	4	8
9	7	8	2	1	6	4	5	3
5	3	1	7	4	8	9	2	6
2	4	6	9	5	3	8	1	7

Score: ____________

237 KILLER

8	5	2	6	3	1	9	4	7
6	4	7	9	5	2	8	3	1
9	3	1	8	7	4	5	6	2
5	8	9	2	6	3	1	7	4
3	1	6	7	4	8	2	9	5
2	7	4	5	1	9	6	8	3
1	6	8	4	2	7	3	5	9
4	2	5	3	9	6	7	1	8
7	9	3	1	8	5	4	2	6

Score: ____________

238 KILLER

7	5	3	4	2	6	9	8	1
4	9	6	8	1	3	5	7	2
1	2	8	9	7	5	6	4	3
3	4	7	5	9	1	8	2	6
5	8	9	2	6	4	3	1	7
2	6	1	3	8	7	4	5	9
8	1	2	6	5	9	7	3	4
9	7	4	1	3	8	2	6	5
6	3	5	7	4	2	1	9	8

Score: ____________

239 *KILLER*

4	9	8	2	6	3	5	7	1
6	7	2	9	1	5	8	3	4
3	5	1	8	7	4	6	9	2
1	8	4	5	9	2	7	6	3
7	6	3	1	4	8	9	2	5
9	2	5	6	3	7	4	1	8
5	1	7	3	8	6	2	4	9
2	3	6	4	5	9	1	8	7
8	4	9	7	2	1	3	5	6

Score: ____________

240 *KILLER*

4	2	6	3	8	5	1	7	9
7	5	8	9	1	4	6	3	2
9	3	1	6	2	7	5	8	4
6	8	5	7	4	1	2	9	3
2	1	9	8	6	3	7	4	5
3	7	4	2	5	9	8	1	6
1	6	2	4	9	8	3	5	7
5	4	3	1	7	2	9	6	8
8	9	7	5	3	6	4	2	1

Score: ____________

241 *KILLER*

2	8	9	4	7	6	5	1	3
5	6	1	3	9	8	4	7	2
3	7	4	2	1	5	6	9	8
7	2	3	1	8	4	9	5	6
9	1	5	6	2	7	3	8	4
6	4	8	5	3	9	7	2	1
8	5	2	7	4	3	1	6	9
4	9	6	8	5	1	2	3	7
1	3	7	9	6	2	8	4	5

Score: ____________

242 *KILLER*

1	4	5	3	8	9	6	7	2
3	7	8	6	2	1	9	5	4
2	9	6	5	7	4	3	1	8
4	6	7	9	1	3	8	2	5
9	8	1	2	5	7	4	3	6
5	3	2	4	6	8	7	9	1
8	1	4	7	9	5	2	6	3
6	5	9	8	3	2	1	4	7
7	2	3	1	4	6	5	8	9

Score: ____________

243 *KILLER*

7	9	8	5	4	6	1	3	2
2	1	6	8	9	3	5	7	4
5	3	4	2	1	7	6	9	8
3	2	7	6	5	9	8	4	1
8	6	9	4	2	1	7	5	3
1	4	5	7	3	8	9	2	6
6	5	3	9	8	2	4	1	7
9	8	1	3	7	4	2	6	5
4	7	2	1	6	5	3	8	9

Score: ____________

244 *KILLER*

7	5	6	8	9	3	1	2	4
8	1	9	6	4	2	3	7	5
2	4	3	1	5	7	9	6	8
1	7	4	3	8	9	2	5	6
9	2	8	4	6	5	7	1	3
6	3	5	2	7	1	4	8	9
3	9	1	5	2	8	6	4	7
4	8	7	9	1	6	5	3	2
5	6	2	7	3	4	8	9	1

Score: ____________

245 *KILLER*

5	2	9	4	6	1	3	7	8
3	4	6	7	2	8	9	1	5
1	7	8	9	5	3	6	4	2
6	9	4	5	8	7	2	3	1
8	1	2	3	4	6	7	5	9
7	5	3	1	9	2	4	8	6
2	6	5	8	3	4	1	9	7
9	3	7	6	1	5	8	2	4
4	8	1	2	7	9	5	6	3

Score: ____________

246 *KILLER*

8	5	9	7	6	1	3	2	4
2	7	3	5	4	9	8	6	1
4	1	6	8	2	3	7	5	9
3	2	5	1	9	4	6	7	8
7	9	4	3	8	6	5	1	2
1	6	8	2	7	5	4	9	3
9	4	1	6	5	8	2	3	7
6	8	7	9	3	2	1	4	5
5	3	2	4	1	7	9	8	6

Score: ____________

ANSWERS: KILLER

***247** KILLER*

4	8	7	9	5	2	6	1	3
2	9	5	6	3	1	7	4	8
1	3	6	4	7	8	9	2	5
3	1	2	5	9	7	4	8	6
7	6	4	2	8	3	1	5	9
9	5	8	1	6	4	2	3	7
8	2	9	7	4	5	3	6	1
6	4	3	8	1	9	5	7	2
5	7	1	3	2	6	8	9	4

Score: ________

***248** KILLER*

6	9	8	1	2	4	5	7	3
1	3	5	9	7	6	8	4	2
7	2	4	8	5	3	1	9	6
9	7	6	4	8	1	2	3	5
8	5	2	6	3	7	9	1	4
3	4	1	2	9	5	7	6	8
5	6	3	7	1	2	4	8	9
4	8	7	5	6	9	3	2	1
2	1	9	3	4	8	6	5	7

Score: ________

***249** KILLER*

6	2	4	8	5	9	7	3	1
5	9	3	6	1	7	4	2	8
7	8	1	2	3	4	5	9	6
2	6	7	1	9	5	3	8	4
4	5	9	3	7	8	1	6	2
1	3	8	4	2	6	9	5	7
3	7	2	9	8	1	6	4	5
8	1	6	5	4	3	2	7	9
9	4	5	7	6	2	8	1	3

Score: ________

***250** KILLER*

7	1	2	8	4	9	3	6	5
3	5	8	2	1	6	9	7	4
9	6	4	3	5	7	8	2	1
8	4	5	1	6	2	7	9	3
1	3	9	7	8	5	6	4	2
2	7	6	4	9	3	1	5	8
5	8	1	9	7	4	2	3	6
6	9	3	5	2	1	4	8	7
4	2	7	6	3	8	5	1	9

Score: ________

***251** KILLER*

7	8	5	4	1	2	6	9	3
3	6	9	8	5	7	1	2	4
1	4	2	9	6	3	7	5	8
6	9	7	2	8	1	3	4	5
4	5	3	7	9	6	2	8	1
2	1	8	3	4	5	9	7	6
5	7	6	1	2	4	8	3	9
8	2	4	6	3	9	5	1	7
9	3	1	5	7	8	4	6	2

Score: ________

***252** KILLER*

4	7	3	9	6	5	1	2	8
6	1	2	7	8	4	3	5	9
8	5	9	1	3	2	6	7	4
9	6	7	2	4	3	8	1	5
2	3	5	8	7	1	9	4	6
1	8	4	6	5	9	7	3	2
3	9	6	5	2	7	4	8	1
7	2	8	4	1	6	5	9	3
5	4	1	3	9	8	2	6	7

Score: ________

***253** KILLER*

7	4	3	1	5	9	2	6	8
6	8	2	7	4	3	1	5	9
9	1	5	2	6	8	7	3	4
5	2	4	3	8	1	6	9	7
1	6	7	9	2	4	3	8	5
3	9	8	6	7	5	4	1	2
2	7	9	5	1	6	8	4	3
4	5	6	8	3	7	9	2	1
8	3	1	4	9	2	5	7	6

Score: ________

***254** KILLER*

7	4	2	5	9	6	8	3	1
8	3	9	4	7	1	5	6	2
5	1	6	8	2	3	7	4	9
2	6	8	9	5	4	3	1	7
3	9	4	7	1	8	6	2	5
1	7	5	3	6	2	4	9	8
9	8	3	1	4	5	2	7	6
4	2	7	6	8	9	1	5	3
6	5	1	2	3	7	9	8	4

Score: ________

255 *KILLER*

8	7	6	4	3	2	1	5	9
9	1	2	6	5	8	3	4	7
4	3	5	7	1	9	6	8	2
6	5	8	9	7	1	2	3	4
7	9	4	8	2	3	5	6	1
1	2	3	5	6	4	9	7	8
3	4	9	1	8	6	7	2	5
2	8	7	3	9	5	4	1	6
5	6	1	2	4	7	8	9	3

Score: ______

256 *KILLER*

7	8	5	4	1	9	2	6	3
2	6	4	7	3	8	5	9	1
9	3	1	5	2	6	8	4	7
6	1	7	8	5	4	3	2	9
8	4	3	9	7	2	6	1	5
5	2	9	3	6	1	7	8	4
4	5	6	1	8	7	9	3	2
1	7	2	6	9	3	4	5	8
3	9	8	2	4	5	1	7	6

Score: ______

257 *KILLER*

7	2	1	3	4	9	6	8	5
8	9	6	5	2	1	3	7	4
5	3	4	8	6	7	2	1	9
1	5	3	6	9	8	4	2	7
2	6	9	4	7	5	8	3	1
4	8	7	2	1	3	9	5	6
9	1	2	7	3	4	5	6	8
6	7	8	9	5	2	1	4	3
3	4	5	1	8	6	7	9	2

Score: ______

258 *KILLER*

7	2	5	8	1	9	3	4	6
9	8	1	3	4	6	7	2	5
4	3	6	2	5	7	9	1	8
6	9	8	1	7	3	4	5	2
5	4	7	9	2	8	6	3	1
3	1	2	4	6	5	8	9	7
2	6	9	7	3	1	5	8	4
1	7	3	5	8	4	2	6	9
8	5	4	6	9	2	1	7	3

Score: ______

259 *KILLER*

2	6	1	8	9	7	4	3	5
4	8	3	5	2	1	7	9	6
5	7	9	3	6	4	2	1	8
3	1	7	9	8	5	6	2	4
8	4	2	6	1	3	5	7	9
6	9	5	4	7	2	1	8	3
1	5	8	2	4	9	3	6	7
7	3	6	1	5	8	9	4	2
9	2	4	7	3	6	8	5	1

Score: ______

260 *KILLER*

3	5	7	8	2	9	1	6	4
8	1	6	5	4	7	3	2	9
4	2	9	3	1	6	7	8	5
9	8	3	6	5	4	2	1	7
2	6	4	7	3	1	5	9	8
1	7	5	9	8	2	6	4	3
7	9	2	4	6	3	8	5	1
6	4	8	1	7	5	9	3	2
5	3	1	2	9	8	4	7	6

Score: ______

261 *KILLER*

1	6	5	4	8	3	9	7	2
3	7	8	9	2	1	6	4	5
4	9	2	6	5	7	8	3	1
6	8	9	5	7	4	1	2	3
2	1	7	8	3	6	4	5	9
5	4	3	2	1	9	7	8	6
7	2	6	1	4	5	3	9	8
8	3	1	7	9	2	5	6	4
9	5	4	3	6	8	2	1	7

Score: ______

262 *KILLER*

2	8	6	7	3	5	1	9	4
7	9	5	2	1	4	3	6	8
4	1	3	6	8	9	7	2	5
8	4	9	5	7	1	6	3	2
1	3	7	4	6	2	5	8	9
5	6	2	3	9	8	4	7	1
9	7	4	1	2	6	8	5	3
3	2	1	8	5	7	9	4	6
6	5	8	9	4	3	2	1	7

Score: ______

ANSWERS: KILLER

***263** KILLER*

6	8	7	9	4	2	5	3	1
5	4	9	6	3	1	8	7	2
1	3	2	5	8	7	9	4	6
7	9	5	4	6	3	2	1	8
8	2	4	7	1	5	3	6	9
3	1	6	2	9	8	7	5	4
9	5	1	8	7	6	4	2	3
2	6	8	3	5	4	1	9	7
4	7	3	1	2	9	6	8	5

Score: ____________

***264** KILLER*

9	8	5	3	7	1	2	4	6
2	4	1	6	8	5	7	3	9
7	6	3	2	9	4	1	8	5
5	3	4	7	6	8	9	2	1
1	7	8	5	2	9	4	6	3
6	9	2	4	1	3	5	7	8
8	2	9	1	3	7	6	5	4
3	5	7	9	4	6	8	1	2
4	1	6	8	5	2	3	9	7

Score: ____________

***265** KILLER*

9	7	2	1	3	8	5	6	4
5	3	1	4	6	9	2	8	7
8	4	6	5	2	7	9	1	3
6	9	5	3	4	1	7	2	8
3	1	7	2	8	6	4	9	5
4	2	8	7	9	5	6	3	1
7	5	9	6	1	3	8	4	2
2	6	3	8	5	4	1	7	9
1	8	4	9	7	2	3	5	6

Score: ____________

***266** KILLER*

7	5	4	8	6	1	9	3	2
9	3	8	5	4	2	6	7	1
6	1	2	7	3	9	4	5	8
1	4	9	6	8	5	3	2	7
2	8	6	3	9	7	1	4	5
3	7	5	2	1	4	8	9	6
8	2	3	9	5	6	7	1	4
5	9	1	4	7	8	2	6	3
4	6	7	1	2	3	5	8	9

Score: ____________

***267** KILLER*

3	5	7	6	2	9	8	4	1
2	6	8	3	1	4	5	9	7
4	9	1	7	5	8	2	3	6
5	8	2	9	4	6	1	7	3
1	7	9	5	8	3	6	2	4
6	3	4	2	7	1	9	8	5
8	1	5	4	3	2	7	6	9
9	2	3	1	6	7	4	5	8
7	4	6	8	9	5	3	1	2

Score: ____________

***268** KILLER*

9	7	6	4	1	2	3	8	5
5	4	8	3	9	7	6	2	1
2	3	1	5	8	6	9	7	4
7	5	2	1	6	4	8	9	3
6	8	4	2	3	9	5	1	7
3	1	9	7	5	8	2	4	6
8	9	7	6	4	3	1	5	2
4	6	5	9	2	1	7	3	8
1	2	3	8	7	5	4	6	9

Score: ____________

***269** KILLER*

5	4	2	6	8	9	3	7	1
8	7	1	4	3	5	6	9	2
3	6	9	7	2	1	8	4	5
1	2	6	5	9	7	4	8	3
7	8	4	2	1	3	5	6	9
9	5	3	8	4	6	2	1	7
2	1	5	9	6	4	7	3	8
4	3	7	1	5	8	9	2	6
6	9	8	3	7	2	1	5	4

Score: ____________

***270** KILLER*

6	7	3	1	2	4	8	9	5
2	5	4	9	7	8	6	3	1
8	9	1	6	5	3	7	2	4
3	6	5	8	1	9	4	7	2
7	8	9	2	4	6	1	5	3
4	1	2	5	3	7	9	6	8
9	2	8	3	6	1	5	4	7
5	4	6	7	8	2	3	1	9
1	3	7	4	9	5	2	8	6

Score: ____________

271 *KILLER*

6	9	8	5	4	2	1	3	7
1	3	4	8	9	7	6	5	2
2	7	5	6	3	1	4	9	8
3	1	6	2	5	9	8	7	4
4	2	9	1	7	8	3	6	5
5	8	7	3	6	4	2	1	9
8	5	2	9	1	3	7	4	6
7	6	1	4	2	5	9	8	3
9	4	3	7	8	6	5	2	1

Score: ___________

272 *KILLER*

5	4	8	6	1	2	9	3	7
3	6	7	8	9	4	1	2	5
9	1	2	5	3	7	8	4	6
8	9	6	2	7	3	4	5	1
7	2	1	4	6	5	3	8	9
4	3	5	1	8	9	6	7	2
6	5	4	3	2	1	7	9	8
1	7	3	9	5	8	2	6	4
2	8	9	7	4	6	5	1	3

Score: ___________

273 *KILLER*

8	5	1	9	4	3	7	6	2
6	4	2	8	1	7	9	5	3
9	3	7	2	5	6	8	1	4
7	1	8	6	9	4	3	2	5
3	6	4	5	7	2	1	9	8
2	9	5	3	8	1	4	7	6
1	8	3	7	2	5	6	4	9
4	2	6	1	3	9	5	8	7
5	7	9	4	6	8	2	3	1

Score: ___________

274 *KILLER*

4	6	5	8	3	1	2	9	7
8	2	1	6	9	7	3	4	5
7	9	3	5	2	4	8	1	6
6	8	7	9	4	2	1	5	3
9	1	2	3	7	5	4	6	8
5	3	4	1	8	6	9	7	2
3	4	8	7	5	9	6	2	1
1	5	9	2	6	8	7	3	4
2	7	6	4	1	3	5	8	9

Score: ___________

275 *KILLER*

3	1	2	5	9	6	8	7	4
7	5	8	4	2	3	6	9	1
6	9	4	1	7	8	2	5	3
1	7	5	2	3	9	4	6	8
2	3	6	8	4	5	7	1	9
4	8	9	7	6	1	3	2	5
5	4	7	9	8	2	1	3	6
8	6	1	3	5	7	9	4	2
9	2	3	6	1	4	5	8	7

Score: ___________

276 *KILLER*

5	6	2	4	8	3	9	7	1
3	7	9	6	2	1	8	5	4
1	4	8	5	9	7	3	2	6
9	5	3	1	7	6	4	8	2
7	8	6	3	4	2	5	1	9
2	1	4	8	5	9	6	3	7
8	2	1	9	3	4	7	6	5
6	9	5	7	1	8	2	4	3
4	3	7	2	6	5	1	9	8

Score: ___________

277 *KILLER*

3	1	8	9	4	5	7	6	2
6	5	7	8	1	2	9	4	3
2	4	9	6	7	3	1	8	5
7	3	4	5	9	8	2	1	6
9	2	5	1	3	6	4	7	8
1	8	6	7	2	4	5	3	9
4	9	3	2	6	7	8	5	1
5	7	1	3	8	9	6	2	4
8	6	2	4	5	1	3	9	7

Score: ___________

278 *KILLER*

5	6	9	2	8	1	7	4	3
4	7	8	5	9	3	2	1	6
1	3	2	6	4	7	8	9	5
9	2	4	3	7	5	6	8	1
7	8	5	4	1	6	9	3	2
3	1	6	8	2	9	5	7	4
2	5	7	9	3	4	1	6	8
8	4	1	7	6	2	3	5	9
6	9	3	1	5	8	4	2	7

Score: ___________

ANSWERS: KILLER

279 KILLER

5	8	6	4	7	3	2	9	1
3	9	4	6	2	1	8	5	7
7	2	1	9	8	5	6	3	4
6	7	9	8	1	2	3	4	5
4	5	8	7	3	9	1	2	6
1	3	2	5	6	4	7	8	9
2	4	3	1	5	6	9	7	8
9	1	7	2	4	8	5	6	3
8	6	5	3	9	7	4	1	2

Score: ________

280 KILLER

8	6	1	2	4	3	9	7	5
9	3	7	6	5	1	2	8	4
4	2	5	9	8	7	3	6	1
3	1	6	8	7	4	5	2	9
5	8	9	3	2	6	4	1	7
2	7	4	5	1	9	8	3	6
1	4	2	7	3	5	6	9	8
6	5	3	1	9	8	7	4	2
7	9	8	4	6	2	1	5	3

Score: ________

281 KILLER

3	5	6	2	8	1	4	9	7
2	7	8	9	5	4	3	1	6
4	1	9	6	7	3	5	2	8
6	2	4	7	1	5	8	3	9
7	3	5	8	2	9	1	6	4
8	9	1	3	4	6	2	7	5
5	6	7	1	3	8	9	4	2
1	8	2	4	9	7	6	5	3
9	4	3	5	6	2	7	8	1

Score: ________

282 KILLER

6	9	5	1	3	8	4	2	7
8	7	4	6	2	5	1	9	3
3	1	2	4	7	9	8	5	6
1	8	9	3	5	4	6	7	2
7	5	3	2	1	6	9	8	4
2	4	6	9	8	7	3	1	5
9	2	1	7	4	3	5	6	8
5	3	7	8	6	1	2	4	9
4	6	8	5	9	2	7	3	1

Score: ________

283 KILLER

1	4	8	7	2	9	3	6	5
2	9	6	3	8	5	1	7	4
3	5	7	1	4	6	2	8	9
8	2	5	6	1	4	9	3	7
6	7	9	5	3	2	8	4	1
4	3	1	8	9	7	6	5	2
7	6	2	9	5	3	4	1	8
9	1	3	4	7	8	5	2	6
5	8	4	2	6	1	7	9	3

Score: ________

284 KILLER

6	5	8	7	9	1	2	3	4
3	4	2	8	6	5	9	7	1
1	7	9	4	3	2	5	8	6
2	8	7	6	5	4	1	9	3
5	9	1	2	7	3	4	6	8
4	3	6	9	1	8	7	5	2
8	1	5	3	2	9	6	4	7
7	2	3	5	4	6	8	1	9
9	6	4	1	8	7	3	2	5

Score: ________

285 KILLER

9	3	1	2	7	6	8	5	4
8	2	6	1	5	4	7	9	3
7	5	4	8	9	3	1	6	2
3	1	7	9	8	2	5	4	6
6	8	2	7	4	5	3	1	9
5	4	9	6	3	1	2	8	7
2	6	3	4	1	8	9	7	5
1	7	5	3	6	9	4	2	8
4	9	8	5	2	7	6	3	1

Score: ________

286 KILLER

8	5	9	2	3	4	6	7	1
1	7	3	8	9	6	4	2	5
4	2	6	7	1	5	3	8	9
5	6	4	3	2	8	9	1	7
7	3	8	9	5	1	2	4	6
9	1	2	6	4	7	8	5	3
6	4	1	5	8	9	7	3	2
3	8	7	1	6	2	5	9	4
2	9	5	4	7	3	1	6	8

Score: ________

287 *KILLER*

1	2	4	6	3	5	9	7	8
3	5	8	2	7	9	4	1	6
7	9	6	8	1	4	2	5	3
5	8	1	4	2	6	7	3	9
6	4	3	1	9	7	8	2	5
2	7	9	3	5	8	6	4	1
9	6	7	5	4	1	3	8	2
8	3	5	7	6	2	1	9	4
4	1	2	9	8	3	5	6	7

Score: __________

288 *KILLER*

5	4	8	9	2	1	7	6	3
1	2	3	4	6	7	9	5	8
6	7	9	5	3	8	2	4	1
8	3	2	7	1	4	6	9	5
4	5	1	2	9	6	8	3	7
9	6	7	3	8	5	1	2	4
3	1	4	6	7	2	5	8	9
2	8	5	1	4	9	3	7	6
7	9	6	8	5	3	4	1	2

Score: __________

289 *KILLER*

5	6	7	9	2	4	3	1	8
4	1	9	6	8	3	2	7	5
8	2	3	5	1	7	6	9	4
7	5	8	4	3	9	1	6	2
2	4	6	8	7	1	5	3	9
3	9	1	2	6	5	8	4	7
1	7	4	3	5	2	9	8	6
6	3	5	7	9	8	4	2	1
9	8	2	1	4	6	7	5	3

Score: __________

290 *KILLER*

2	9	6	4	5	1	8	7	3
8	1	3	9	6	7	5	2	4
5	4	7	8	3	2	1	6	9
6	7	9	3	4	5	2	1	8
3	5	2	1	8	6	4	9	7
4	8	1	2	7	9	3	5	6
1	6	8	7	2	4	9	3	5
9	3	5	6	1	8	7	4	2
7	2	4	5	9	3	6	8	1

Score: __________

291 *KILLER*

5	8	3	6	2	7	9	1	4
4	6	7	9	8	1	5	2	3
1	9	2	5	3	4	8	7	6
8	1	6	2	5	3	4	9	7
9	7	4	1	6	8	3	5	2
3	2	5	7	4	9	1	6	8
2	4	9	8	7	5	6	3	1
7	3	1	4	9	6	2	8	5
6	5	8	3	1	2	7	4	9

Score: __________

292 *KILLER*

7	6	2	5	8	9	3	4	1
3	9	1	2	6	4	5	8	7
8	4	5	1	3	7	2	9	6
5	8	6	3	4	1	9	7	2
9	1	7	8	2	6	4	3	5
4	2	3	9	7	5	6	1	8
2	5	4	7	1	3	8	6	9
6	7	9	4	5	8	1	2	3
1	3	8	6	9	2	7	5	4

Score: __________

293 *KILLER*

8	5	9	4	6	3	2	1	7
7	4	2	5	9	1	8	6	3
1	3	6	7	2	8	5	9	4
4	6	5	8	1	9	3	7	2
9	1	8	2	3	7	6	4	5
2	7	3	6	5	4	9	8	1
3	9	4	1	8	5	7	2	6
5	2	7	9	4	6	1	3	8
6	8	1	3	7	2	4	5	9

Score: __________

294 *KILLER*

4	5	8	7	6	9	2	1	3
6	7	1	4	2	3	5	8	9
9	2	3	5	1	8	6	4	7
8	4	5	1	3	7	9	6	2
7	1	6	9	4	2	8	3	5
2	3	9	6	8	5	1	7	4
5	8	7	3	9	1	4	2	6
1	9	4	2	7	6	3	5	8
3	6	2	8	5	4	7	9	1

Score: __________

ANSWERS: KILLER

***295** KILLER*

6	7	8	2	5	1	3	9	4
5	2	9	3	7	4	6	1	8
1	3	4	9	8	6	2	5	7
3	6	5	4	9	7	8	2	1
4	8	1	6	3	2	9	7	5
7	9	2	5	1	8	4	6	3
8	4	7	1	2	9	5	3	6
9	1	3	8	6	5	7	4	2
2	5	6	7	4	3	1	8	9

Score: __________

***296** KILLER*

4	9	6	5	8	3	7	2	1
7	1	2	4	9	6	8	3	5
3	5	8	2	1	7	4	9	6
8	3	4	1	2	5	6	7	9
6	2	1	7	4	9	5	8	3
9	7	5	6	3	8	2	1	4
1	4	7	9	6	2	3	5	8
5	6	3	8	7	1	9	4	2
2	8	9	3	5	4	1	6	7

Score: __________

***297** KILLER*

3	8	9	4	7	2	6	1	5
6	5	7	9	8	1	2	3	4
2	1	4	6	5	3	8	9	7
5	6	8	3	9	7	1	4	2
7	9	2	1	6	4	3	5	8
4	3	1	8	2	5	7	6	9
8	7	3	5	4	6	9	2	1
9	4	6	2	1	8	5	7	3
1	2	5	7	3	9	4	8	6

Score: __________

***298** KILLER*

6	7	4	8	5	9	2	1	3
8	2	5	3	6	1	7	4	9
3	1	9	2	4	7	8	5	6
7	5	8	9	2	3	4	6	1
2	9	1	6	8	4	3	7	5
4	6	3	1	7	5	9	2	8
5	8	2	4	9	6	1	3	7
9	3	7	5	1	2	6	8	4
1	4	6	7	3	8	5	9	2

Score: __________

***299** KILLER*

5	8	4	6	3	7	1	2	9
3	6	2	4	9	1	5	8	7
7	1	9	8	5	2	4	6	3
1	4	3	9	7	8	6	5	2
2	7	8	5	6	3	9	1	4
9	5	6	2	1	4	7	3	8
4	3	5	1	2	9	8	7	6
8	2	1	7	4	6	3	9	5
6	9	7	3	8	5	2	4	1

Score: __________

***300** KILLER*

7	6	8	2	5	9	4	1	3
3	2	4	7	1	8	5	6	9
9	5	1	4	6	3	7	8	2
8	1	7	3	9	6	2	5	4
5	4	2	8	7	1	3	9	6
6	9	3	5	2	4	8	7	1
4	7	6	1	3	5	9	2	8
2	8	9	6	4	7	1	3	5
1	3	5	9	8	2	6	4	7

Score: __________

SCOREBOARD

	POINTS SCORED
Extreme Sudoku:	
Squiffy Sudoku:	
Sudoku 16:	
Killer Sudoku:	
Total Score for Entire Book:	

Remember – if you can't complete a puzzle you score zero points!

Total Points:
Under 1,600 = Sudoku Sergeant
1,600–3,200 = Sudoku Major
Over 3,200 = Sudoku General

Sudoku Sergeant: Well done, soldier! You've made it through the Sudoku battlefield with flying colors. Keep up with your training and see if you can increase the speed of your deadly Sudoku skills.

Sudoku Major: A very impressive score. We salute your bravery in the face of Extreme Sudoku fire. You're well on your way to being a well-decorated Sudoku veteran.

Sudoku General: Congratulations – an incredible score! You have attained the top Sudoku rank, defeating everything in your path. Be alert though, and make sure you remain at peak Sudoku performance – others will always be waiting in the wings to shoot you down.

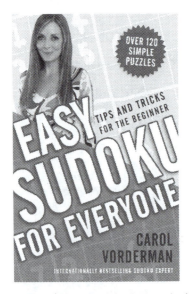

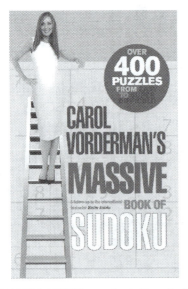

Printed in the United States
by Baker & Taylor Publisher Services